IT'S THE REGIME, STUPID!

IT'S THE REGIME, STUPID!

A REPORT FROM THE COWBOY WEST ON WHY STEPHEN HARPER MATTERS

BARRY COOPER

KEY PORTER BOOKS

Library and Archives Canada Cataloguing in Publication

Cooper, Barry, 1943-
    It's the regime, stupid! : a report from the cowboy west
on why Stephen Harper matters / Barry Cooper.

ISBN 978-1-55470-156-8

    1. Harper, Stephen, 1959-. 2. Canada--Politics and government--21st
century. 3. Federal-provincial relations--Canada. I. Title.
FC640.C66 2009   971.07'3   C2008-906784-3

ONTARIO ARTS COUNCIL
CONSEIL DES ARTS DE L'ONTARIO

The publisher gratefully acknowledges the support of the Canada Council for the Arts and the Ontario Arts Council for its publishing program. We acknowledge the support of the Government of Ontario through the Ontario Media Development Corporation's Ontario Book Initiative.

We acknowledge the financial support of the Government of Canada through the Book Publishing Industry Development Program (BPIDP) for our publishing activities.

Key Porter Books Limited
Six Adelaide Street East, Tenth Floor
Toronto, Ontario
Canada M5C 1H6

www.keyporter.com

Text design and electronic formatting: Jean Lightfoot Peters

Printed and bound in Canada

09 10 11 12 13 5 4 3 2 1

Printed on 30% recycled paper

Preserving our environment

Key Porter Books chose to print the pages of this book on recycled paper and saved these resources:

energy	water	greenhouse gases	solid waste
10 million BTUs	20,578 L	595 kg	317 kg

15 trees were saved for our forests

Printed by **Webcom Inc.**
on Legacy TB Natural 30% post-consumer waste.

Estimates were made using the Environmental Defense Paper Calculator.

FSC

Mixed Sources
Product group from well-managed forests, controlled sources and recycled wood or fiber

Cert no. SW-COC-002358
www.fsc.org
© 1996 Forest Stewardship Council

To the memory of my pioneer forbears:
From the Province of Ontario (1870)
From the Dominion of Newfoundland (1910)

CONTENTS

AUTOBIOGRAPHICAL PRELUDE

Eastward I go only by force; but
Westward I go free.
—HENRY DAVID THOREAU

On the thirteenth of May, 1998, Alexander (Sandy) Soutzo and I left the Ricardo Ranch just southeast of Calgary at 8:00 a.m. and drove into the sun for three hours to the Medicine Hat Feeding Company, where a couple of thousand head would come under the auctioneer's hammer that afternoon. Soutzo was looking for black baldy replacement cattle, and he had learned that Aldo Pederzolli was getting out of the business. Pederzolli had a good reputation as a stockman and his cows would be worth looking at. They would be worth buying if the price were right. "Black baldy" is the name ranchers give to the first-generation cross between Aberdeen Angus and Hereford, the two most popular British breeds. They are almost always black with white faces, though occasionally red calves are born even from Black Angus cows, and combine the hardiness of the Angus with the mellow disposition of the Hereford.

They are vigorous, with a pleasant nature and a strong character, and are excellent converters of feed to meat. Black baldies are a good fit for conditions in southern Alberta. The second filial generation, conventionally called brockle-faced, have slightly diminished hybrid vigour but are still excellent beasts. Soutzo considers them the most sought-after replacement cows, and he was in the market. It all depended on the bids.

Soutzo and I had played rugby together at school, front row, *les frères du jock*, we called ourselves then, and had taken quite distinct educational and domestic paths since school. Soutzo had assumed the operation of the ranch from his father several years earlier. Like most ranchers, he ran it as a business, and unlike putative knights of the range paid relatively little attention to the romance and nostalgia associated with cowboys. And yet, running Ricardo Ranch, which was originally part of the cattle empire established over a century ago by Senator Pat Burns, makes nostalgia and romance unavoidable. The setting, the valley of the Bow River a mile downstream from the Deerfoot Trail crossing, with a long view of the Rockies, is straight from central casting. In fact, the ranch had been the scene of a couple of TV movie shoots.

Sandy had removed the tailgate from his new F150 to gain an extra two miles per gallon (no one knew how many kilometres a litre that worked out to). The route took us through the rolling hills of the Blackfoot Reserve, now called the Siksika Nation, to Gleichen, where we joined the Trans-Canada for the run to the Hat. It was a glorious morning. The geese were back on the sloughs, antelope ran on the horizon, and coyotes loped across the prairie, occasionally stopping to turn and look back at our speeding efficiency.

Arriving a little after 11:00 a.m., we had an hour or so to look at the livestock, shiny in the warm spring sun, muscular, nervous, and stupid. They were every bit as good as Sandy had hoped. If there were not too many buyers from the commercial operations to drive the price up, it should be a good day.

The auction market is a family-run affair. Lyle Taylor, the owner, also runs a concrete-cutting business and a lighting business in town. He works the stockyards, he says, for relaxation. His brother Lorne was then the local MLA and Minister of Science and Technology in the Conservative government of Premier Ralph Klein. Delvin Stuber, a big triangular man with a lot of weight above the belt and not much below, managed the year-round business. With four thousand head sold on a good day, at around a thousand dollars each, it is a high-cash-flow business, and a reasonably profitable one. It is also straightforward: the price at auction is the market price. No one quarrels with it or complains.

Soutzo took up a position in the middle of the amphitheatre, high in the back. He could survey others as they bid, but they would have to crane their necks to see him, an indignity cowboys prefer to avoid. The cows and calves were brought in as lots of four or six pairs accompanied by the unintelligible chatter of the auctioneer. Only the price was clear. Bidders nodded, winked, raised a finger or an eyebrow to signal a bid, and the auctioneer moved on: "Eight hundred; eight and a half; nine; nine-fifty; a thousand. Do I hear eleven? Eleven. Eleven and a half. Going. Once. Twice. Sold to Mr. Sampson for eleven hundred Canadian dollars!" For some reason Sandy is known as Mr. Sampson, and he had just purchased twelve head at $1,100 each. One of the men working the pit recorded the successful bidder's name and the price agreed on. At the end of the sale, buyers settled up with a cheque. Sandy then hired a waiting cattle liner, saw it loaded, and told the driver where to deliver his passengers.

The sale had gone well. Sandy picked up what he wanted at a reasonable price and Aldo was happy too. They met in town for a drink at the Eagle Restaurant, across from the Pattison Funeral Home and Crematorium. Aldo was buying. Eagle's specialty was a 22-ounce T-bone with potatoes and garlic toast for $13.95. Lucas, the owner, complained that no one "eats big" any more. Aldo agreed and said that's why his cows were under 1,300 pounds. "Strip steaks mean smaller carcasses," he said, "no one works any more. No one pitches hay on a ranch. It's all done by machinery. So nobody eats big." Besides, New Age cowboys know that lots of protein and carbohydrates make for bad food combining and gas.

After an early supper, we headed west into the sunset. When we arrived back at the ranch, the cattle had been unloaded. We had driven 590 kilometres on three-quarters of a tank of gas. Removing the tailgate worked.

The conversation during the six hours of the trip covered most of the topics in this book. Soutzo's persuasion convinced me to write it, and to write it as an essay, a personal set of reflections on the widespread experience of political malaise in recent Canadian history, which I attribute to changes in the Canadian regime. Even though I am a certified political scientist, I have reduced the subtle qualifications of scholarship to a minimum. Second thoughts have been suppressed in order to articulate a point of view that is, by intention at least, coherent to the point of boldness. After all, the purpose of an essay is to push the envelope, to argue as far as an argument will go, and then to consider what it all means. Like a conversation, which is a kind of oral essay, it does not aim so much at proving a point or reaching an agreed-upon conclusion as shedding light on a problem. Facts are useful because they make the problem appear in the world. Literally, they create the phenomena that are analyzed to grasp a meaning. So far as I know, there are no new facts presented here—and some of the arguments have been made elsewhere.

It should be clear from the genesis of this essay, riding shotgun in Soutzo's pickup, that I have not written it *sine ira et studio*. I am not sure that anyone ever attains that Weberian ideal. Certainly Max Weber never did.

We all have to begin somewhere. I begin by recollecting a few experiences that remain part of the biography of my consciousness. They have remained with me because, for reasons not entirely clear, they are important sources of excitation in the way I look at things, mainly political things. To put it crudely: I have written this from the position of the cowboy West, including the afflictions of *collum rubrum*, where a drive to the Hat and back is all in a day's work.

One preliminary observation. This is not a book about Stephen Harper the individual, nor of Stephen Harper the political leader and initiator of certain public policies regarding which we may say "yea" or "boo." It is about the Canadian regime and, with luck, what a Harper government may mean for Canada.

My paternal and Ontario-born grandfather married a native-born Albertan from Millarville, southwest of Calgary, who claimed remote descent from Captain Cook; my maternal grandfather, from Heart's Delight, Newfoundland, despite marriage to a woman descended from the Loyalists of New Brunswick, always looked upon Canada as a slightly foreign and malign place. For Grandfather Cooper, the CPR was anything but the embodiment of the national dream. My earliest memories of how my family fit the wider world were that they moved west into it, exploring what was out there. There was a Canada from which the entire family came, but it was "back east"—a term that to me conveyed both backwardness and stodgy immobility. Something had been rejected in their exodus but more had been gained by leaving.

I am by habit a westerner, rather than a (central) Canadian, a Canadian of the Great Lakes drainage basin, or, for reasons that are explained below, a Laurentian Canadian. Learning about that Canada was accommodation to somebody else's option, not a second nature. The first political conversation I recall was between my two grandfathers and my dad, in a log cabin on a fishing trip into the Chilcotin when I was about five. None of them was clear about what "social credit" actually meant in British Columbia. It was not the Alberta variety, that much was clear; and it had nothing to do with socialism. It was a mystery, as British Columbia often is for Albertans.

I uttered my first political statement about a year later. My mother was driving my sisters and me to visit relatives on the ranch of one of my uncles, west of Nanton. The highway south from Calgary for most of the drive was parallel to the railway tracks. We gradually overtook a freight train and I announced proudly, "Look, Mum, it's the goddamn CPR." She reached over and whacked me on the side of the head and told me never to use that word again. After my tears evaporated, I was puzzled, not knowing I had uttered a blasphemy. I was just using what I thought was the full name of the railway, because that was what my grandfather and uncles always called it.

When I knew my great-grandmother, she was blind. She spent her last years in a rocker. My cousins and I at Christmas would gather at her feet and ask her to tell stories. "Tell us the story of the Indian," we would ask in unison. She would reach out to lay her hand on our faces to see who was there. My cousins would shy away, but I enjoyed her soft old hands and loved it when she said, "Little Harry, little Harry." (My dad's name was Harry.)

She had been a rancher's wife before the wire—the time of the open prairie before the land was hemmed by barbed wire. Her husband was often away for weeks on a roundup. It was customary, especially in spring, for a few Indian families to gather around the settlers' ranch houses to be fed and cared for at the end of winter. Sometimes, as on this occasion, it coincided with the roundup and the men would be away.

The story goes that the Indian families had left, and only a half-dozen young men remained at the ranch. The convention was that they would stay outside and the ranchers would bring them bread and bacon. This day, however, one of the young men wanted to come into the house, and my great-grandmother told him he could not. He came in anyway, and she reached for the shotgun on the mantle; pointing it at him, she told him to leave. He advanced on her and received both barrels. His friends removed the corpse with apologies and left. Eventually the Mounties took her statement and that of the other Indian men.

This story thrilled us all. It was a Wild West cowboys-and-Indians yarn. Later, when I was a teenager I remember telling my dad what Great-Grandmother had said. He was horrified. "No," he said, "she didn't shoot anyone. She shooed the Indians outside with her broom." I knew what I heard and it had nothing to do with brooms. Not until I was in my twenties did I understand what my dad was up to. It was not political correctness *avant la lettre*. My great-grandmother, young at the time and pretty, was afraid of being raped, and she defended herself. In the 1950s, rape was not discussed or even thought about, which is why Great-Grandmother's shooting turned into my dad's shooing.

There was, however, one story about a shooting that could not be euphemized. My great-uncle Stanley ranched west of Nanton. He would come into town once a week to buy sausages at Denoon's meat market and have a few drinks. One time, after more than a few, he climbed back on his horse, pulled out his gun, and fired off a few celebratory rounds. The last one went through the brain of his ride. This was a cautionary tale about the dangers of strong drink, not gun control. In fact, as my colleague in the History Department at the U of C, Warren Elofson, has shown, the Alberta cattle frontier was not much different than Montana or Wyoming so far as gunplay was concerned.

In Vancouver where I grew up, we studied the Latin language and Roman history in junior high at Point Grey. In the midst of the Cold War, which we knew to be a contest between us and the bad guys in the Soviet Union, we saw a replay of the Punic Wars. My friend David Collier and I agreed one rainy afternoon in Grade 7 that it would be appropriate if the part of

Rome were played by America: "*Delenda est Carthago*," said Cato. "*Delenda est Sovieticus*," said we tiny cold warriors. Earlier in life we had both been upset and indignant when, at the Kerrisdale Theatre, Movietone News showed F-86 Sabres being shot down over Korea. From Roman history I learned as well that the Rome that fought Carthage turned into something else, a world empire. It was as grand, our history teacher said, as the British Empire. He also told us that Rome lost something when it took an imperial turn: that was the lesson of Shakespeare's *Julius Caesar*, he added. It never occurred to us that the British or American empires lost anything by growing big and strong. We took pride in it.

As had happened to my father and uncles, I was sent to boarding school on Vancouver Island. They had gone to Brentwood, which in my day had not been rebuilt after the fire in the late 1940s, so I was sent to Shawnigan. In Grade 11 I won a trip to Ottawa, an "Adventure in Citizenship" sponsored by the Rotary Club in Duncan. It was my first exposure to the east after infancy, and the reward for triumphant rhetorical overkill disguised as a debate on the question "Should We Trade with Red China?" I argued the negative side with great indignation and little common sense. This visit to the national capital, however, was to a place stranger by far than Seattle or San Francisco, cities from which several of my school friends came and which I had visited many times. I returned home with the first book in French that I was not compelled to read: *Pourquoi je suis séparatiste*, by Marcel Chaput.

At the University of British Columbia (UBC) I first read Herodotus and Thucydides. From the former came the major divide between Greeks and barbarians. This recapitulated the insight from junior high of the division between us and them with the additional conceit that "we" were Greeks and our adversaries were barbarians. But then, on reading Thucydides, I learned that the Greeks can turn barbaric—and the Macedonian barbarians, or half-barbarians, started behaving like Greeks. Nothing seemed to be set in stone or amber where the politics of antiquity was concerned.

Could the same be true of Canadian politics? Alan Cairns and Donald Smiley, two of the most insightful students of Canadian federalism ever, implicitly raised just such a question. Smiley introduced undergraduates to the centralizing implications of the now-forgotten post-war tax-rental agreements. On one occasion he rescued me from the persistent questioning of Walter Young, who did not approve of my undergraduate honours essay, which applied Robert Michels' "iron law of oligarchy" to the communist leadership of the United Fishermen and Allied Workers' Union. I had to join the union in order to work summers on the boats, having abandoned a promising career as an under- or non-paid cowboy in Alberta.

The classes of Alan Cairns raised a different kind of question. He taught a great deal about the Canadian and the British law of the constitution. One day he asked: why is it that in British Columbia, where the government is Social Credit and the opposition is NDP, they both are called "third parties" by the national media? No one knew. His implicit message was clear: we in the West can see things invisible to those in Toronto, Montreal, and Ottawa. We still can and do.

During World War II, my father was a medical officer in the RCAF, stationed mostly in Alaska, of all places. The division between our civilized forces and the barbaric enemies of Japan and, more remotely, of Germany, was a given of my youth. I first saw Germany the summer before I went to graduate school, travelling on a Eurail pass with one of my friends from school, Chas Pentland, who spent his academic career at Queen's, teaching international relations. His German was polished; mine was rudimentary. We were both amazed, however, at the uniforms of the officials staffing the German Federal Railways. Their self-importance and (to us) their military uniforms—red hats with tall peaks—made us think of the ss, with which we were familiar from the movies. As the trains pulled away from the stations, we would on occasion yell out the window: "Achtung! Herr Hauptoberplatformleutenant! Du bis mit Dummheit beladen." This may not have been recognizable German, but it allowed us to come to terms with the orderliness of the central European other. We reflected profoundly about Mittel-Europa and of Asia beginning at the Landstrasse in Vienna, as Metternich had once said.

This groping and pompous silliness, no less than the stories told by my grandparents and parents, was an untutored way of coming to terms with the character of regimes. The Federal Republic, as Aristotle might say, had given a different political form to the German people from that provided by the Nazis. Hannah Arendt had explained to my undergraduate mind that the Nazis had made evil a boring and everyday way of living. The plump burghers among whom we moved were, if anything, guilty and abashed, not arrogant or evil. About the same time, the other great political evil of the last century, the Soviet Union, was explained not by the Sovietologists but by novelists—a mediocre one, Arthur Koestler, and then by a great one, Aleksandr Solzhenitsyn.

In 1973, I organized a conference on Canadian political thought at York University, the first place I had a long-term job. Some of my colleagues and a few of the participants, including our keynote speaker, C.B. "Brough" Macpherson, queried whether Canadian political thought existed. Since I was teaching a course on the subject, I was confident it did. The conference was not entirely a success, though it confirmed in my mind that I came from a different country than scholars such as Macpherson, no less than my Toronto pals, who for reasons I could not fathom supported the NDP. I did, however, meet Rainer Knopff and David Bercuson, who later became members of the legendary Calgary School, about which more must be said below. Of course, it did not exist even notionally then.

The only other experience of interest associated with York is that, as noted, it was there I first taught a course in Canadian political thought. This was about the same time Don Forbes was doing the same downtown at the University of Toronto. The approach I took was based on the work of Eric Voegelin and on the dictum that one must begin with the self-interpretation of society and "proceed by critical clarification of socially pre-existent symbols." What this meant in plain English was that anyone interested in the reality of Canadian politics had better pay attention to the language, the myths, and the symbols by which Canadians gave meaning to their varied existences as Canadians. This meant reading a lot of Canadian as well as western history and literature and figuring out the difference between Susannah Moodie's bush garden and a thirty-quarter grain farm or a fifteen-section ranch. I concluded that some novelists could be more insightful than even the best conventional political scientists in expressing or articulating political reality. But like Plato or a press release from the PMO, they have to be interpreted in order to be understood.

To the extent that the basic disputes have been settled in any given political order, the result is a "regime." A regime indicates who rules but especially what type of human being rules and is sufficiently admired that he or she has the right to enforce and coerce a specific way of life, if that should prove necessary, and to bask in public legitimacy, like fat seals on a rock in the sun. We will see that the question of the regime—especially in a democracy—is inherently problematic and contentious. It is enough to note in the present context that, until recently, most Canadians have had reason to be careless about their government. Indeed, for many of us, it was not really our government but the politicians'. Or, as political scientists used to say, the elites were in the business of "accommodating" one another. Such an attitude is, unfortunately, typical more of subjects than of citizens. In quiet times, when elites are creative rather than repressive, it may be acceptable to live as a subject, but at other times it is not. Today it is not, at least not for Albertans.

Once, not too many years ago, Canadians thought the future both would be continuous with the past and, most likely, would bring more of the good things of life. Today, we know that the range of options is more extensive than that. Things can go very wrong. Moreover, most Canadians have discovered that whereas the elites, especially the political elites, have accommodated themselves to one another well enough, they have somehow also changed the country in ways of which no one is proud.

We begin with reflections on how things changed for the worse. Under the influence of such melancholic humours, one is compelled to think about what the government (chiefly, but not exclusively, the federal government), has done and what it might do in the future—for better or for worse. It should come as no surprise that I welcomed the result of the 2006 federal general election, and the 2008 one even more. But this was less for partisan reasons than for patriotic ones. Perhaps the Conservatives led by Stephen Harper could help give Canadians, including westerners, something in which they could take pride. Their predecessors were certainly skilled at serving the interests of some, but the cost in national self-respect was high. One of the most difficult tasks of modern politics, harmonizing pride and interest, is a question to which we return, more than once. Such sobriety-inducing considerations—first, that Canada has changed for the worse, and second, that all is not lost—direct us away from recollecting the historical foundation of Canadian politics laid down from earlier experiences and toward the present question: the nature of the Canadian regime, which is *not* a historical question. It also seems to be an empirical necessity to begin an investigation such as this on the basis of political experiences and the knowledge we gain from daily life.

I must confess that some of these questions occurred to me when I thought about the string of victories put together by Jean Chrétien. Like many Albertans, the sheer stupidity of our fellow citizens in Ontario who voted for what, to western eyes, appeared as an unredeemable and corrupt regime was difficult to understand. Many Albertans found it difficult to accept as well and so made plans to invoke the Clarity Act and found a new regime outside the degeneracy they apprehended in the Canadian one. Whether matters are as corrupt as they seem, the question is still there: what has happened to Canada? And why? Pondering that problem, which began on the cattle-buying trip of 1998, led to this book.

A word of warning: to understand the significance of the title of the first chapter, it is necessary to think through some political philosophy. That is not to everyone's taste or capacity. It may make your head hurt, but it provides the most solid foundation available for the subsequent discussions, which are closer to the common sense of public policy. It offers an account of why we do, in fact, get the political leaders we deserve and, in light of what Canada has become, why the wisdom of Pogo, the grand philosopher of my childhood, rings true: "We have seen the enemy, and he is us."

CHAPTER ONE

WHY REGIMES MATTER

"The cause of the laws is the regime."
—LEO STRAUSS

For the past generation the average Canadian has been complacent. Canada has existed more or less for a century and a half. If you see the country as one result of the breakup of the "first" British Empire, it has lasted even longer, and unlike the American fragment, Canada has been spared a civil war. We have a constitution that has been debated and interpreted for generations. So we really ought to be familiar with our political core, the purpose of our living together.

At the same time, a robust common sense would have us conclude that perhaps we are in fact all too familiar with our political core, and its illusiveness is a harbinger of its non-existence. Apart from carping academics, we have the serious testimony of a famous leader of the Quebec secessionists, Lucien Bouchard, that "Canada is not a real country." Perhaps he is correct. But then, what kind of country is it? At the very least one might say that those who ask such a question are not complacent, that, indeed, our self-understanding is often darkened by self-dissatisfaction. Even so, when we raise the questions "What do we stand for?" or "What are our political purposes?" we are raising the issue of the meaning of the Canadian regime. It is not self-evident that raising such a question should, by itself, induce deep anxieties beneath a cold sweat.

In contemporary political science, the word *regime* is used to translate the Greek *politeia*. In English the word also carries a sense of regimen, of a way of doing things, such as going on a diet or adopting an exercise program. This is why we can speak of a person's constitution as well as the constitution of a nation. In a political context, it refers to a way of life that is in part formed and conditioned by a specific kind of government. Sometimes regimes are understood to be civilizations or cultures. Thus one can speak of a clash of cultures and of cultural wars, to say nothing of the recently famous clash of civilizations. A regime, as John Stuart Mill said, is "something which is settled." In antiquity, regime politics was the focus of the founders of political science, Plato and Aristotle. They and many others agreed that the regime was the basis for the whole life of the political community and that the greatest influence on the character of the regime was *paideia*, education in the most comprehensive sense of the term, which today includes music, TV, and the Internet as well as history, engineering, and study of the law.

According to Socrates in the *Republic*, the best regime, which is either a monarchy or an aristocracy, is ordered by a desire for goodness and excellence. Second is timocracy, rule of honour-lovers, men who are filled with ambition and, generally speaking, desire victory as well. Third is oligarchy, the rule of the rich who order their lives through the pursuit of wealth. Democracy is the rule of the free who simply desire to be free and, so to speak, random in what they desire. In a democracy, even domestic animals have lost their sense of obedience to their human masters and roam feral in the streets. Finally, there is tyranny, the rule of the entirely unjust who are consumed by a desire to inflict injustice for its own sake. Corresponding to the several regimes are several personalities, so that, for example, the honour-loving man, the timocrat, will succeed and rule in a timocratic regime but not in an aristocracy or a democracy. This is why, for Plato and Aristotle, the key question "Who rules?" included the question "What is the character or personality of those who rule?" That aspect tends to be forgotten today, but it is central.

The classics were not relativists. There really is a hierarchy of noble and base pursuits that are independent of human will and the mysterious intuition of "values." There is a story about Winston Churchill that illustrates this point. When Prime Minister Herbert Asquith heard that Churchill had never read Aristotle's *Ethics*, he loaned him a copy. When it was returned next morning, Asquith asked if Churchill had learned anything from it. "Nothing that a gentleman would not already know," he said. When we consider the more familiar statements of Canadian politicians regarding public happiness, it is important to recall that not only are they not gentlemen (or ladies) but that they really know no better.

There are some fascinating ways to apply classical regime theory to Canadian politics. Aristotle wondered whether, when a democracy replaced an oligarchy, it was just for the new regime to repudiate the debts of the oligarchs. Likewise,

Canadians might wonder whether Adscam was the result of the action of the Government of Canada, the Liberal Party of Canada in Quebec, or a few rogue individuals. For the moment, we can postpone answering such questions. The point is, the answers we arrive at carry implications for how we understand the regime. Similarly, when Aristotle considered the justness of a policy, it involved more than popularity or whether transfers between the rich and the poor mollified the latter; the reasonable, who might be rich or poor and who made intelligible arguments, also had a voice. When Aristotle discussed geographic extent or population size and national character, his arguments dealt with problems that conventionally we collect under the heading of federalism, of a "distinct society," or of the politically correct characteristics of a so-called first nation.

To summarize: the regime is, concretely, a ruling group that embodies and defends what its members think is most distinctive and most important about the political community, which is, in classical terms, its collective opinion about the best way of life. Moreover, support for the regime is itself not merely an opinion that, for example, the UN once considered Canada to be the best country in the world. It also sustains the open honouring of the individuals who embody that way of life and the enthusiastic acknowledging of their right to legitimate rule. The individuals and the principles are both *cherished*. The actual institutions of government thus provide a visible and practical expression of what way of life is considered best. In short, there is more to the regime than the law of the constitution, however important formal documents may be.

The comprehensive character of the regime explains, in a way that may be surprising to contemporary Canadians, why the Greeks were so concerned with poetry and music. In a nut-shell, the poets were constrained by the regime to give their audiences what they wanted, rather like TV producers. The problem of music in a very general sense matters for the Canadian regime as well because music, and the interpretation of music, provides compelling evidence regarding Canadian self-understanding, Canadian self-interpretation, and the health of the Canadian soul.

Take the example, or, if you like, the case of Warren Kinsella. In his 2001 memoir, *Kicking Ass in Canadian Politics*, Kinsella confesses to his great affection for Jean Chrétien (perhaps *Kicking* should be changed to *Kissing*) and the many dirty tricks he has played on behalf of Chrétien and the Liberal Party of Canada. Kinsella was for many years the executive assistant to David Dingwall, the first among Chrétien's "Roman Guard," to use the apt term of another of Chrétien's companions, Eddie Goldenberg. This is interesting enough, but greater insight into the kind of person who rises high in the Liberal organization and who befriends the prime minister is given in his later reflection on his musical education, *Fury's Hour: A (sort-of) Punk Manifesto* (2005).

Kinsella's description of himself in the Calgary of the 1970s is that of "a rabble-rousing punk," hanging with "the anti-social bunch of punks that made up our band, the Hot Nasties" for whom "getting arrested for inciting a riot was *pretty fucking cool.*" Being punk, he said, "was about pissed-off young people shaking things up and having a bit of fun, and maybe chang-ing a few attitudes (and redressing a few injustices) along the way." Kinsella still admires punks "for their refusal to conform." (But, of course, they do conform: who could mistake a punk for an accountant?) Kinsella goes on to ask, "What is it that all punks [and, we would add, all politicians of a certain kind] share irrespective of race, religion, gender or partisan affiliation?" And he answers: "All punks are pissed off at something." In the end they are pissed off at reality, or as Kinsella says, "at George W. Bush, for being born."

Kinsella said that he "looked for inspiration in the direction of Joey Shithead of DOA" and, one must add, he found it, particularly in Mr. Shithead's inspiring words, his "maxim," Kinsella calls it, which "best captures the pith and substance of it all. Punk is about being *angry* about something (like politics, like parents, like pop music) and *doing something* on your own ... to fix it." The great problem for teenagers, Kinsella says, is "it's all fucking bullshit." And the response, "disappointment, anger, or both," is followed by the solution: "You break things, you take drugs, you punch someone out, you join something."

Normal parental therapy for precious narcissists such as our young Warren is to tell him to read a book or play hockey and, one way or another, to get a life. The more serious problem with anger as a motivation for anything, even when sublimated into political *ressentiment*, is that it is also a means of obliterating both reason and spirituality. When people such as Kinsella are enraged, they lose touch with reality. But this peep into Warren's world is not intended to analyze Kinsella and his services to the Liberal Party of Canada. Rather it serves to illustrate the classic view, that imaginative literature, poetry, music, and, conceivably, dance, painting, and opera, reflect the spirit of the regime, the dominant principles and opinions of the regime under which it was conceived and produced. In classical times, poets who lived under tyrants would sing their praises, and poets living in democracies would celebrate freedom and liberty—the prejudices of their respective audiences. The terms have changed today but the relationship between the regime and the imaginative support of it has not. The most important kind of poetry, as the next chapter argues, is myth. Regimes are animated by myths, by stories we tell ourselves about ourselves. Part of the problem of the Canadian regime is that we have several, and they conflict. We will see that conflict is inevitable.

In contrast to the animating myths of a regime, which tend to be unreflective, even accidental, the justification of specific policies tends to be deliberate and based upon thought and a conscious decision about what the public good effectively is. This is not to say that mistakes are impossible and that prejudices never arise, but only that deliberation and argument have also played a role in the creation and maintenance of the Canadian regime.

The great eighteenth-century political scientist Vico was right: human beings make their history, which means that Marx, who taught that history, and economic history in particular, makes human beings, was dead wrong. The implication is that the nature of the Canadian regime matters because it influences the way Canadians live—in the past, today, tomorrow. Criticism of the regime is not really a partisan matter because the same regime has persisted in Canada (arguably) since the end of World War II despite changes in partisan office-holders. At the same time, it seems unlikely that Canada could engage in regime change without a significant break in the long-term dominance by the Liberal Party of Canada of the federal government. The reason is simple:

political parties have to reproduce themselves. What counts is not corruption or honesty per se, but the logic by which an organization reproduces and thus maintains itself. In a regime such as has been established by the Liberal Party of Canada, the only vice is disloyalty. It is for this reason that I confess I am a self-conscious but not (I trust) blind partisan. If I support Conservatives more than Liberals, it is because the Liberals have given up on liberalism. Like the NDP, which never believed in liberalism, the Liberals now also strongly believe in directing the affairs of citizens, which is to say, turning them into subjects not of the monarch but of the bureaucracy that rules in the name of the monarch. It may, of course, turn out that the Conservatives believe this too, notwithstanding occasional remarks to the contrary by supporters and leaders of that party. If so, they will simply have added the vice of mendacity to their burden of office.

One of the arguments to be made below is that the basis for the political practices analyzed by the Gomery Commission was laid down in the post-war institutional transformation of Canada. Every system, every regime, fosters if not the economic victory at least the economic advantage of certain kinds of human beings over other kinds. That includes bureaucrats as well as capitalists and proletarians. Moreover, all regimes tend to follow their own internal logic to the end, toward an extreme. This invariably leads to abuse, but it also makes the principles of the regime easier to see. It is in this sense that Adscam and Gomery exposed in a bright light the principles of what the Canadian regime had become over the past half century. Thus, for example, if the recent Liberal government did not already have the power to grant such favours as led to

Adscam, it would not attract from within the Montreal advertising world and the bureaucracy the kinds of people who were specialists in seeking such favours and administering them. The questions we shall explore are these: what were the policy and institutional changes that, eventually, enabled Adscam to be accomplished? How did Adscam come to express the Canadian regime? And what, if anything, is to be done? Or can be done?

As a preliminary answer to the questions this entire essay tries to answer, consider briefly the argument made by Eddie Goldenberg, a man who for most of his adult life has held the cloak of Jean Chrétien. He called his book *The Way It Works* and not *The Way It Worked* because the lessons he learned "will continue to apply regardless of which political party is in government or in Opposition and which prime minister is in office." That is, his is a book about the Canadian regime as understood by one of its experienced functionaries. He neither expects, nor wishes, it to change.

First among the purposes of the regime is dealing with Quebec or, to use the language of regime self-interpretation, "national unity." Ten of Goldenberg's twenty-two chapters deal with Quebec. The book opens with his account of the greatest triumph of the Chrétien government, saying no to the United States over joining Canada's closest, and in many respects only, ally in its invasion of Iraq. Nearly 300 pages later we learn that the decision on Iraq was driven by Quebec isolationism and its long-standing tradition of free riding and pacifism. Goldenberg really does think (as his boss does) spending on the military is a frivolity and not a means to defend the national interest. Real politics, he says, is more about "getting the job done," as he put it, than playing by the rules, namely the law of the Constitution. Thus he was pleased as punch about the vast "educational package" that wrapped together the Canadian Institutes of Health Research, the Canada Millennium Scholarship Foundation, the Canada Graduate Scholarships, and 2000 Canada Research Chairs, even though all of these programs were in areas of provincial constitutional responsibility. His conclusion was almost predictable: "Government will continue to work best when issues are put in their proper context, when value is placed on historical perspective and institutional memory," which is to say, government will work best in the future when it works the same way it did in the recent past. My view is that government has not worked at all well for those same reasons.

In major respects, political regimes correspond to ways of life. The use of the verb *correspond* may suggest a chicken-and-egg problem. Let us admit it. But then the question is not deciding where to begin but simply deciding to begin somewhere. Almost always there is overlap between the formal government and the ruling culture. In Canada, the latter means referring to the CBC and the vast number of institutions that comprise the government- (or rather, taxpayer-) funded "culture industry" from the Canada Council to Hockey Canada. As an example of the term *ruling culture* consider the career and some writings of the recent viceregal couple, Adrienne Clarkson and John Ralston Saul, who, in many respects, exemplify the nadir of the regime.

By appointing Adrienne Clarkson to be the twenty-sixth Governor General of Canada, Jean Chrétien completed an innovation of twenty years earlier when Pierre Trudeau elevated an NDP political retread, Ed Schreyer, to the same post.

Roméo LeBlanc, Jean Chrétien's previous appointment, was possibly the worst example, being at the time a senator whose son was working in the Prime Minister's Office. Although Adrienne Clarkson had never been elected to office, her career in the CBC made her a Liberal cheerleader lacking only pompoms and a short skirt. In her memoir, a splendid combination of saccharine sentimentality and hard-nosed revenge, she is disingenuous enough to say both that she does not "believe fame gets you anywhere" and that Chrétien "did not associate me with television." The fact is, fame got her the job, and to pretend that Chrétien knew, for instance, that she was the author of *A Lover More Condoling*, is preposterous.

Much of the immediate commentary that greeted Clarkson's appointment focused on the details of a life that has been both admired and despised. Her daughters are unmentioned in her coy entry in *Who's Who in Canadian Women*, but her hobby, collecting wild mushrooms, is. At CBC her support crew dismissed her: "She didn't carry the sticks." In other words, she didn't help out on the production side of the cameras.

Shortly after settling a long-standing dispute with her neighbour over planned renovations, which might have thrown shade upon the study of her partner, John Ralston Saul, Clarkson married him. In this she followed the precedent of her immediate predecessor, who made honourable his long liaison with Diane Fowler in the same fashion. It remains a matter of speculation whether such acts are concessions to decent opinion or are designed to mock respectability by drawing attention to the supreme hypocrisy of the deed. Either way, Rideau Hall is evidently worth a mass. In Clarkson's memoirs, she allows that her understanding of a model couple is that of

Simone de Beauvoir and Jean-Paul Sartre, with Ralston Saul, one assumes, in the role of the raunchy Jean-Paul.

Her current husband has received almost as much attention as she has. Though eight years her junior, John Ralston Saul, whom I like to think of as Rosedale's JR, is at least as distinguished a celebrity as his bride. Unlike her, he has won fame in print, not TV, and so is accountable to a higher standard than the mass diversions provided by CBC. At the press conference called to announce the appointment, Chrétien was nevertheless able to take the full measure of the man. JR, he said, "wrote about politics and so on, and sociology and whatnot."

Such an appraisal is strongly at odds with Ralston Saul's own understanding of his wide-ranging genius. His manner is assured; his rhetoric, certain. He pronounces without hesitation on Quebec poetry and the nature of referenda, on the differences between Plato and Socrates, and between true and false populism, and much, much more. Such a mind cannot avoid being aware of its own powers and the impression it creates on others.

In fact, however, a book such as *Reflections of a Siamese Twin: Canada at the End of the Twentieth Century*, is superficial, glib, and intellectually undistinguished. It is, however, a sad portent because, first of all, the author has become a celebrated guide to our present discontents—not for Canada alone but (in the estimation of one authority) for "the planet." The importance of his *oeuvre*, therefore, is that the author has been accepted and promoted by the authoritative and very public intellectuals of our times. The point of my own dismissive judgment is not simply to puncture a balloon: Ralston Saul, unimportant in himself, is a portent of the exhaustion of elementary analytic skills among leftist intellectuals. The book's success and the celebrity of its author are portents for which the media-savvy left has become a choir, the views of which on selling water, the Free Trade Agreement, or gun registration are entirely predictable, and quite out of tune with opinion beyond lovely, genteel Rosedale. Accordingly, the response to the news that one of their own had made it to Rideau Hall was greeted with joy in the Rosedale national newspaper, the *Globe and Mail*. Jeff Simpson was simply giddy: "Rideau Hall may never be the same." Michael Valpy gushed, "We know her," and Hugh Windsor reminisced fondly about the good old days at U of T when she was SAC vice-president. For these *gauchistes de fauteuil*, condemned to live, if not in the shadow of the CN Tower, at least within sight of it, it was all too perfect.

Likewise Madame's inflated views of her office (she saw herself as "the guarantor of responsible government in our parliamentary democracy"), her lavish taste for the amenities her office could command (especially travel), the breathtaking ignorance that, quite simply, she did not, as Governor General, have official views, her defence of the Chrétienistas (and disdain for the Paul Martin faction) were also portentous: the culture of narcissism has an elite as well as a common manifestation. Her sense of entitlement was combined with a vicious appraisal of any who might question it.

The most amusing aspect of the ruling culture is what those who are part of it, including Eddie Goldenberg, take to be its redeeming virtue: the understanding they have of Quebec. "Only in Quebec," said Madame, "have I seen that Canadians truly understand that culture is an expression of their highest aspirations as human beings.... The rest of Canada should just stop envying and start emulating Quebec." Two observations regarding such sincerely held precious nonsense are in order. First, not all of the rest of Canada envies Quebec for their "aspirations as human beings" because they have understood the significance of Adscam. It did not take place in Manitoba, and yet it remains the fullest expression of what the Canadian regime has become. Second, it is precisely the allegedly envious boors in the rest of the country, led by the cowboys and rednecks of Alberta, who have been handed the bill and are paying for this exquisite culture that the sophisticates of Quebec enjoy so well. To members of the ruling culture, not paying your own way, not "carrying the sticks," is a large part of what makes it attractive.

The institutional corruption of the Canadian regime is relatively recent. Time is important in the study of regime change, but so is space. Not much experience in the world is needed to grasp that human beings, who certainly look alike physically, can live very differently. Consider East and West Germany in 1957 or North and South Korea today. There are parts of Canada where a handshake can still seal a deal. Canadians once were warriors at least as bellicose and ferocious as Americans: remember the First Special Services Force, called the "Black Devils" by the Germans at Anzio in 1944. Over the next half century something changed in the arrangement of offices and honours that both conditioned and fostered a specific set of myths and stories, loves and hates, fashions and assumptions that outline the aspirations of the young and the standards of decent conduct for mature citizens. The entire system of incentives and disincentives, which established the tone, the climate of opinion, or the political culture of Canada, changed in the course of a generation. What happened?

The answer is found not in nostalgia but in looking at the trail of evidence. There is not much point in regretting the lost opportunities of 1947 or of 2003, because democracies have no character except what together the regime and the citizens provide them at any given time.

The fact is, any democracy seeks to realize several competing and even incompatible goods: freedom, of course, but also security and prosperity. If I pursue only one such good, others grow recalcitrant and pigheaded and pursue an opposed policy with such single-mindedness that cooperation becomes impossible. Pigheadedness is not unknown in Canadian political life, as both Kinsella's sublimated punk rage or Clarkson and Ralston Saul's absurd self-importance shows.

The character of genuine and so moderate liberal democrats disposes them to a government that works for them, not the other way around. They want a few laws, applied impartially, and they want to be rewarded for their efforts, not by the favour of others. They want to share a country with decent, not vicious people and, if necessary, to overawe their enemies. This modest wish list is remote from the experience of most of humanity most of the time. That Canadians take such a regime for granted does not lessen its fragility. Nor does it contradict the most prominent feature of democratic regimes, a changing character that reflects changes in what its citizens love. In *The City of God*, St. Augustine (following Plato) said: to discover the character of a people, observe what they love. What do Canadians love? Do they love the same things in Alberta and

Quebec and PEI? And if so, what? How do Canadians express their loves?

Depending upon the character of citizens, different kinds of offices and honours are needed to bring to prominence certain kinds of men (and women) and to suppress others. Laws are just the most authoritative way of legitimatizing some kinds of behaviour and condemning others. Hence the importance of loves and hates, of fashions and things avoided by those who set the tone and shape the climate of opinion. Regimes are embodied by what the Brits first called the "establishment."

In Canada the establishment consists of the men and women whose lives and achievements have been so ably and lovingly chronicled, described, discussed, and analyzed in many books by Peter Newman. The establishment also includes the officials, particularly the senior management, in the Ottawa mandarinate, and in the provincial bureaucracies. Business and non-profit groups that depend on and profit from connections with government are included, not least of all because they tend to see eye to eye with public officials. It extends to universities as well: by and large the Department of Political Studies at Queen's is usually in, and Political Science at the University of Calgary (I must sadly report) is usually out—at least until very recently.

For their part, the movie stars and pop singers, the rich socialites and decorated generals, the princesses and prime ministers, reflect the regime to the people. Gisele MacKenzie expresses a different reality than Shania Twain. Todd Bertuzzi says something different about Canada than Gordie Howe. And yet they are all models for young people and so shape their characters.

Regimes are especially influenced, however, by the personalities and character of political leaders. They are important in
part because of the effects of leadership by example, by precepts and exhortations, and by the power of the purse. They
are the people in society who actually deploy incentives and
disincentives. They create different paths to the top, which
favour different kinds of people. This is something that neither
Marxists nor public-choice economists easily understand. To
put it crudely, the meaning of free markets will differ for people of different ethical dispositions. Consider Conrad Black:
his reputation prior to his trial in Chicago in 2007 was rather
different than it was afterwards. The question of example was
highlighted in a phrase used in the Gomery report, "culture of
entitlement." It was given an iconic and formular expression in
the words of David Dingwall, who explained hotly to a parliamentary committee looking into his expenses as head of the
Canadian Mint (a tidy sum of over three-quarters of a million
dollars): "I'm entitled to my entitlements."

In the first place, a culture of entitlement is a culture of
grasping and seizing. In German, to seize or to take, *kriegen*, is
also the word for war, *der Kriege*. So when David Dingwall
declared he was "entitled to his entitlements," he was following
the logic of war: reward your friends, crush your enemies, and
take what you can. Included among his entitlements were car
payments, golf club memberships, and reimbursement for
chewing gum and coffee. Dingwall was speaking the truth,
which raises an interesting political issue: how to characterize
a regime where taxpayers pay for the chewing gum of the head
of a Crown corporation? A culture of entitlement at the bottom
means the old distinction between the deserving poor and

sturdy beggars can no longer be made. There are fewer and fewer people who, like the wolf in Aesop's fable, would prefer to eat meagrely what they earn than share the bounty of the heaping dish of the dog and the dog's collar.

Regime change is sometimes more obvious with foreign than with our own governments. In Japan today, rulers tend to be people who know how to study for, and get high marks in, exams dealing with production and service delivery; they are different kinds of people than those who made it to positions of power in 1936 and against whom my father donned the King's uniform to fight. Likewise, the Soviet Union in 1947 was Stalin "written in large letters," as Aleksandr Solzhenitsyn once said. When Stalin's successors no longer had the heart or the stomach to rule by terrorizing the party and then unleashing it to terrorize the rest of the population, the days of the Soviet regime were numbered. So too the change from the leadership of the Liberal Party from Jean Chrétien to Paul Martin carried hints of a change in regime, as Adrienne Clarkson clearly sensed. When Martin announced the Gomery Commission, for example, spokespersons for, or representatives of, the old regime, such as Alfonso Gagliano and Eddie Goldenberg, made it very clear they thought Martin's move was particularly ill-advised. In this respect, change of regime preceded change in government.

So far the focus has been on character and myths to live by, but political institutions also matter. Laws regulate family life, for example, by determining whether the state or charity provides health care to the indigent. The state influences educational research and qualification criteria for lawyers and veterinarians by financing institutions such as universities.

Eventually the state—which is to say, concretely, the bureau-cracy—becomes the arbiter of truth. Think of so-called global warming. More prosaically, when governments award the big contracts, for everything from frigates to Band-Aids, they create winners and losers. This raises another question: what kinds of character do bureaucrats promote? By way of illustration, there was no such thing as a "social worker" before the government started spending money to institute such a thing—including university faculties to make them "professional," even though what they profess is hardly articulate.

In the opposite social role, so to speak, stands the soldier. In antiquity, the soldier is the citizen: *miles est civis*. It is hardly an exaggeration to say that the ability to fight and to win at war is the greatest expression of character. If the habits of a people do not result in a victorious military, that people will quite properly disappear and disappear without lamentation. As Churchill said, every country has an army, either its own or somebody else's. In a democracy, the regime sets the tone for military institutions as for other ones so that the character of the military is strongly influenced by the character of the political leadership. It is certainly true that by dispensing with the military a people will never know its importance in the formation of citizens. A major step in that direction has been taken when it is forgotten that civilian control of the military also means participation in the military by prominent civilians. It is significant, for example, that the percentage of MPs with military experience has declined from over 30 per cent during the two decades after the end of World War II to under 2 per cent today. It is significant as well that General Rick Hillier, a soldier articulate to the point of flamboyance, was chosen chief of defence staff by Paul Martin and kept on by Stephen Harper. It meant the military was no longer viewed as Boy Scouts with rifles as Martin's predecessor believed.

Other institutions influence the regime as well. The governing assumption of federalism is that citizens will be concerned chiefly with local or provincial interests. This was true especially for James Madison, whose "Federalist No. 10" remains one of the great studies on comparative federal theory. In contrast, when people pay more attention to political matters that have nothing to do with local affairs, such as bilingualism in northern British Columbia, and involve obedience to rules, about which they had no say in their formation and can do nothing to change, then, to quote Tocqueville, they are isolated "and then dropped one by one in to the common mass." The point is not whether official bilingualism is a good thing that will enlighten the backwoods loggers of Terrace. Rather, to the extent that the Official Languages Act is administered in Terrace by minions whose first allegiance is to Ottawa and, to the extent that the good people of Terrace submit to their rules rather than resist them, their sense of citizenship and responsibility is bound to atrophy.

Responsible citizenship will be replaced, moreover, as sure as the sun rises in the east, with the discretionary rule of bureaucracy. It can be measured by the reluctance of the government ever to punish its employees for harming citizens. Justice Gomery found, much to his surprise, that such reluctance was widespread and perhaps total. It turned out to be impossible to enforce the Financial Accountability Act. As a result, the act was not enforced. So when a thug auditor from Canada Revenue Agency laughs in your face, the logic of a rational response explains why so many Russians still long for Stalin: he at least threw the bones of the direct oppressors to his subjects. And here is born the earliest of servile thoughts: to get along, go along. Nurse your grudges against sadistic government accountants stinking with resentment and hope that eventually their day of retribution will come. These are not the attitudes of self-respecting citizens, but mirror images of your cynical bureaucratic antagonist.

Harvey Mansfield, who may well be the best living political philosopher (after all, somebody is), has characterized the problem of the modern regime, we noted above, as one of balancing pride and interest. It constitutes, as the French say, a *problématique* where regional fiscal transfers and equalization payments meet up with the political correctness of employment equity. The intensity with which debate over the latter issue is conducted was brought home to me long ago in 1986 when, as one relatively inexperienced in such matters, I was asked (who knows why?) to speak to a collection of "employment equity" officers of several large public- and private-sector bureaucracies who had been assembled at the former Windsor Station in Montreal by CN Rail. This gathering was described as bringing together persons of wide-ranging and divergent views. Mine were in a minority and, for the first time, my remarks were met with prolonged booing and shouted calls to sit and keep silence, which was rather fun. The *rapporteur*, an angry woman, Doris Anderson, summarized the discussion of the workshop, Equality in the Economy (1986), with the remark: "Many participants were aware of the difficulties which Professor Cooper's position presents to the advocate of economic equity and made some attempt to answer his objections." With all due respect to my co-panelists and to the audience, their attempts to answer my objections were a failure. The reason for their failure, precisely, is that they did not consider the importance of pride (including their own), so focused were they on promoting the interests of others, in this instance, the "disadvantaged."

To put this dispute into perspective, consider that one of the fundamental insights of economics is that your pride, your prickly sense of self-respect, even of self-importance, can be costly to you because it makes you, perhaps temporarily, lose sight of, or forget about, your interest. For an economist, freedom is all about interests. Political freedom, however, is also a matter of pride. It is important to be clear about this difference.

Interests are desires that, *ex hypothesi*, anyone would have in a given situation. They are normal, not idiosyncratic; they tend to be quiet rather than excessive. In the first instance, or most generally speaking, your interest appears opposed to your pride. It is often in your interest to surrender your pride to a bigger interest. Perhaps you lose your independence, but so what? Of course, to be independent is to choose, but choosing can be expensive and dangerous at times. Why not let someone else choose for you? Interest, understood as the heart of politics, makes this possible insofar as you assume two things: first, that you do not choose your interest; and second, that you are a "rational actor." Consider the question "Why bother to vote?" Except on those once-in-a-million occasions, your vote won't count in the sense of being decisive. You won't be missed. In short, a system of interests proceeds on the premise that virtue is unnecessary and so proves it unnecessary. It may well be in your interest to be a slave or, just as an economist might say, it's in your interest to be a free rider. It is impolite to talk about slaves, and the "free-rider problem" in economics does not properly illuminate the political issue. Instead of slaves, let us call such persons "dependants."

But there is still the problem of the "you" in whose interest it is to surrender your pride. There must be a *something* that you hold on to without qualification as to whether it is in your interest to do so—otherwise there would be no "you" to have an interest. That residual something is pride. Most people do not think it is in their interest to be slaves. Why not? Remember Aesop's dog and its collar. If their interests are served, why is servility not a reasonable attitude? Perhaps in refusing slavery, they are not such rational actors after all. Economists have difficulties dealing with this question, but their difficulty does not abolish the political problem: how to deal with interest in such a way that it also includes pride, which in turn seems at least on occasion to be opposed to interest. The short answer is to be found in respect for the constitution, which is in your interest because it helps you get what you want, and it expresses your pride because you can properly take pride in self-government.

To return to the Montreal meeting: supporters of employment equity and lefty-liberal intellectuals generally believe it is in your interest to act against your interest if it is in support of the "disadvantaged" or, better, the "least advantaged" (because we all must have some "advantages"—but they never ask: Where do advantages come from?). The result is to render the least advantaged into dependants, and that is a political problem because it insults their pride by making it impossible for them to exercise their own rights.

The problem, which is common to left-wing economists as well as their right-wing cousins, is that, professionally speaking, they are all unacquainted with what the Greeks called *thymos*—spiritedness, anger, pride. They are of the view that no one wants to be boss and so they pretend that no one can be boss, even as they act in practice like the boss. This is why my former colleagues at the Fraser Institute universally believed that following the precepts and prescriptions of economics will make you better off. Historically the claim has been that economics will provide a substitute for virtue. Marxists think an increase in virtuousness will happen automatically after the more or less inevitable revolutions; free marketers say virtue does not matter, which is to say being better off is already to be better because prosperity provides choice and choice is good. When anti-market moralists insist that it matters *what* people choose they are echoing, usually quite faintly, a seventeenth-century debate that was won decisively by the economists.

Back then, the opponents to the economists argued on common-sense grounds that you should not have faith that good times will last. Not even an Alberta energy boom lasts forever. As Aesop's fable of the ant and the grasshopper teaches us, bad times show up, so that failing to expect the inevitable brings grief. The traditional, pre-economics argument was that it made sense to trust in virtue and what secures virtue more than in the chance and fortune of good and bad times. This is what the original argument was about.

The economists won in part because they discovered or rather invented the business cycle. Bad times were not inevitable provided the business cycle was properly managed. To do so, the state had to monitor the economy so as to know what was going on. As a result there has emerged a new tension or contradiction in modern political economy: what are the criteria by which we judge a government? It was central, for example, to the Canadian general election of 2006: do we judge government performance by whether we are better off (vote Liberal and ensure prosperity continues) or by whether our rights are protected (vote Conservative and ensure an end to Liberal thievery; and, oh yes, we Conservatives will ensure prosperity, too)?

The most pretentious claims are made by Keynesians (apart, of course, from those made by socialists, which are too silly to be taken seriously). They argue that appropriate intervention in the business cycle will ensure benefits forever. Keynesianism became the ruling orthodoxy in post-war Ottawa, but government interventions have had unanticipated consequences that have made the economy even less controllable. This does not mean that intervention has declined or that non-Keynesian or pre-Keynesian economics is the answer. If you rely on the market, you take what it gives you. The only guarantee it will improve your lot is the guarantee of a questionable economic theory that, in turn, is based upon assumptions concerning interests, on the one hand, and the substitution of liberty for virtue on the other. In other words, political science has reservations not with respect to Keynesianism but with respect to economics as such.

Constitutional government, I noted, combines pride and interest harmoniously. The origins of this form of government lay in the aftermath of the sixteenth-century wars of religion in Europe and the political settlement of the religious question. The lesson learned by European states conducting international and civil wars of religion half a millennium ago is that the state is not in the business of saving souls. The care of souls is, for modern constitutional regimes, the concern of private individuals in civil society. Sometimes people forget to care for the souls of others, or even for their own souls. On occasion they seek a substitute in caring for bodies, especially the bodies of the "least advantaged."

This was a problem from the beginning, with Thomas Hobbes who, followed by John Locke, may be considered the founder of modern constitutionalism. Hobbes's account of the privatization of religion was that it was necessary to avoid public religious partisanship that had been rendered uncontrollable because of the promise of posthumous rewards to angelic combatants. Hobbes was of the view that fighting over an invisible realm of perfection is both futile and senseless. He proposed in place of God a human sovereign whose chief purpose is to assure peace. The condition for both peace and human sovereignty is the abandonment of supernatural perfection. Hobbes's "reasonable" account of the state of nature, as distinct from the unreasonable dreams of divine revelation, which we now call "spirituality," was intended to provide the grounds for both liberalism and constitutionalism.

The essential feature of liberal constitutionalism is that governments are limited. By Hobbes's account, which was sugar-coated but not essentially altered by Locke, natural liberties or natural rights need to be protected by governments because, in nature, they are insecure. The state of nature is a state of war, said Hobbes, and life is famously "solitary, poor, nasty, brutish, and short." Insecure natural rights become secure civil or political rights because, the story goes, governments are

constituted for no other purpose. Once rights have become protected, or as the American constitution says, "secured," by
governments, governments limit themselves by respecting the
difference between securing and exercising rights. For example,
under a liberal constitution you have a right to seek housing
under fair terms but you do not have a right to fair housing.
Likewise the right to free speech cannot specify what is to be
said. In short, rights are formal, whether they are secured by
government against itself or against individuals.

The premise of a constitutional regime is thus that nature is
more important than nurture, culture, custom, background,
and history. Limited government assumes that human beings
can overcome deprivation with the equipment, as Aristotle
called it, that they have been given or at least born with. With
opportunities, individuals can succeed in overcoming their
own past. There is always the possibility of a "fresh start," unless
it is refused—but then who is to blame? One conclusion seems
inescapable: any regime based on rights, which is to say, any
constitutional regime, must be willing both to tolerate the free
exercise of rights and to be pleased with the result. This harmony of pride and interests is expressed, as we noted above, as
cherishing the regime.

The great danger to a regime of rights is not that the government will suppress them and turn into a tyranny but that it
will subvert them and turn rights into entitlements. An entitlement is something that is awarded by government even if
unneeded and without respect to cost. It is a challenge to the
liberal and constitutional understanding of rights because it
breaks down or bridges the crucial distinction between a right
that the government exists to protect and its exercise, which is

the task of individuals. To a degree—and the degrees will vary—an entitlement is a guaranteed right, a right the exercise of which is more or less assured by government and to that extent is exercised by government. For example, the right to look for a job is transformed by "Employment Insurance" to the right, if not to a job, then to the proceeds of somebody else's job—a taxpayer, for example. The role of the government is to transfer the money from the taxpayer to the person so "insured," acting thereby as a job-holder and creating dependence along with entitlement.

When the state acts instead of, and on behalf of, individuals, it creates dependency. Alan Cairns has called this regime the "embedded state" (see Chapter 4, below). Dependency is a disposition to depend on others, and especially on government, to secure one's own well-being. More than welfare dependency is involved: in the first place, the growth of dependency on government provision of entitlements is not confined to the poor or to notional Newfoundlanders on pogey. Subsidized farmers, servants of the Canadian Wheat Board, students who receive "loans" from government to attend university, and wealthy widows whose assets are sequestered in tax shelters are all turned into dependants because, even though they are capable of doing things for themselves, they expect the government to do it for them.

There is an additional and more restricted meaning as well. It refers to what taxpayers are expected to give government so that you, as a government official, are entitled to large expense accounts. You are entitled to spend taxpayers' money on partisan projects. You are entitled to reward your friends with government contracts. There is, in other words, no question of abuse and getting away with it. This is business as usual. In the rather unusual case of David Dingwall, he understood he was entitled to have taxpayers pick up his golf tab, his limo expenses (no taxis, please; we are Liberal VIPs), and a cool grand a month dedicated to his BMW 530 lease. This kind of entitlement sent Madame Clarkson on her extensive travels.

The result, as Cairns himself observed, is a people so fragmented they cannot see themselves as a whole because they need to spend all their efforts defending their entitlements against their erstwhile fellow citizens. Of course, the entire system of entitlements, dependency, and the embedded state is said to serve the interests of the alleged beneficiaries. But as noted above, by having another serve your interests you are deprived of any sense of pride in exercising your own rights. The ultimate effect is not just fragmentation but the fostering of a nation of losers and whiners. Weakness is celebrated by being the focus of public attention, and those who contribute to the income of the disadvantaged are neither acknowledged nor thanked. When they live in Alberta they are, furthermore, denounced as rednecks filled with greed. This is not a recipe for widely sought but ever-illusive national unity.

Cui bono? Who benefits from a culture and a regime of entitlements? The most obvious answer is this: those, especially in the ruling culture, who promote programs of entitlements. Certainly they benefit far more than the targeted beneficiaries, whom we call the alleged beneficiaries. The real beneficiaries, the program promoters, may be excused from the accusation that they are promoting dependency on the grounds that they know not what they do save for the fact that they also claim, usually, to be intellectuals or at least competent administrators whose programs are connected to ideas—of "social justice," for example. One way or another, they are presumed to know what they do—unlike politicians, who are said to be governed by expediency, and unlike the alleged beneficiaries of entitlements, who are presumed to be incapable of exercising their rights owing to their disadvantaged backgrounds. This explains why intellectuals are so willing and so proud to advocate for them and why administrators are so pleased to exercise their rights for them. Both sets of people assume that the alleged beneficiaries are incapable not just because of their disadvantages, but because they can never overcome them: once a slave, always a slave. Of course, the alleged benefactors are never so rude as to say that. They just act on the basis of what such a statement reveals.

Some of these insights were brought home to me at another conference, this one held at UBC in the fall of 2000. My friend Tom Flanagan had just published *First Nations, Second Thoughts*, a splendid and award-winning analysis of the great flowering of dependency and entitlements associated with Indians. There were Indians present, some of whom were lawyers as well. Alan Cairns, author of his own study of the Indian question, called *Citizens Plus*, was also there. The Indian lawyers and the lawyers for Indians were, like punks, uniformly angry. Cairns assured me this was normal on such occasions. One well-dressed and very attractive woman lawyer (the men took much less care with their grooming) was especially incensed at Flanagan's book.

"You wanna know what it's all about?" she said. "Well, I'll tell ya. This is what Flanagan says: 'We won. You lost. Get over it. Get a job.' I mean, it's that crude! God! Talk about insensitivity."

In the question-and-answer period I addressed the lawyer with the following question. "I don't wish to appear insensitive, as you claim Doctor Flanagan to be," I began. "And I must compliment you on your accurate and succinct review of his book. My question is: what exactly do you find wrong with his argument?" Cairns laughed, but the pretty lawyer did not. She accused me of being from Calgary.

There is a serious issue involved. No one has a stake in what they are given. Thus when the Russians gave tanks to Syria, they were soon enough out of commission because the Syrians never bothered to change the oil or even go to the trouble to learn how. By giving Syrians tanks, the Russians ensured both dependency and incompetence. That is the secret burden of Canadian aboriginal policy. As with affirmative action or employment equity, aboriginal policy is also a "regime question" because it reveals something about the Canadian federal government—Ottawa. All such policies are inherently underhanded because they cannot serve the purpose for which they are ostensibly designed unless that purpose is denied. That is, the point is to help those who are "disadvantaged" and so considered by those who can discern such matters to be incapable of helping themselves. But this can never be admitted. We want to help people—Indians, for example—because we think people are equal and so deserving of equal treatment under the law. Thus do we always begin with affirming the formality of equality. But if we actually do help them, we assume they are in fact unequal, at least insofar as they deserve special or unequal treatment. So, in order to help but not insult, you have to deny you help even while helping under the table.

Specifically with respect to Indians, instead of treating individuals as citizens, that is, people who can do things for themselves, they are treated as victims, as people who have had things done to them and who seek things from others. Indians deserve help because they are legally equal to Canadians, but they need it because they are not. The only consistent explanation of how this is possible is to accuse Canadian society as a whole of prejudice, racism, and possibly "cultural genocide." Of course, there are people prejudiced against Indians but they will not change their minds when they are called racists. And when those who are not racists are accused of being racists, what then? They are insulted. The insult is excused by being softened into an apparatus of racism, of "institutional racism" or, to use a less ugly and aggressive term, of "systemic discrimination."

This abstraction, namely systemic or institutional discrimination, carries with it the great advantage of never actually having to name anyone as a racist, which would provide an occasion to create clarity when the accused fought back. Maintaining ambiguity permits an appeal to a diffuse sense of guilt that resides in the hearts of most Canadians when they see poor and miserable fellow human beings suffer. But it is no way to show respect to, or coexist with, fellow citizens. Worst of all, it does nothing but perpetuate the grief and poverty it claims to wish to remove. It also falsifies what changes have taken place for the better, including education in residential schools, and effectively denies the genuine goodwill Canadians today have toward Indians. As a result one can expect, eventually, the climate of suspicion and accusation so long nurtured to bear fruit. Eventually, that is, most Canadians are likely to regard the whole business of aboriginal policy as a colossal waste of money and nothing else.

Special status has the additional consequence of encouraging irresponsibility by explaining that Indians have only the rest of the world to blame for their problems and never themselves. Even if it is true—and one must be naïve beyond measure to believe it—accusation is no way to fix things because it is always difficult to reform those whom you blame. Besides, why not do something yourself? Why not do so even in the face of Canadian opposition—if in fact it is there? Why expect lawyers to do it for you—especially pretty non-Indian lawyers hired with non-Indian taxpayers' money? Why, indeed, should Indians expect Canadians to change their attitudes when Indians are perfectly capable of changing their own attitudes and doing something on their own? It is both futile and insulting to everyone to expect Canadians to fix the problems of Indians.

Finally, such "help" by Canadians extended toward Indians encourages a patronizing and perhaps maternalistic attitude on their part toward Indians. If Canadians don't hold Indians to the same standards as other citizens, how can anyone ever expect them to perform well? Such an attitude obviously reinforces the notion of Indian inferiority and encourages them to see themselves as victims capable only of passivity and complaint. Making claims on Canadian society for all their suffering and need is to highlight nothing but inadequacy. If Indians want respect, it can be given only on the basis of what they have contributed as citizens to Canadian society and what they will contribute tomorrow. Whining about what was taken from them eventually invites contempt. Nor is much to be gained by exalting the sensitivity of Indian culture, its attachment to "the land," and all the other malarkey taught by Canadian cultural anthropologists to ensure they, too, have special subjects to study. If Indians need to live in the bush to protect their cultural experiences, that is well and good. But they should not expect, say, brain surgery, which is hardly part of Cree culture, to be available in Cumberland House. The greatest contribution Indians can, in fact, make is to remind Canadians that democracies can also commit injustice. But that does not mean they must dwell on nothing else. As the pretty lawyer said in summarizing Flanagan's book, but this time without irony: Get over it.

Indians may see special status, Cairns's notion of "citizens plus," as attractive. They may see the presence of him of the lofty title, Grand Chief Phil Fontaine, at a First Ministers' conference as evidence of their power. In fact, there is nothing shocking in any group using bureaucratic politics to advance their interests. But there is nothing edifying either. It may be justified but it can hardly be dignified. This is why it must also be said that many Canadians see it as a free ride for them paid for by somebody else—that is, having a grand chief at the table on somebody else's dime is also a measure of his dependency. It is said in response that having Indian leaders sit next to Canadian politicians is a good role model for young Indians, but ask yourself: Do we need more celebrity big shots who happen to be Indians? Is promoting such people as role models actually promoting their merits? Or rather, is the role they model simply to be patronized by real leaders? An honorific grand chief is fine and dandy, but we all know the real big chief is a premier or a prime minister. Why not an Indian premier? An Indian PM?

The long-term failure of Canadian aboriginal policy is but a symptom of a wider disorder. If you do not take responsibility to exercise your rights, whatever rights you may have do not result from having contributed to the country. Indeed, they flow not from your strengths and talents and abilities but from your weakness, your needs, and your disabilities. How then can you deserve your rights? And if they stem from weakness, how can you ever say anything—for who brags of their disabilities? And who listens to whining for long? In short, when rights are taken to be entitlements, they culminate in the right to feel dissatisfied. The joyless quest for joy, as Strauss called bourgeois liberalism, is recapitulated in the unhappiness that comes from defending what is indefensible: special status, not just for Indians, but for everyone. Because we are all special, we all must have prizes. Or, as a first minister from Atlantic Canada once said regarding transfer payments to his region: Justice demands that every province has a per capita income above the national average. He did not think he was making a joke.

For Aristotle, democracy meant ruling and being ruled in turns. This was the essence of citizenship because citizens share equally in the privileges and the responsibilities of the regime. In contrast, a regime that operates chiefly by rules and administration, which is to say, by bureaucrats, trains not active citizens but patient subjects. For Aristotle, justice meant treating equals equally and unequals unequally. Today justice means fairness, as John Rawls has proclaimed to the world, and has been echoed by the Supreme Court of Canada. And such fairness demands dependency on the state to allocate it right and left. It sustains an ethos not of equality and the desire to excel among your peers but an ethos of losers animated by anger and its sweet stepchild, resentment. There is politics here, but it is not great politics. It is seamy, slutty politics that teaches citizens to view cooperation as a zero-sum game and to regard the volunteer as a fool. To the degree we have become a nation of dependants, we must ask ourselves: Why survive? It cannot be out of pride, for no one can be proud of their dependency. The question is especially poignant where the myth of survival is central to regional identity—as is argued in the following chapter.

The regime matters in Canada because character matters. What the government does to deal with shootings on Yonge Street or at Jane and Finch, with pogey in New Brunswick, or with Indians in the Territories shapes the expectations and thus the character of citizens, and reciprocally the character of citizens shapes the expectations of what governments can do, or at least do legitimately. That is why the nature of the regime in this country matters and why we must look at character as much as at the Constitution. The short answer to the question of why the regime change begun by Paul Martin and Stephen Harper matters is that their character is unlike that of those who preceded them in office over the past quarter century.

CHAPTER TWO

MYTHS OF DISUNITY

"Nations do not make myths. Myths make nations."
—F.W.J. SCHELLING

*"Ontario is the heart of Canada ... no group identifies more
closely with Canada than Ontarians."*
—DALTON MCGUINTY, PRIME MINISTER OF ONTARIO

The 1993 national elections brought into focus for the first time since the 1920s the connection between regional identity and the representativeness of the party system. During the 1920s, the combination of the farmers' parties, the Progressives, and the Maritime Rights movement put considerable strain on the customary "brokerage" role of political parties in Canada. Instead of trading off regional and other interests within the government, these interests, fortified by ideological visions, clashed openly across the floor in the House of Commons. In some respects, the twenties were the golden age of regional protest parties. Notwithstanding this challenge to traditional party government, the Liberal Party of Canada under Prime Minister Mackenzie King was able to swallow and digest or perhaps merely eclipse and suppress regionalism. As a consequence of this adroitness, King transformed the Liberal Party of Canada into what Reg Whittaker was the first to call the Government Party. The 1993 eclipse of the Progressive Conservatives and the replacement of the two constituent elements of that party by the western-based Reform Party of Canada and the nationalist Bloc Québécois provided Prime Minister Chrétien with a problem and an opportunity not dissimilar to that faced by King during the 1920s and 1930s.

Changes in the political economy of the West and in the structure of federalism over the past several decades made Chrétien's task more difficult than King's. In the event, Chrétien's aggressive personality and the traditions of Quebec politics in which he was schooled resulted in dissatisfactions similar to those that followed on the government of Brian Mulroney in 1993. Dissatisfaction with Mulroney's style, as well as with some of his policies, and mistakes made during the campaign account for the 1993 defections of many voters who had previously supported the Conservatives. At the same time, it was not preordained that the beneficiaries during the 1990s would chiefly be the regional parties. There could have been a Liberal resurgence in the West and Quebec, but there wasn't. The Liberals, too, are or were a regional party, the region being concentrated in Ontario, but the "regionalism" of Ontario is peculiar insofar as it is expressed as a (pseudo) pan-Canadian myth.

Ever since the celebrated 1969 essay of J.M.S. Careless in the *Canadian Historical Review*, Canada has been described as a nation of "limited identities." Limited identities are expressed in regional myths. I argued in the previous chapter that a regime is more than the formal, external, or elemental institutions of governance and law. It includes purpose and meaning, which necessarily are symbolized and expressed in rituals, stories, and myths. In this way what begins as policy and the subject of ordinary history—CPR freight rates, for example—ends as myth: for my grandfather and his sons, the CPR could do nothing right. Or, as Northrop Frye once said, history aims at telling what happened and myth tells what happens all the time. Sometimes this stable, more or less taken-for-granted, everyday, typical context is called "political culture." Political cultures, like myths, are often distinct and occasionally opposed to one another. As David Elkins put it, with respect to "British Columbia as a State of Mind," political cultures differ in "the range of actions deemed appropriate, possible, plausible, or decent."

Difference with respect to what is decent, however, can quickly become opposition to indecency. The reason is not moral but is inherent in the polarizing character of political myth. Myths are stories that tell us who we are, where we have come from, and to what we are called. It divides people into "us" and "them" by creating a group self-understanding or "identity." Those that are remembered across the generations are effective; those that fade into oblivion are not. Almost always, effective myths involve struggle, *agon* as the Greeks would say.

Political myths are pre-eminently expressed in imaginative literature. As po-mo critics would say, literature is "privileged." In English-speaking Canada, discussion of Canadian literature began in Queen Victoria's time. Most of it dealt with the low profile good literature had in the general life of the nation. As with most "progressivist" interpretations, the assumption was that literature (and the other arts) will come... later. Later, when the railway is funded. Later, when the prairies are settled. Later, when CBC Radio is established from sea to sea. Later, when CBC-TV is established from sea to sea to sea. Later, when the Canada Council supports writers properly. Later, when American culture is banished. The excuses may vary, but culture is always postponed until the times are more propitious. But the times never seem propitious.

This view of culture is itself an attribute of Canadian culture. It is also drivel. Take the least economically advanced, which is to say the least rich, people on earth—Inuit, pygmies, Mongolians, Trobrand Islanders: have they no culture? The answer is found in the demand for Cape Dorset sculptures.

To understand political culture in Canada, we begin with the annual commentaries made for many years by Northrop Frye in the pages of *The University of Toronto Quarterly*. These essays provide a comprehensive discussion of the cultural question in Canada. There are two reasons to begin this way: first, he is the best we've got; but second, he got it brilliantly wrong.

"Culture," he said, "is born in leisure and an awareness of standards," but pioneer conditions make leisure rare, the memory of which lingers long after pioneer conditions have vanished. This is why Canada has produced no Shakespeare or Goethe, which is not a bad thing, at least not for our present purposes. Consider a hockey analogy. One-timing a sharp pass from the slot into the five-hole is not easy. You can see how tough it is by watching the Brandon Wheat Kings try to pull it off. Watching the Canucks or the Oilers make it look easy is misleading. Likewise, the absence of great Canadian literature makes it easier to see what great literature tries to be, which

Frye said, is to draw us toward the centre of literary experience. With the less-than-great-literature of Canada, we remain aware of the author's social and historical setting. That is, CanLit tells us about Canadian life; it gives an undistorted voice to our imaginative experience.

Culture has political implications in Canada because, high or low, it is an expression of identity. For foreigners who have never been concerned with identity because it is so self-evident, Canadian concerns seem artificial, self-pitying, and self-indulgent. "But," Frye went on, "it is with human beings as with birds: the creative instinct has a great deal to do with the assertion of territorial rights." Culture, he said, is "vegetable" because it grows from roots; it doesn't move around like a cat but stays put like a carrot. Thus, the question of "Canadian identity" or of "Canadian culture" is not, properly speaking, a *Canadian* question at all, but a local, and at most a regional, one. So Frye asked the obvious question: What can there be in common between an imagination nurtured on the prairies and one nurtured on the urban plains of southern Ontario or the tree-shrouded valleys of southeastern British Columbia? Let there be no misunderstanding; the answer to Frye's rhetorical question is "None."

Chief among the questions that culture does answer is "Where is here?" To which may be added the divisive derivative one noted above, "Who are we?" The short answer is this: *we* are those who know where here is; *they* don't know because they are not from here but "from away" (as they say in Newfoundland). The "knowledge" of we and they, of here and away, and of all the subsidiary things that are implied by this strange knowing comes not from an awareness of facts but from a story, a myth in the very old sense of that term. To put the point abruptly, when someone says, "I am a westerner," or "I am a Newfoundlander" he or she means *something*. Often literate Canadians—Noah Richler in *This Is My Country, What's Yours?* (2006), for instance—find regional identity puzzling. After playing with the conceit of being from Nowhere in a conversation with artist Lee Henderson, Richler said, "Another way to put it would be to ask you where you think you are from." Henderson replied: "I'm from western Canada. I'm definitely from western Canada." Richler ended the paragraph right there, struck dumb. He had nothing further to say.

But we cannot leave it there. Henderson's remarks require interpretation. He was making an imaginative or metaphorical identification of place and meaning. He was answering the question "Where is (my) here?" To understand Canadian regionalism properly one must take into account not only voting data and economic interests but also literary texts and speeches that express regional imaginative consciousness. Or, as I said in the last chapter, our pride in being a Newfoundlander or an Albertan. Only in such words can one find questions of meaning presented. In short, the significance, purpose, or meaning of regimes, therefore, is expressed in stories—from informal stories passed on from the elderly to the young to official stories enunciated by the great newsmakers of the day. In between are the stories of poets and novelists, journalists and historians. This is why myths of regional identity, of regional pride, count.

When one reads this literature and the interpretation that critics have made of it, one discovers several important things. First of all, there isn't much of it. It is possible to read a very large percentage of Canadian literature and every scrap of CanLitCrit with a comparatively small investment of time. If literature does indeed reflect to the reader a discourse on identity, then the size of the corpus of Canadian literature and its relative neglect suggest that Canadians have not wanted to find out who they were or where is here.

What, then, is to be said of the other famous Canadian problem, national unity? According to Frye, "Unity is national in reference, international in perspective, and rooted in a political feeling." The distinction between regional identity and national unity speaks to the heart of the Canadian regime. For Frye, national unity is found in "the east-west feeling... expressed in the national motto, *a mari usque ad mare*." If the tension between unity and identity dissolves into its poles, the result is either "the empty gestures of cultural nationalism" or "the kind of provincial isolation which is now called separatism." The east-west feeling, he said, has developed historically along the axis of the St. Lawrence drainage basin. The provincial isolation called separatism referred to Quebec. Suitably qualified, Frye's observation undoubtedly applies to western regionalism, political culture, and myth.

The devil is in the qualifications. First, it should be emphasized that the tension between cultural identity and national unity is not just unresolved for the time being, but is incapable of resolution. Second, the "east-west feeling" is not necessarily a positive one. Consider, for example, the motto of Canada quoted by Frye: *a mari usque ad mare*. This is taken from the Vulgate translation of Psalm 72:8: "He shall have dominion also from sea to sea and from the river unto the ends of the earth." Hence the name, Dominion of Canada, stretching from the "river" of the St. Lawrence unto the "ends of the earth," which can refer only to the land north and west of the river. It would be news, insulting news, to the inhabitants of these parts that they lived at the ends of the earth. Third, unity is not only distinct from uniformity but is opposed to it. Political unity rejoices in dissent and in variety of outlook, tradition, and myth.

In part, Frye's understanding of Canadian unity is expressed in the celebration of linguistic duality, and clearly the symbolism can include Albertans and Newfoundlanders, who are overwhelmingly English-speaking. At the same time, however, the symbol of bilingualism expresses most perfectly an important aspect only of the old colony of Canada, Upper and Lower Canada, Canada East and Canada West, the Canada of the St. Lawrence valley, not the entire country. To distinguish the identity of Canadians living in what was the old colony of Canada from the identities of other Canadians, I propose to employ the venerable term *Laurentian*. As is indicated below, it refers not just to the approach to Canadian history celebrated by the great Ontario historians of the mid-twentieth century, Harold Innis, Donald Creighton, and A.R.M. Lower, but to an important regional myth.

Frye emphasized clearly the distinction to be drawn between unity and uniformity; for westerners such as I, the connection between national unity and decentralization is self-evident. Consider this charming political anecdote told by Patrick Martin, Alan Gregg, and George Perlin in *Contenders: The Tory Quest for Power* (1983). On March 25, 1983, Joe Clark, of High River, Alberta, described William Davis, of Brampton, Ontario, as a "regional candidate" for the leadership of the Conservative Party, which leadership Clark eventually won. On

June 7, four days before the leadership convention, Premier Davis hosted a dinner at a Toronto club, the Albany, for 150 people who had helped in his bid. In his remarks to his supporters that night, he commented on Clark's statement, which had been festering in his mind for the ten weeks since Clark had uttered it. "I am not a regional candidate," Davis said. "I believe in Canada, not a community of communities," a term that Clark had borrowed from Frye and had used to describe his understanding of Canadians' limited identities. As one observer noted, "Davis's eyes filled with tears as he spoke of his commitment and his audience was visibly moved." The image of a weeping Ontario premier, and of the hearts of his adamantine political supporters at the Albany Club swelling with patriotic pride, is an index of the power that comes from the identification of a genuine but limited "Canadian" identity with the non-existent, but evocative, pan-Canadian alias. A westerner would be puzzled or amused by all the emotion or just write it off as Toronto-centric parochialism, like Noah Richler's silence, unable to confront a genuine challenge to its own self-understanding. No westerner, not even the accommodating Mr. Clark, could have taken Premier Davis's words at face value.

The difference between Davis's Laurentian and Clark's western image of Canada can be brought out theoretically by considering the limited applicability of what Frye regarded as the "essential element" of unity, the "east-west feeling." In *Divisions on a Ground*, a 1982 collection of his writings on culture, Frye wrote:

In Canada there is a single gigantic east-west thrust down the St. Lawrence, up the Great Lakes, and across the prairies, then through whatever holes a surveyor could find in the Rockies to the west coast.... One enters Canada through the Strait of Belle Isle into the Gulf of St. Lawrence, where five Canadian provinces surround us, with enormous islands and glimpses of a mysterious mainland in the distance, but in the foreground only sea and sky. Then we go down the waterway of the St. Lawrence, which in itself is only the end of a chain of rivers and lakes that starts in the Rockies. The United States confronts the European visitor: Canada surrounds and engulfs him, or did until the coming of the airplane.

Notice the omissions. First, the Maritimes, and especially Halifax and the neutral Yankees of Nova Scotia, its history stretching south to "the Boston states" and beyond, to the Caribbean and east to Europe, are eclipsed. Second, the history of the West prior to the history of Canada's interest in the West is symbolically non-existent; the Hudson's Bay Company was not named after the St. Lawrence River. Third, the desire of westerners in the twentieth century, prior to the Free Trade Agreement, for a north-south connection as well as an east-west one is ignored, as is the mere fact of the many flights across the Pacific in more recent years. Vancouver is an international Pacific Rim city as remote from Laurentian experience as Seattle or Valparaiso.

Frye gave compound expression to error in his conclusion a few years before to the first edition of the *Literary History of Canada,* by introducing the notion of the *Canadian* imagination, characterized, he said, by "what we may provisionally call a garrison mentality." The earliest maps showed only real forts, and later cultural maps showed only imaginary ones. The garrison of a fort is a closely knit, because beleaguered, society, held intact by unquestionable morals and authority. Motives count for nothing. One is either a fighter or a deserter. As Margaret Atwood, one of Frye's most gifted pupils, put it: "The central symbol for Canada—and this is based on numerous instances of its occurrence in both English and French Canadian literature—is undoubtedly Survival, *la Survivance*." The point of garrison life is to survive. Garrisons are also sites of military and administrative rule.

The problem with Frye's (and Atwood's) interpretation is that it is impossible to maintain *both* that identity is regional, local, and imaginative, *and* that there is a Canadian identity expressed imaginatively in a Canadian literature. If one holds to the first insight, the survival of the garrison, which is by all arguments the symbolization of an identity of some kind, becomes an expression of a national identity. But there is no national identity: there is no Laurentian feeling in British Columbia; the dim memories of such a feeling on the prairies, which owed their existence to the rule of the Hudson's Bay Company, became, under the impact of the National Policy of Sir John A. Macdonald, mostly hostile as I learned unambiguously as a kid. Janice Kulyk Keefer, who has examined in great detail the self-understanding of Maritimers, called Frye's Laurentian understanding of Canada a "demotion" of the Maritimes and of its own interpretation of itself. In fact, it is an insult to Maritimers, all the more significant for being accidental. Likewise the imagery, myth, and symbols of Newfoundland are different again from the Maritimes and the notion of "Atlantic Canada" is nothing but a term of administrative convenience invented by the Ottawa bureaucrats after Newfoundland was lured into Canada. Imaginatively, "Atlantic Canada" is non-existent.

Recall Frye's imagery: Canada has no Atlantic seaboard; arrival in Laurentian Canada is a recapitulation of the story of Jonah being swallowed by the whale. For the people who actually inhabit Newfoundland and Maritime Canada, such images simply do not express the reality of their experience. Not only does the country have an Atlantic seaboard, but the experiences native to it constitute, to use the title of Archibald MacMechan's early study, the "headwaters of Canadian literature," where the adjective refers to a political not an imaginative category—rather akin to "post-colonial" in this respect.

Frye's Laurentian imagery implied that, because a search for imaginative Canada could never start with the Maritimes, what one found there (if anything) was unlikely to be "Canadian," in the Laurentian mythic sense. If the Maritimes were, in one way or another, to be swallowed by the Laurentian/Canadian whale, that happy event would signal the region had at long last become imaginatively "Canadian." Maritimers (and Newfoundlanders) see things rather differently. Their parochialism is a defence against imaginative "Canada," to say nothing of the West. According to Keefer, the "historical type" native to the Maritimes is "that of the pawn or born loser." If so, such a literary figure is the appropriate expression of historical experience: the exiling of the Acadians, the reception of exiles from the Thirteen Colonies and from the Scottish Highlands. Even if one traces the social patterns of twentieth-century Maritime experience to an otherwise admirable and genteel eighteenth-century conservatism, the fact remains that stagnation and decadence remain the most prominent features of pre-modern communal life to have survived into the present. Maritimers are not the only losers, however.

Laurentian Canadians are even bigger losers, but as was Frye, they are loath to admit it. Consider: Frye made a useful distinction between unity and identity, which he then promptly surrendered with his evocation of a national identity expressed in a national literature that makes articulate the garrison mentality. Dennis Duffy, another literary critic, explained why. In his 1982 study of the literature of Upper Canada and Ontario, *Gardens, Covenants and Exiles,* Duffy declared that although he set out to write "another CanLit theme book," the works he considered made imaginatively articulate not Canada and not even the contemporary political unit of Ontario, but the heartland of Upper Canadian Loyalism, the wedge of land between the Ottawa River and Lake Huron. In that place the myth of exile (from the American colonies), covenant (loyalty to the Crown), and return to a garden (the transformed wilderness) fully expressed the regional identity of an imaginative "Canada." To be more precise: "Canada," understood as a symbol of identity and not as a political body, is centred in the Loyalist heartland, is full of garrisons anxious about survival, and is indeed moved by warm feelings of a meaningful east-west axis, which, thanks to a benevolent God or to history, they happily and quite properly control. This "Canada," which is imaginatively real, is, however, imaginatively unconnected with even the Loyalist Maritimes, as Duffy pointed out. It is even less connected with the West.

By confusing Canada, the imaginative reality centred in the Loyalist heartland, with Canada the political reality, imaginative "Canada" betrayed its own regional identity and destroyed the possibility of an alternative political reality that might have grown from other and non-garrison experiences. This is what Joe Clark sensed in his identification of Bill Davis with Ontario regionalism. Historically this is why the inhabitants of the Red River Settlement did not greet the representatives of Canadian administrative rule as the bringers of light, culture, and civilization, which was how the newcomers understood themselves. The story of this cultural conflict, which is the foundation myth of the West, has been played out time and again. Recall, differences in culture and in identity and their eventual opposition are what myths express. They are not lies but stories that evoke and shape the meaning of individual and of collective lives.

To employ Frye's terminology consistently: there is, indeed, a "Canadian identity," and it is located in Ontario. The political unit, Canada, of course embraces the Loyalist heartland but a lot more as well. Just as there is no pan-Canadian identity, neither is there a pan-Canadian culture. This is not to say that believers in "Canadian identity" and "Canadian culture," in the precise (and restricted) sense of the identity and culture of the Loyalist heartland, do not mistake themselves for bearers of a pan-Canadian, sea-to-sea equivalent. They makes this mistake all the time, just as Frye promised and as the epigraph to this chapter from Ontario premier McGuinty illustrated.

In contrast, national unity is a matter of will: the many become one when confronting an external and threatening other. Historically, this condition has arisen spontaneously under the circumstances of war, but never in post-Confederation Canada. Wartime conscription crises were crises, not occasions for national unity. Today support for the Afghanistan mission varies across the country and is notably low in pacifist Quebec. Nor has the threat of the United States' economic control, which, if it is a danger at all, falls far short of war, caused a unity of will in response. Nor, it hardly needs to be said, has unemployment, inflation, or any other element of fortune or of domestic incompetence created national unity; nor have public policies such as medicare or multiculturalism. The reason is obvious: no country is made by the services it consumes, but by sacrifice, by having done great things together, as has been said. The greatest of things citizens can do together, we argued in the previous chapter, is fight for what makes them citizens. That is something Canadians have never done, however bravely they have fought as junior partners in honourable coalitions. In short, only in the presence of a real enemy can such a thing as *la nation une et indivisible* exist. But Canada, the peaceable kingdom, has never experienced the requisite enemy.

Why, then, the persistent calls for national unity? One explanation identifies the will to unity with the national interest. This sentiment is expressed, with nauseating regularity, by whining phrases such as "If only Canada were united, then...." Then all things would be possible. The century would be ours. And so forth. But this, too, is drivel. Remember: genuine Canadian garrison identity is confined to the Loyalist heartland of Ontario, and Loyalism was forged by two crucial historical experiences: by the successful rebellion of the Thirteen Colonies and the consequences, the foundation of the United States and the expulsion of the Loyalists. The second crucial event was the War of 1812. That war experience confirmed the covenant made with the royal authority. Canada survived, a genuine garrison facing a genuine enemy, united in fact, until 1837; united still in the imaginative aspiration of old Ontario. This is the reason that so much current "Canadian nationalism" is a questionable combination of anti-American sentiments and Ontario-first policies.

Other analysts of a non-existent Canadian identity have evoked notions of self-doubt or disappointment. For them the fate of John Franklin, who perished of starvation while failing to find the Northwest Passage in 1847, expresses nobility, like the moral superiority of the Loyalists looking down their very long noses at the Yankee rabble. In fact, it is just a loser's myth. A refusal to participate in the loser's myth is, in the end, why the tear in the eye of Bill Davis at the Albany Club looks so kitschy to westerners.

The story of a French linguistic, cultural, ethnic, historical, or religious garrison can be accommodated by the Laurentian myth as easily as a Loyalist one. The foundation myth of nationalist Quebec, which can be, politically speaking, either sovereignist or federalist, took on recognizable form in the wake of Lord Durham's famous *Report* (1839). Durham shocked a generation of French-Canadian political and intellectual leaders by pointing out the inherent bad faith of being themselves urban and educated liberals, liberals of the Enlightenment, but who then appealed to the non-liberal sentiments and emotions of their rural and ignorant Church-bound, pre-Enlightenment supporters. It was bad enough of Durham to expose the intellectual swindle of the *Patriotes*. Far worse was his patient explanation that the obvious solution to this ongoing political problem was more, not less liberalization. The first major response came in 1840 when François-Xavier Garneau published

Louise: Une légende canadienne; five years later his *Histoire du Canada* began to appear. The *Histoire,* in particular, set the pattern for nearly all subsequent French-Canadian historiography and inspired a school of patriotic poetry and the plot lines of innumerable third-rate historical novels. It was a simple story: the malicious English sought to suppress the virtuous French, and yet goodness survived among the French, and endured, and one day would triumph. The key to survival was to cling to tradition, to change nothing, and to resist the temptation of "English" liberalism. Liberalism was a temptation because, as Durham said, it promised prosperity.

The formular novels of the mid-nineteenth century disclosed a variation on the following story: a young French-Canadian man abandons the farm, lured by an urban *anglaise* temptress. In the city he is degraded: he learns to swear, drink, smoke, and brawl but is saved by a virtuous French-Canadian girl who brings him back to the rural paradise, saves his soul, and, by raising a family, ensures continued survival. The most famous variation on this theme (slightly altered in detail) was Abbé Groulx's *L'appel de la race* (1922). Groulx is conventionally identified as the spiritual patron of later Quebec nationalism.

A generation after Groulx, the contrast between the corrupt but rich urban English and the virtuous but poor rural French had turned into the contrast between rich corruption and poor virtuousness *within* the city. If it was not God's will that only the rural poor were virtuous, then another explanation had to be sought. Sociologically inclined historians explained the relative poverty of French Canadians in 1950 by way of the conquest of New France nearly 200 years earlier. The logic was simple: the English are a majority in Canada and majorities rule in their own interest, which meant suppressing the French for two centuries. The logic of Groulx and Garneau overwhelmed the need to examine evidence contrary to the thesis. Indeed, historical facts, if chosen with sufficient care, could easily confirm it.

By the 1960s and with the decline of the Church, which had its own sociological and historical causes, the Quiet Revolution proclaimed the triumph of pluralism, secularism, materialism—in short, the rather mixed ethical bag that constitutes liberal democratic political life in industrial and technological societies. Birth control, along with sexual permissiveness, small families, and easy divorce ended the Catholic vision of life as something widely supported and believed in in Quebec. No longer was the expression *maudits anglais*, damned English, to be taken literally, but the villain remained. Borrowing from the revolutionary fantasies of Sartre and Fanon, the doctrine of decolonization explained why it was righteous to feel, not morally superior to the English, but angry at them. The duty of the French Canadian (or Quebecker, as was increasingly the preferred self-definition) was to rebel, with violence, against the hated pseudo-masters, the English. These were the days when Pierre Vallières' *Nègres blanc d'Amérique* was an expressive text. By the mid-1960s, the conventional dogma of the terrorist Front de Libération du Québec, the FLQ, and of their supporters was expressed with great conviction in pamphlets and books; in public debates, poetry, plays, and demonstrations; in TV specials; and, on occasion, by direct action.

Revolutionary consciousness turned out to be as stupid in Quebec as in France and the result was merely bombs, murder, and the comedy of public posturing. Anglophobia and writing

in *joual* were considered political acts. The story of de Gaulle's
"*Vive le Québec libre*"—or rather, "*Vive le Québec L-I-I-I-I-B-R-E*"—
speech, the conflicts between Prime Minister Trudeau and
Premier Lévesque, the FLQ crisis, and the subsequent constitu-
tional gavotte, were the fallout, now all familiar tropes in
Canadian history.

The mythic element in Quebec nationalism, however, is
often overlooked. As with all such spiritual realities, it is sustained by a series of ancillary sacred symbols by which the
ordinary, commonsensical, and pragmatic political world is
joined to a greater source of meaning, the sacred community of
Quebeckers, beyond which lay only mundane but hostile powers. As Mordecai Richler observed with his usual and mordant
good humour, when the streets of Montreal were filled with
crowds on St. Jean Baptiste day, the *fête nationale*, heartily
chanting "*Le Québéc aux Québécois*," they did not have in mind
men and women by the name of McGregor or Cohen, Ng or
Manfredi. In the same spirit, when the sovereignist Quebec
Party lost the first independence referendum, Premier René
Lévesque (like the Loyalists) declared a moral victory because
the real Quebeckers, the one true church, had supported independence; his successor, Jacques Parizeau, who led the Quebec
Party to a second referendum defeat, this time by a much
smaller margin, again claimed a moral victory and darkly and
explicitly blamed "money and ethnics" for the loss. Indeed,
Premier Parizeau's evocation of the "true" sacramental community is palpable even in translation. "Okay," he said,

> if you like, let's stop talking about the francophones of
> Quebec. We'll talk about us. At 60 percent we voted

for it.... Don't ever forget that the three-fifths of what
we are have voted "Yes." It wasn't quite enough, but
soon, it will be. This country is ours. Soon we shall
have it.

Those who are not "us" must be "them." In nationalist symbolism, "they" are "English Canada," including the "ethnics,"
the only attribute of which is to be other than "us."

The problem, of course, is that Quebec will *not* vote for
independence even though the state in Quebec has taken upon
itself rights and obligations unknown to other provinces.
Moreover, the talk by political leaders concerning the status of
Quebec or of Quebeckers as a nation, inside Canada or not,
and of whether nation and *la nation* translate one another
(they do; Eugene Forsey used to quote General de Gaulle on
this question) is as conceptually vague as the remark made by
Gilles Duceppe in response to Prime Minister Harper's
announcement that Quebeckers were a nation within Canada:
"We are what we are." This is rhetoric of which Popeye would
be proud: "I yam what I yam." More seriously, if Duceppe had
a greater sense of history and of law, he would have seen in
Harper's motion a statement akin to that of Chief Justice John
Marshall of the U.S. Supreme Court in his 1831 judgment in
Cherokee Nation vs. Georgia. The nation, Quebec, like the
Cherokee nation, "is not a foreign state in the sense of the constitution" but a "domestic dependent nation" that is in "a state
of pupilage." The lineaments of dependency in Canada today
are not military, as they were with the Cherokee, but economic,
as is the pupilage of contemporary Quebec.

A final symbolic dimension, beyond the evocation of the

spiritual community and its differentiation into the children of light and the children of darkness, is an apocalyptic vision that provides an intelligible account of past events, an understanding of the current crisis, the promise of future resolution, and the relief of an eventual arrival. It does so, moreover, from the perspective of a participant in the field of spiritual conflict and political struggle. On all sides of any serious discussions of Quebec nationalism can be found an enthusiastic embrace of an intramundane religious sensibility. On the one hand, the transition from the French-and-Roman Catholic myth of Abbé Groulx to a modern secular, indeed a queer and po-mo, myth has been completed. This makes Pierre Trudeau one of the last political intellectuals for whom the old nationalist myth, the old political religion of Abbé Groulx, was significant enough to be worthy of his opposition. The current discussion, between federalists and sovereignists, occurs within a much diminished experiential context.

The only question worthy of attention nowadays seems to be whether the Quebec nation is more perfectly actualized within Canada or independently. Lucien Bouchard expressed the limited spiritual horizon when he observed that "even the Quebec federalists are nationalists." Whereas the sovereignist nationalists seek political independence from Canada as the solution to present difficulties and justify their aspirations with a myth of an ethno-nationalist garrison, the federalist nationalists find hope for the future in "renewed federalism" of some sort and justify their aspirations with a garrison myth of their own: two founding peoples or perhaps nations must hang together so as not to hang alone.

The two-founding-peoples myth (or the two-or-more version of John Ralston Saul) supplies the federalist nationalists with their own account of a contractual basis to the political nation. Its great flaw, as many people have pointed out, is that it conflicts abruptly with the premises of liberalism and the formality of legal equality. A federalist nationalist, such as Charles Taylor, arguably the most internationally acclaimed public intellectual in the history of Quebec, for example, is compelled to distinguish between "deep" diversity and "thick" cultures and what can only be called "shallow" diversity and "thin" cultures. To his credit, Taylor senses that this distinction is insulting to those endowed with shallow and thin cultural distinctiveness. On the sovereignist nationalist side there are fewer hesitations and greater reliance on abstract accounts of the course of history. Fernand Dumont's *Genèse de la société québécoise* (1993), for example, reads like a secular Hegelian historical theology "proving" that the perfection of Quebec society is the Quebec state. Unfortunately, nothing has changed. Dumont's myth is still a loser's story, like that of the Loyalists.

The great constitutional squabbles of the 1980s and 1990s, which fatally undermined the credibility of the myth of the two founding nations, also undermined Dumont. One thing for sure: a sense of nationhood cannot be conferred by the Government of Canada, as the Harper government has tried to do. It must be earned, by blood, sweat, and tears, not simply by high wages, whining, transfer payments, or subsidies to Bombardier. I say, give me an honest, manly separatist any day of the week to these smarmy confidence men! The problem is, there are none to be found. This is why Jacques Parizeau planned to declare independence quickly had the sovereignists won the 1995 referendum. He knew perfectly well what he never could admit: the entire confidence game could not withstand rational scrutiny. The same is true on the other side: the honeyed words of the federalist nationalists lead not to a pluralistic and peaceful state ordered by the moderate virtues of civic constitutionalism and procedural liberalism, but the creation of a new mystical body politic where individuals become constituent elements of an organic suprapersonal whole that the rest of us will be duty-bound to despise and reject, as we did with Meech Lake.

In contrast to the decadent anguish of Quebec's myth of *la survivance* and the increasingly parochial garrison myth of the Loyalist heartland lies the other major mythic evocation, the West. Literary critics have nearly all emphasized the importance of the landscape and of its impact on the mind of western explorers, fur traders, and settlers. A few have noted explicitly that the garrison mentality is not prominent in western fiction. Notwithstanding the actual existence of Hudson's Bay Company forts and caragana palisades around prairie homesteads, the West is not a transplanted imaginative Ontario garrison.

The prairie landscape extends spatially, as one critic said, "from the dryland to the Promised Land," that is, from Manitoba and Saskatchewan to Alberta. Imaginatively, Alberta is the quintessential West, the far West—and as the signs at the edge of town proclaim, Calgary is the heart of the new West. In this context, British Columbia, as Edward McCourt said in his classic study, *The Canadian West in Fiction* (1949), is the "near East." In fact, the mythology of British Columbia is more complex than that, but the point I wish to make is that there are alternative identities west (and east) of the Laurentian centre.

For our purposes, changes over time are more important

than changes over space. The historical dimension of western identity consists in variations in the response of European groups and individuals to a non-European landscape. The new land did not have an impact on an empty head but on a conscious one filled with old words such as meadow, red deer, and snow that proved inadequate to the reality experienced. Only recently have cultural geographers and historians devoted much attention to the problem of how the western landscape was articulated by the pre-settlement explorers. After the early explorers, who were more interested in markets than landscape anyhow, descriptions turned technical or fictional. From the start, the West has felt the impact of the most advanced contemporary technologies. Moreover, unlike the technologies of Laurentian Canada, western ones were concerned directly with resource extraction, not industrial manufacturing. At the same time, however, they were subordinated to central Canadian administrative control. Consider the prairie town. The "hugeness of simple forms" that Wallace Stegner described congealed in towns into the mass production of identical elevators, banks, and railway stations, a main street called Main Street, and a dirt road beside the tracks called Railway Avenue. It was as if the CPR had one blueprint and people had to fit it. Even so, western identity, such as it is, has been made articulate by imaginative writers who found meaning, not its absence.

The earlier settlers and the earliest writers clung to the "inappropriate" cultural forms they left behind. Instead of the lived reality of the frontier experience, the literary imagination tended to see the West as part of an imperial civilization whose most idyllic fictional characters, the policeman, the preacher, and the teacher, were its agents. When, during the 1920s, the "realistic" novels of F.P. Grove or Sinclair Ross began to dis-place the romantic pastoral adventures of an earlier day, a new awareness of western experience had achieved articulate form. The chaste, sunlit, and superficial garden myth was rejected along with the spirit of empire. Constriction and isolation, the dark effects of conquering rather than cultivating the land, became major themes of western literature. The closest the West ever came to creating a garrison mentality was probably in a Depression-era novel such as Ross's *As for Me and My House* (1941). And even with this splendid book two things ought to be recalled. First, when it was published it sold only a few hundred copies; and second, those who certified it as a "prairie classic" were critics for whom garrison literature was most familiar, which is to say, Laurentian Canadians. Certification was as much a political as an artistic judgment.

Contemporary western literature, W.O. Mitchell, Robert Kroetsch, W.P. Kinsella, Jack Hodgins, Aritha van Herk, or Guy Vanderhaeghe, for example, offers less a rejection of sentimental romance, as did Ross and Grove, than a self-conscious new begin-ning. The possibility of beginning anew is what brought people west; it still does. The habit of new beginnings is part of western consciousness, and as many critics have argued, comedy is the appropriate expression of such an experience. The same can be said even of Margaret Laurence, whose great novels are almost never considered to be western, and the rich array of B.C. writers who are hardly known beyond the provincial borders. Even the mundane experience of homesteading and the elevation of the necessity of frontier independence to a virtue was tempered by the contrary necessity of cooperation. The contradiction of sturdy independence with the need to cooperate can be reconciled only through comedy. Just think of cowboy poetry.

We need not be diverted by the charms of literary theory to make the following modest conclusions regarding western self-understanding: (1) the West has not been part of imaginative "Canada"; (2) there is scant evidence of a garrison mentality; (3) survival is not the dominant theme save under extreme and adverse conditions; and (4) it soon enough gives way to the spirit of new beginnings.

Sometimes the different visions of the country are connected to conflicting interests. A few years ago Saskatchewan premier Allan Blakeney told a surprised audience at the Canadian Club in Toronto that the only natural resources extensively regulated by the federal government were those that were western staples: oil, gas, uranium, and wheat.

> We in the West find it passing strange that the national
> interest emerges only when we are talking about
> Western *resources* or Eastern *benefits*. If oil, why not
> iron ore and steel products? If natural gas, why not
> copper? If uranium—and we in Saskatchewan may
> well be Canada's biggest uranium producer in a few
> years—if uranium, why not nickel?

Premier Blakeney's ironic rejection of the myth of the nation was sustained by a western vision: why should the "national interest" always serve the interests of the inhabitants of southern Ontario? One could adduce a similar stance from the early speeches of Premier Peter Lougheed, particularly during the period of the National Energy Program, before he became a certified national statesman. And likewise the

"Green Shift" of Liberal leader Stéphane Dion looked to westerners as nothing but another revenue transfer from west to east, this time conducted under the guise of the moral panic called environmentalism.

On occasion, rejection of the garrison myth, particularly when heavily freighted with conflicting regional interests, has led to a rejection of the forms of parliamentary government. The conventional understanding of western politics is based on the obvious: the usual alternation of Liberal and Conservative governments, which is almost the rule elsewhere in the country, has been modified beyond recognition west of the Ontario frontier. Many of these western parties are, no doubt, "protest parties." Most political analysts see no need to ask the next question: what are these parties protesting against? And why have the Liberals or the Conservatives been unable to capture that protest and turn it into permanent or at least long-term support for their own party? Or, if they do capture the "protest party," as the Conservatives conceivably may have done under Brian Mulroney and Stephen Harper, or the Liberals may have done with the Progressives during the 1920s, why don't the voters remain loyal, once they have been captured? Why did the Progressive voter switch to the CCF or Social Credit? Why did the western Conservatives desert to Reform? What lies ahead if Harper creates a "national" Conservative party?

These questions relate less to conventional classifications of "party systems" than to historical patterns and mythical accounts of them. Once the "national" myths, the "national" policies, and the "national" parties are out the window, westerners are liberated to take pride in being non-Laurentian Canadians. This is why they have pursued a multi-pronged strategy, both inside and outside the Liberal and Conservative parties, to find a political vehicle to represent their interests and their vision in the national government. The reason is clear enough: the Canadian regime has been subverted to serve eastern sectional interests.

One of the main conventions of parliamentary government is the ability of the legislature to control the executive by granting or withholding supply. This ability depends on the prior ability of the legislature to raise funds. But the chief source of provincial finances, namely the benefits derived from natural resources, were withheld from the North-Western territorial government and from the successor prairie provincial governments until 1930, though the demand was on record from as early as 1884.

The timing of the Natural Resources Transfer Acts, however, could not have been worse inasmuch as the entire country was about to endure a decade of severe deflation. The prairie provinces were the hardest-hit part of Canada so that, even if the provinces did control their resources, they brought in little revenue. The chief consequence of the absence of responsible government from the prairie provinces for the sixty years prior to 1930 was that political leaders were deprived of the education in parliamentary government and an understanding of the regime that their colleagues in the east had experienced for at least a generation before 1870. Instead of being merely neophytes in the arts of parliamentary democracy, prairie politicians, for two additional generations, were stunted by the federal government. In response they sought alternative forms of self-government, which is to say they strove to create a regime that more adequately expressed their political aspirations than did the parliamentary regime controlled by Ottawa and animated by the Laurentian myth. Hence the rejection, from time to time, of parties and even of parliamentary governments in favour of non-partisan government and "populism."

These demands to change, to reform, or even to destroy parliamentary government have never been wholeheartedly supported across the West. Even during the miserable seven lean years of the Great Depression, when the CCF and Social Credit were on an upward curve, the two old parties still attracted the support of over half of the electorate. Even so, the logic that explains western support for populism is obvious. Having been excluded from the political education that accompanies the operation of responsible government, and having been persistently out-voted and out-muscled by the operations of the party system and the first-past-the-post electoral system, a significant number of westerners found in populism a coherent explanation for their condition. In one way or another, populism identifies public virtue with the will of the people, and the people are one. From this assumption, which to a populist is a self-evident verity, they drew the conclusion that divisions and conflicts are, in principle, artificial and manufactured by self-interested and mischievous outsiders. From the Progressives during the 1920s to the unreconstructed Reformers of today, "the common sense of the common people" (to use the formula that opens the Reform Party's 1993 Blue Book) has been strongly contrasted with the manipulative and Machiavellian activities of the "elites," mostly Laurentian elites. The Reform Party proposed to put its populism into practice by advocating direct democracy through the great trinity of initiative, referendum, and recall. But direct democracy and the legal and constitutional changes required to enact populist measures are wholly incompatible with the operations of parliamentary government. Most populists either ignore this awkward problem or they don't know it is there.

The most significant conflict in mythologies so far as the Canadian regime is concerned is between the West and Laurentian Canada. But it is not the only one. We have already indicated the resistance of Maritime Jonah to being swallowed by the Laurentian whale. There are several subsidiary conflicts as well: between Newfoundland and Laurentian Canada; between Newfoundland and the Maritimes; between the Maritimes and the West; and so on. To consider only the last example: if western Canada cleaves to a comedic mythology of "next-year country," to use the title of Jean Burnet's splendid study of society around Hanna, Alberta, the comparable image of the Maritimes may well be that of a region that, in the words of W.H. New, is "everyone's half-forgotten past and no-one's future." Or as Keefer put it, the Maritimes exemplify "a dry-eyed recognition of longstanding deprivation," which is a defence against imaginative "Canada," and "an expression of wounded pride," or as she said, a "loser ethos."

The political consequences of the difference between next-year country and a loser ethos for contemporary Canada usually appear in a context of controversy and polemic in which statistics on income or unemployment feature prominently. In making sense of these indicators, a somewhat more profound conflict of interpretation comes to light. On the one hand, Maritimers have long maintained a hostility to Confederation; on the other, outsiders have long been puzzled by the post-Confederation economic ineptitude and inertia of the region. It can't just be the end of sailboats! Only recently have Maritimers begun to question the desirability of federal transfer payments to the region, though their fellow citizens from other parts of the country, and from the West in particular, have long held serious reservations about the deliberate creation and maintenance of economic dependency by the federal government. To a westerner there is nothing glorious in being a Moosehead-swilling local whose highest aspiration is to collect pogey to the max. And Maritimers have paid the cost of dependency in the coin of diminished self-respect. To his credit, Stephen Harper reminded his fellow citizens living in the region of the regrettable consequences of embracing a loser ethos. To his political regret, his delivery of this home truth was not appreciated, not least of all because he reminded them of something shameful.

This account of the tensions between the several regional myths or regionally based images and understandings of the shape of the Canadian body politic is far from complete. My main concern, however, is to report on how things look from here. If this chapter is persuasive, you will have learned of the fraudulence of "Canadian culture" or "Canadian identity." This is not a new question in Canada. Over a generation ago George Grant argued, in *Lament for a Nation* (1965), that both Canadian political independence and, good Laurentian that he was, Canadian "identity" had already been lost. I am not so sure, but I do know that nationalist, that is, imaginatively "Canadian," myths are viewed by westerners or Maritimers with suspicion or contempt. Those who reject the appeal of Ottawa do so, generally speaking, because they wish to be more at home where they are. Grant's lament for a nation, for the imaginative reality of Loyalist, Laurentian Canada, was no more than the lament for an anachronism as well as a region of the political unit.

Grant explained the demise of Canada by reference to the homogenizing universality of technology, as distinct from the natural and the particular. But consider the dilemmas of those who wish to save baby seals or the culture of Eskimos or even to stop what they believe to be human-caused climate change. Because they must cleave to the natural and act against the technological by means of technology, they can never be consistent and so are not really serious. Moreover, it is by means, precisely, of the technological that they are free within nature. This is why it would take one with great comic talents to explore fully the significance of saving baby seals by landing on ice floes and growlers with helicopters and green spray paint. Likewise there is a profound absurdity of a poetic sensibility discovering a spiritual void in the successful operation of a high-tech wheat farm. Contemporary western literature often expresses a dream of origins, a dream of home that may never have been and to which contemporary westerners can certainly never return. But in the same way that it makes no sense to try to refute a poem, no more than a sense of eastern alienation can be gained by pointing out the "romantic" nature of this imaginative contemporary western reality. Its reality, not its reasonableness judged in light of external criteria, carries meaning and political weight.

This chapter began by drawing attention to the stress under which Canadian governments have found themselves in recent years. It would be foolish to think that the appearance of regional identities by way of the party system beginning with the 1993 election was fortuitous or to predict that western regional myths could serve as forces for political education for the whole country. It would be even more foolish to attempt to foresee the consequences of the 2006 or the 2008 election, whatever may be one's hopes that Canadians can, in fact, be educated by the Harper government, which is a Conservative government. But what is the conservatism informed by western political myths? What is cowboy conservatism? That is our next question.

CHAPTER THREE

COWBOY CONSERVATIVES?

"The impossibility of conservatism in our era
is the impossibility of Canada."
—GEORGE GRANT

We just saw that competing myths of identity as well as the more mundane conflicts in interest lie at the heart of the Canadian federal regime. The "garrison mentality" is both appropriate and important to the Loyalist heartland of southern Ontario. The Loyalists were the losers of the American Revolution and the original conservatives of the continent. Compared to the successful revolutionaries, how could it be otherwise? American loyalty to the Crown would have conserved the British Empire. Beyond loyalty, however, of what did their conservatism consist? And how is it related to the Loyalist myth? Perhaps most important, what were the experiences that found appropriate expression in the Loyalist myth? So far as the perspective adopted in this essay is concerned, it has often been said of the "Calgary School" that it is "conservative." An important issue, therefore, will be to discover, if possible, just what conservatism means in the Canadian and especially the western Canadian context. To put the question stupidly: are cowboys conservative?

Answering that question immediately raises a problem: there is no agreement among Canadian scholars about whether conservatism exists in this country and, if it does, how it may be characterized. There are, of course, learned debates that draw upon the arguments of Burke and Locke, Adam Smith and "classical republicans." There is the notional "red Tory," an oxymoron to most British and American conservatives, said to describe a faction of the Progressive Conservative and now the Conservative Party. A "red Tory," according to Gad Horowitz who invented him in 1966, is a conservative with "odd" socialist views (or a socialist with "odd" Tory ones). There are "business liberals" who are indistinguishable from "business conservatives" as well as temperamental conservatives who are said to be prudent and thoughtful rather than idealistic and rash. The conservative is said to honour a received good today more than the hope of a greater good tomorrow. This makes him or her a hindrance to movement and change, and to the movers little more than a custodian of the quaint and backward, a guardian of amenities not yet ready for destruction.

Thoughtful individuals who call themselves conservative are not much help either. Raymond Aron, for example, used to say he was a liberal, that is, a conservative; the conservative economist Milton Friedman believed in "classical" liberalism, which has nothing to do with a classical liberal education. Conceptually, liberals promote liberty, which in turn is what conservatives seek to conserve. In other words, we will not find much insight into what conservatives might be—let alone cowboy conservatives—by the minute dissection of allegedly conservative (or liberal) texts, though we have to consider a few.

Let us, then, consider history. It is well known to political historians that both liberalism and conservatism, however they understand themselves, are reactions to the phenomenon of revolution. The early responses were less radical than the later ones. When England had made its adjustments to the Glorious Revolution by about 1690, the institutional structure of an aristocratic Parliament was still intact, as were the mores of a Christian commonwealth, in the form of a national Church. Later, the American Revolution, despite the rhetoric of Enlightenment, still preserved much of the institutional and Christian spiritual climate of the British *ancien régime*. The famous American separation of church and state was intended to foster, not stifle, Christian practice. Observers from Tocqueville to the latest public opinion survey have shown that it worked. That is, in both the English and American revolutions considerable institutional conservatism ensured continuity.

With the French Revolution, in contrast, the radical and anti-traditional faction triumphed with such severity as to split the French nation more or less permanently into a secular or laicist fragment that claims to preserve the "gains" of the revolution, and a conservative fragment that still resists the destructiveness of the revolution and tries to recover or salvage the pre-revolutionary heritage. It is also worth noting that the terms *liberal* and *conservative* were first applied to politics during the French revolutionary times. Finally, among the European states there was the German Revolution. The institutional structure had been broken beyond repair during the Thirty Years War; the country had been forged together by power; worst of all, the modern spiritual movements—economic materialism, biological racism, quack psychology, unbounded faith in technological domination—had next to no traditional opposition. Romanticism, which began in opposition to these modern spiritual movements, ended as their ally and made matters even worse with the National Socialists.

The pattern of revolutionary political change and conservative or liberal response was, as just indicated, part of *the* historical disruption of North America, the successful rebellion of the Thirteen Colonies and the founding of the United States of America. By this argument, the origins of Canadian conservatism, however that is understood, are coeval with Canada. Because the conservatism of French-speaking Canada is tightly bound to the contingencies of ethnicity, seventeenth-century Catholicism, and culture, I will limit the discussion to English-speaking Canada. Specifically, those origins lay in the consequence of the political judgment that King George III was not a tyrant. It is an understandable, if regrettable, fact that American historians have, until recently, more or less subscribed to the view of the revolutionary Patriots, that the Loyalist was a "tory" whose head was in England, whose body was in America, and (as the brutal and tasteless Patriotic joke goes) whose neck should be stretched.

As a result, the Loyalists' arguments have been deliberately submerged or simply forgotten by American historians, especially by those who believe with Harry Jaffa that "American Conservatism is... rooted in a Founding which is, in turn, rooted in revolution." But if the Patriots were conservative, what then were the Loyalists? The simplest answer is to ignore them, as most American conservatives do.

For their part, because the Loyalists read the same books as the Patriots in search of a justification of their practical decision regarding (alleged) British tyranny, they were ideologically as liberal or as Whig as the revolutionaries. It was not until after the War of 1812 that the Loyalist successors began extensively to document not the immediate experience of the Loyalists during the Revolution but stories that cohered as the Loyalist myth. That is, a generation or so after the American founding, Canadian historians seek and find evidence of "Canadian conservatism." This is not contradicted by the deep love the Loyalists had for America and by their support of the colonists' grievances. American-born Loyalists removed to England, such as Thomas Hutchinson, former governor of the colony of Massachusetts, were heart-sick exiles longing to return "home." Incidentally, Hutchinson's use of "home" to refer to Massachusetts contrasts markedly with the usage of the Fathers of Confederation a century or so later. For them, "home" was always the U.K.

Reasonable men might differ on the interpretation of Locke or of his relevance to the passage of the Stamp Act (1765). Despite a common set of texts from which to argue, there were obvious differences in interpretation. To generalize the differences, the Locke of the Patriots and, later, the American Locke was simplified, rationalized, and enlightened, a Locke shorn of tradition. The Locke of the Loyalists, inherited by Canadians, was perhaps more complex, a Locke who, for example, genuinely considered Hooker judicious. That is, the Loyalists found a Locke who respected more than he repudiated in the pre-liberal past. Whether the Canadian or American version is a more accurate interpretation of how Locke understood himself is a separate question that for our purposes does not matter. Even so, it should come as no surprise that a regime that understood its own existence as the beginning of a *novus ordo seclorum* would claim as its inspiration a Locke whose words were compatible with their initiatives.

The conflict in interpretations is brought out in Hutchinson's remarkable "Dialogue between an American and a European Englishman," written in 1768. It is one of the few texts of the period that elevated the dispute beyond the context of immediate controversy and clash of interests. *American* said he could "easily conceive" that there are certain fundamental principles that, when a government ignores them (as the Patriots said of the British), the people so governed are freed from the obligation to obey. Because there can be no government deciding its own case as to when it has abandoned its own principles, "every man's own conscience must be the judge and he must follow the evidence of truth in his own mind and submit or not submit accordingly." This was a clear Lockean version of the "right of revolution" arising from the government creating a state of nature where "all obligation to submit ceases."

To this argument *European* replied: "Such a compact as you suppose would be a mere rope of sand," and challenged *American* to provide instances. In general the Loyalist arguments commonly had recourse to historical evidence and praised the stability provided by venerable institutions. They worried over the lack of cohesion implicit in a community ordered by self-interest but saw no conflict between liberty and authority. The power that upheld the one enabled the other to flourish. Despite reliance on a common set of texts, then, the same words, when uttered by one's opponents, were effectively a different language and certainly conveyed a different meaning. The American Revolution and its result, two constitutional regimes, at least in their beginnings, were not, however, about interpreting Locke. The most one can say is that actions taken on the basis of antithetical interpretations of Locke had significant consequences for the practical initiation of a conservative regime in Canada.

Thus Joseph Galloway, a Loyalist, wrote regarding the First Continental Congress, "I do not differ from them in opinion, that America has grievances to complain of; but I differ from them in the mode of obtaining redress." According to the Loyalists, the difficulties between the colonies and Britain stemmed not from British tyranny or British conspiracies and designs but from a lack of flexibility in the British constitution. Despite his fondness for Locke's whipping boy, Robert Filmer, the Patriot Rev. Boucher agreed with Hutchinson on this point. "Our Constitution," he wrote, "admirable as it is, is not it would seem, wholly adapted to all the Purposes of Government in large Adjuncts of the Empire neither foreseen, nor provided for, when this Constitution was formed." In sum the Patriots argued that Locke's categories regarding revolution were applicable to the Americans' circumstances; the Loyalists denied it. All, including Hutchinson and Boucher, agreed that Britain had erred in its colonial policy during the 1760s and early 1770s. The practical or as Machiavelli would say, the effective, question was: did those errors constitute tyranny?

To the Loyalists, the argument led plainly to a negative conclusion. According to Locke, a state of war or of force without right may arise either in civil society or within a state of nature.

When anyone is subjected to force without right, they may have recourse to the laws of nature. The Declaration of Independence asserted that the British government sought to reduce the colonies under absolute despotism, a condition in which they might be subject to unlimited force without right. Evidence that the "long train of abuses and prevarications" amounted to Locke's force without right was not, however, universally compelling. The conclusion drawn by the Loyalists was that the Patriots were not Whigs but republicans, and Whigs had a stock of arguments left over from the mid-seventeenth century to deal with the ancient heresy of republicanism: it led to levelling and rule by the poor in their own interests, which was democratic and lawless tyranny. Moreover, it was viable only if republics were small. After the revolution this was, of course, a topic of hot contention between Federalist and anti-Federalist writers.

The Loyalists did not accept the analogy drawn by the Patriots with Locke's account of 1688; then the country changed rulers but remained more or less united, whereas a short century later the issue was, to use an American term of the 1850s and 1860s, one of nullification and secession. That is, to the Loyalists, the Patriots nullified laws they did not like and then seceded when they were not allowed to act independently. No Loyalist familiar with this argument would have been surprised by the arguments of the South prior to the War between the States. Such an interpretation sustains the view that the revolution was the "first American civil war." In Canadian language, the Patriots were separatists, but serious ones, unlike those of twentieth-century Quebec, because they were willing and able to fight, and, in the words of signers of the Declaration, to "pledge to each other our Lives, our Fortunes, and our sacred Honor."

Rebellion would, the Loyalists said, open the door to a general disorder even when justified by honeyed and hypocritical words. These sentiments were exposed in a political poem of 1773:

> May supreme laws, by subjects be disputed?
> Then say they're wrong, the Sovereign is refuted.
> If so, could laws restrain and make them budge,
> When they themselves in their own case must judge?
> Confused Anarchy is most exerted,
> When Order, Rule and Laws are thus inverted.

What followed from such sentiments was suspicion that their opponents were deceptive. With the discovery of hidden designs in their words came the insight that treacherous deeds were bound to follow. The practical matter of betrayal and actions taken (on both sides) in light of it, not disputes over the meaning of Locke, sustained their disputes well into the future.

In 1967, Bernard Bailyn offered an account of the conflict between Patriots and Loyalists that helped to explain the symmetry of their arguments with respect to one another. According to him, colonial American "political culture" consisted of "a pattern of ideas, assumptions, attitudes and beliefs given distinctive shape by the opposition elements in English politics." Specifically, the greatest political evil was considered to be ministerial "corruption" or "influence." For all its faults, corruption, in fact, amounted to the grease that kept the wheels of the British government in motion in the days before the existence of political parties. Rotten boroughs, pocket boroughs, Crown patronage, legions of placemen: these were the substitutes for party discipline. Whatever may be said against "corruption" and "influence," Hume's observation, that it was "necessary to the preservation of our mixed government," and so a force for ensuring a stable transition from monarchy to a parliamentary regime, seems indisputable.

Considered from a North American perspective, however, matters looked much more sinister. The basic assumption was that politics in America resembled politics in Britain at least with respect to its major structural feature, the balanced constitution. By analogical reasoning, the colonial governors were akin to the monarch and the two chambers of the colonial assemblies were akin to the two Houses of Parliament. The formal similarity of the structure of government masked a fundamental difference in their modes of operation. What produced harmony in England produced discord in America. Bailyn indicated in detail how this institutionalized disorder operated, but the fundamental flaw was that the executive alone had legal power but lacked the means, namely "corruption" and "influence," to tame the commons because of the constraints imposed by orders from London. What influence existed in America was spread from the imperial capital, London, not the mansions of the colonial governors. The effect was to strengthen the democratic element in the local mixed constitution by enhancing its power while leaving legal authority in the hands of an increasingly unpopular, and so impotent, executive. As Bailyn said, "Swollen claims and shrunken powers, especially when they occur together, are always sources of trouble." Assuming that the analogy between Britain and British North America was reasonable, assuming as well the rhetorical stance of the British opposition, the result was an almost inevitable drift toward an extreme position.

In Britain, the criticism of corruption served to warn the body politic of dangers that threatened the balance and equipoise of the British constitution. In America, the same language constituted an obvious explanation of an imbalance that had already taken place. This same rhetoric, seen from Britain, however, appeared to be a threat to the British constitution because it implied the engrossing of the "democratic" element, which happened to be overseas. At the very least the resulting deadlock did not enhance mutual understanding, to say nothing of the conflicting interests of the parties to the dispute.

A similar kind of engrossing, we will argue, but not of the democratic element of the Canadian regime, has resulted in centralized, non-responsible power and, as in the eighteenth century, large-scale corruption. Unlike the earlier circumstances, however, the existence of parties to apply grease to the machinery of government rendered that corruption less excusable.

Behind the similarities in rhetoric lies the similarity of reality experienced at the western edge of empire, whether British or Canadian. From the days of the Plymouth Colony, the inhabitants of the new world, and later of its pioneering westward vanguard, had to govern themselves. At the beginning of America, the Mayflower Compact (1620) created a body politic not only for "the Glory of God" and the "Honour of our King and Country" but also for "our better Ordering," which is to say, for the building of a decent political order with "just and equal laws," that is, laws that apply equally to all.

By 1641, the Massachusetts Body of Liberties established what is, in effect, legislative supremacy. There was no reference to the King and his honour being served by the reconstituted body politic because the King and his friends and ministers were not present to govern the colonists. By 1689, Parliament had forced the Bill of Right on the King. As Eugene Forsey used to delight in pointing out to bewildered bureaucrats, it remains part of the Canadian constitution. A short century after the Bill of Right, the rebellious colonies declared they had no need for a king at all. From the *Mayflower* experience to the Revolutionary War, much of English-speaking America was driven by the practical necessities of self-government. Those same necessities, whatever the legal formulations of sovereignty in what became British North America, gave a distinctive regional cast to the practice of prairie politics, as well.

The myth of the red Tory was kept alive, especially in the Loyalist heartland, by stories of exile and the modest assistance afforded the refugees by the imperial crown. The view that the state was a positive power, a guardian of the integrity of the body politic, and a protection against evil has persisted, especially among the protectionist left. Paradoxically, the bitterness and hardship of exile intensified the Americanism of the Loyalists without altering their allegiance to a United Empire. They dreamed of re-establishing a continental empire in the old southwest, the present midwest of the United States. Because they had been defeated and expelled by men who spoke in extravagant terms of liberty and democracy, for many years they denied there was any virtue in either democracy or republican government, even when such claims conflicted mightily with common sense and the manifest experiences of daily life.

The British, who prided themselves on the antiquity and legitimacy of their liberties, could not easily accept that they had lessons in these matters to learn from events in America. Accordingly, they saw the causes of the rebellion not in the metropolitan threat to British liberty in America but in recognizable defects of colonial government. The constitution was unbalanced owing to a weak executive and badly skewed in favour of democracy. These faults would be corrected by the Constitutional Act of 1791. In drafting the act, the Home Secretary, William Wyndham Grenville, sought to create in British North America the "image and transcript" of the British constitution. Those words borrowed from William Pitt the Younger were often repeated by Governor Simcoe, who was charged as well with putting them into practice.

The experience of armed defence of their homeland in 1812 and of the grim post-war business of punishing treason and sedition taught the leaders of Upper Canada that the political order they cherished was threatened from within as well as by the foreign policy of the United States. In the post-1812 regime can be found the genuine experiential roots of Frye's garrison mentality. But the War of 1812 also brought an end to local particularism in the province of Upper Canada and introduced an expansive purpose to Canadian conservatism. Economic development such as the building of the Welland Canal was combined with restrictive land policies designed to ensure the growth of a pool of landless labourers, which in turn would contribute to a social order akin to that of Britain. The role of the Crown or of the state in formulating and carrying through this policy was central. And yet, at the same time, economic change undermined the conditions for balance and the pursuit of contentment, stability, and moderation by focusing the aspirations of British North Americans more on prosperity than on the virtues previously associated with Loyalism.

Durham's liberal analysis of the causes of the rebellions of 1837, his liberal recommendations to forestall any repetition, and the growing crisis of federalism in the United States severally and in combination required a response from Canadian political leaders. Canadian historians have argued persuasively that the commercial ambitions of the Montreal merchants and the political convictions of the Loyalists of Muddy York, now Toronto, were two complementary aspects of the same political purpose, "the defence and extension of British interests in North America," as Donald Creighton, the late dean of Laurentian historians, put it. These men saw the United States as a rival and Britain as an ally, and to that extent there existed continuity with the conservatism of the late eighteenth century. But the rivalry and the alliance were no longer grounded in political principle, or even in practical political differences, as with Patriots and Loyalists: all sides were engaged in economic expansion so that conflicts took the less edifying form of squabbles over the defence and extension of market shares.

Specifically, the Grand Alliance of 1854, which created the Liberal-Conservative Party, eclipsed the substance of the old Loyalist conservatism even while it preserved the continuity of form. With Sir John A. Macdonald's vision of a transcontinental empire, a strong united commercial state, the long confusion of the middle decades of the century was resolved. The initiatives that followed, which relied on the new railway technology and the administrative structure of the National Policy, aimed first of all at prosperity. If that were assured, the purpose of the nation would likewise be safeguarded, and with it the fortunes of Macdonald's Conservative Party, if not conservatism in the older sense. That is, we agree with Creighton, biographer of Macdonald, that "nineteenth-century Conservatism in Canada is not what Burke and his successors and commentators thought it ought to be in theory, but what Macdonald and his principal associates made it in practice." But then we are bound to enquire: What *did* they make it in practice? Whatever it was, the empire building of Macdonald and of his Liberal-Conservative associates was not clearly on the side of preserving what remained of the pre-modern aspects of Canadian political life.

This did not mean that the older, somewhat principled conservatism as found in the debates over Locke between Loyalists and Patriots had disappeared, but it surely was eclipsed. As Janet Ajzenstat has tirelessly argued, by the middle of the nineteenth century Canadian political thinking had become liberal and democratic and in that respect very close to American political thought. Only the narcissism of small differences can preserve the myth that contrasts communal, deferential Tory Canada with individualistic, democratic America. Ajzenstat has driven an empirical stake through its duplicitous black heart.

What, then, of the tattered remnants of Canadian conservatism? It is always possible to identify conservatism with the political rule of businessmen. After all, they defend their own interests and thereby serve as a kind of prophylaxis against the seductive obscurities and moralistic visions associated with welfare liberalism and, even more, with socialism. Conservatism, Canadian conservatism included, once meant more than that. Moreover, the business liberal also acts from a spirit of meliorism, finding reason to change whatever he cannot find a better reason to preserve. Then again, if we look to the fate of a genuine conservative argument, such as that made by John Farthing a half-century ago in *Freedom Wears a Crown* (1957), it is hard not to agree with George Grant that conservatism is futile or absurd because it is so far removed from the realities of a progressive technological society such as our own.

I have indicated, perhaps indirectly, my belief that the real conflicts of current Canadian politics are over federalism. In this respect at least, the Americans' Northwest Ordinance of 1787 seems to have allowed for a more orderly expansion of federal institutions because the American transcontinental march never lost touch with the realities of self-government experienced by the Plymouth Colony. In fact, the writ of the King and even the presence of a few redcoats did not absolve the western frontier of the Canadian empire from the necessity of self-government, but it did mean that, viewed from Ottawa, Montreal, or Toronto, prairie politics looked downright unruly because eastern legal and social practices did not quite fit with a novel animating spirit.

When Canada gained control of the North-West, it assumed a legal responsibility for a large and sparsely populated area. J.R. Mallory, a distinguished political scientist of an earlier generation, made the pointed but somewhat enigmatic observation that the western provinces "were provinces not in the same sense as were Ontario and Quebec, but in the Roman sense." Because Mallory's readers are not likely today to be as cognizant of the implications of the "Roman sense" of a province as they were in 1954 when he wrote *Social Credit and the Federal Power in Canada*, we have to ask: What is the Roman sense? A Roman *provincia* was distinguished by two major attributes. First, it was a locale where *imperium*, administrative power, was exercised by an agent from Rome. Second, unlike Roman inhabitants of Italy, those of the "provinces" paid tribute to the imperial capital. Moreover, as the etymology *pro-vincere* suggests, the "provinces" were territories conquered on behalf of Rome.

This is why Prime Minister Macdonald was not unjustified in describing the West, in fact if not in law, as a "Crown colony" of Canada. According to British law, a Crown colony was a possession of the Crown that was under the direct control of a governor appointed from London (or Ottawa). There may or may not be legislative assemblies, but always the Crown has the right of veto and the option of imposing direct legislation by order-in-council. Now, it was not and it is not inevitable that subjects of a Crown colony object to subordinate status. (Consider the attitudes of the inhabitants of Hong Kong before they were handed over to the People's Republic of China in what HRH the Prince Charles called a "Chinese take-away.") Rather, objections to subordinate status arise as a result of individual human wills and personalities. In particular, the Red River resistance of 1869–70, however comic and ineffectual it was, was also sufficient to initiate a continuing struggle against subordination. The initial consequence of Roman provincial status involved not subordination, which was simply a fact, but the western attitude to it, namely insubordination and resistance. That, too, is what Macdonald made of conservatism in practice.

The economic and political deals that stitched together Confederation were of great importance to the country as a whole. Historians have investigated in detail the economic rivalry of Montreal and Toronto, the balancing of the

Intercolonial Railway that brought the Maritimes into Canada and into the orbit of Montreal with the mortgaging of the North-West to Ontario. In the West, Confederation was annexation, and not an act that was unambiguously welcomed. The initial and explicitly political resistance of 1869–70, which was centred in the Metis society but supported by non-Metis as well, was continued by the new settlers from Ontario against whose numbers the Metis originally fought. That is, the attitudes of the same agricultural settlers who destroyed much of Metis society overcame the ethnic base and spatial limitations of Red River but preserved the Metis attitude of resistance. Again historians have been faithful custodians of the facts surrounding the Dominion Lands Policy, the National Policy, the "monopoly clause" of the CPR, the 1911 election, the Progressive Movement, the farmers' political movements and governments, Social Credit, the Social Gospel, the CCF, and so on. Moreover, these political phenomena occasionally have been interpreted as elements of a pattern that continued through the Reform Party and the Canadian Alliance and combined an acceptance of the political and economic institutions of Canada with resistance to political and economic controls.

It is always a temptation to exaggerate the importance of one's subject as a consequence of one's interest, training, or imaginative capacities. Even so, it seems to me that the political significance of western resistance has usually been underemphasized. Not that the facts are unknown, but they have been wrongly understood. To begin with, the malign consequences of Macdonald's imperial and "conservative" ambitions in practice have eclipsed the basic experience of colonists on the western edge of empire, namely the necessity as well as the attractiveness of self-government. This issue has been ignored in Canada in favour of half-baked half-truths, from saving the North-West for the British Empire and from the Americans to bizarre notions that the inhabitants of the North-West were too few, too ill-educated, too foreign, too different, and too stupid to govern themselves. Such is the attraction of imperial rule over "Roman" provinces.

Most of the accounts known to me that are concerned with prairie politics pay little attention to the self-interpretation of individuals who actually take part in political life, nor do they discuss the symbolic context within which the meaning of public affairs has taken place. That is, the dimension of public life expressed as myth has too often been ignored. The symbolic expressions of public life, however, matter a lot.

Western political resistance grew from what used to be called Dominion policies, the policies of old Laurentian Canada animated with what to westerners was a stifling garrison mentality. The intended and actual effect of those policies was to ensure the subordination of the West to, and exclusion from, central institutions of political power. Our initial focus is on Alberta, the west of the West, and the most famous of the texts generated by the (Laurentian) Canadian Social Science Research Council to explain, and thereby to domesticate, the creative activities of Albertans, namely C.B. Macpherson's *Democracy in Alberta* (1953).

This most famous deployment of eastern intellectual power was not the first. A generation earlier, the "Frontiers of Settlement" series, sponsored by the Carnegie Foundation, produced an interesting and still useful collection of books dealing with the settlement and economic development of the prairies in an effort to develop a "science of settlement," as Isaiah Brown, director of the American Geographical Society, called it. Between the 1930s and the 1950s, the Rockefeller Foundation supported the "North American Regionalization Project" or the "Northern Plains" inquiry. This investigation produced some interesting files at the Rockefeller Foundation Archives in Sleepy Hollow, New York, and three conferences—in New York City; Lincoln, Nebraska; and Saskatoon, all of which were devoted to surveying a "plains sensibility," but no major publications. All these initiatives were devoted to understanding western experiences. One need not be a devotee of Foucauldian "power-knowledge" to understand that administrative control was at least as important as disinterested social science. Nowhere is that dual purpose more obvious than in Macpherson's famous book.

Leo Panich, himself an *homme de gauche*, declared *Democracy in Alberta* to be "the best political analysis in the Marxist tradition undertaken in Canada." Professor Panich taught at York University in Toronto for many years. Two westerners who, at the time, sported equally impeccable leftist credentials, John Richards and Larry Pratt, in their book *Prairie Capitalism* (1979), corrected this "uncritical" endorsement by pointing to several serious inaccuracies in Macpherson's understanding of the class composition of Alberta. He neglected, for example, the economic activity whose existence is annually celebrated in the Calgary Stampede, the cattle industry. Cowboys everywhere and especially in universities inevitably find this omission worthy of rebuke. Worst of all, Macpherson's book set the stage for a half-century of unflattering interpretation of Alberta and the

West. Because it cannot be ignored, it must be corrected.

The title, *Democracy in Alberta*, was ironic. Macpherson argued that democracy in Alberta was degenerate and warned darkly that a "Bonapartist dictatorship" was forestalled only by "windfall revenues" from oil. As early as 1953, then, the argument that combined envy at the resource revenue of the province with distaste for the way that Albertans conduct their political affairs was fast congealing into a cliché. After inviting his readers to muse on the spectre of a Bonapartist dictatorship, Macpherson surfed his own three waves of criticism. The first dealt with Henry Wise Wood, William Irving, and the United Farmers of Alberta, the UFA; the second looked at Social Credit, in theory and in practice; the third criticized the party system in Alberta.

Each wave was worse than its predecessor because they successively grew farther away from the insights afforded by Marxism and the applications implied by them—because, Marxists say, Marxism combines both theory and practice. The great problem, it seems, is that Albertans were largely farmers, and farmers never get it right. Farmers, unlike intellectuals at the University of Toronto, are hardly ever Marxists. Why should they be? Macpherson never explains.

As for Social Credit, it was no more than an expression of *petit bourgeois* class anguish, whether it was discovered among oddballs and misfits in the U.K. or among farmers on the western plains. By definition, it seems, such people are "uprooted" and members of "insecure sections" of society. The undeniable fact that Premier William Aberhart looked confident Macpherson attributed to "intellectual limitations" and his lack of "sophistication," a sophisticated way of saying he was (to use a cowboy expression) dumber than a sack of hammer heads.

So too were his credulous followers. In short, he was a lucky but bumbling ignoramus.

A more obvious interpretation of Aberhart's actions than the combination of cunning and stupidity was provided by the course of political events themselves. Eleven days after receiving the assent of the Lieutenant Governor, the Credit of Alberta Regulation Act, the Bank Employees Civil Rights Act, and the Judicature Act Amendment Act were all disallowed by the Dominion government. To Albertans at least, this was part of a familiar pattern. As Eugene Forsey, who was neither a strong defender of provincial rights nor an enthusiastic admirer of either Social Credit or William Aberhart, but who was a decent and honest scholar, remarked: "The revival of Dominion control over the provinces is really the revival of Dominion control over such provinces as try to do things which the dominant economic interests of Canada dislike." In the end, even Macpherson had to admit as much. Social Credit was "directed against the federal parties" because the old party system was still an active means by which outside interests "confused, divided, and ruled the people."

The conclusion to be drawn from the disallowance of the several acts passed by the Alberta legislature was that the federal principle in Canada did not operate through central institutions such as the Senate, as the Fathers of Confederation may have anticipated, but through the provinces, and that Alberta politics ought to be considered in that light. According to Macpherson, however, the significant conclusion we are meant to draw concerned the party system, not federalism, which was the object of the third wave of criticism.

Because Albertans were *petit bourgeois*, they were capable

only of rebellion "against eastern imperialism but not against the property system." Because property relations are the true test of true radicalism, the self-understanding of the farmers must be wrong. They were, he said, "deluded" or, in Marxist language, they were afflicted with false consciousness. Farmers *think* of themselves as independent, but they *are* not, or at least they are not independent enough to prevent their own false consciousness of their dependence. The political consequences of *petit bourgeois* false consciousness were most easily seen in what he called a quasi-party system, which led to the deterioration of democracy and the danger of a Bonapartist dictatorship.

Whatever the limitations of Macpherson's class analysis, it is not a reflection of his ignoring the facts. Looked at in light of political practice rather than that of economic theory, functionalism, or Marxist class analysis, the most significant aspect about democracy in Alberta during the period considered by Macpherson was the amount of political activity in the province. The political activity of Social Credit was less a matter of giving imaginary roots to the rootless or delusions to the deluded than of making visible and articulate the body politic of Albertans. It has, moreover, stood the test of time. So, of course, has what might be called the Macpherson agenda. The same visceral dislike of Alberta politics can be found in any number of "studies" of Premier Ralph Klein and his alleged revolution, to say nothing of ill-disguised envy at the sheer unfairness that the exploitation of the natural resources of the Western Sedimentary Basin has proceeded chiefly in Alberta. Macpherson may be gone but unfortunately his arguments have not been forgotten. In his deeply flawed book can be found the source of the other great cliché of western politics: alienation.

Alienation has found its greatest expression in the other major way (besides Marxism) by which scholars ignore the self-understanding of a political community, namely the survey. The first survey of the North-West was begun on September 8, 1869, when Lieutenant Colonel John Dennis, an Ontario provincial land surveyor, set up his transit and began marking the ground along the Manitoba–U.S. border. Two days later and ten miles west of the Red River crossing at Pembina, his assistant, Milner Hart, began marking the first principal, or Winnipeg, meridian. On October 4, A.C. Webb, following Dennis's instructions and trespassing on Metis lands, was stopped "by Half Breeds, 17 in number headed by Louis Ariel." Riel or one of his companions placed his moccasined foot upon the chain as it was being dragged forward. The survey did not resume until the summer of 1871. The objective was to divide by law 200 million acres of arable land into a million and a quarter homestead units, a quarter section each. The meaning of a survey (literally, to look over from above, to supervise) is that it deploys a technical knowledge across an otherwise unformed space, transforming it into a grid that can then be manipulated according to pre-established rules for specific purposes. In the Dominion Land Survey, the unbroken prairies were mapped into law for the purposes of the Dominion, namely settlement.

The same strategic structure governs the deployment of opinion surveys. Technical knowledge is used to generate information according to pre-established procedures for specific purposes. Most opinion surveys map respondents' answers to pre-set questions into data for the purpose of creating what is to count as knowledge. The chief difference between surveying land and surveying opinion, apart from the instruments used, is that land forms change at a rate many orders of magnitude slower than opinions. Neither is simply "scientific" or disinterested.

Like the Dominion Land Survey, opinion surveys are deployed from above. That is, they are meant to represent individual attitudes and "social facts" in a universal context. Elaborate testing of the instruments used to measure attitudes, that is, survey questionnaires, is intended to ensure comparability over time and space. The importance of the *form* of statistical data, however, is often ignored. Statistical laws of probability are valid only for large numbers of items or long periods of time. Political meaning or excellence, however, is disclosed only in those rare events and acts that light up, usually quite briefly, our everyday, normally distributed existences. This means that statistical analysis of politics eliminates significant areas of its own subject matter, namely excellence and *virtù*, by turning rare and meaningful events into error variance.

The limitation of survey research matters because, first, much of what has been published about Albertan "provincial nationalism" as a "political culture" is so sharply polemical as to be worthless except as evidence of academic resentment, and second, even subdued data analysis introduces an anti-political bias that systematically denigrates excellence. For example, the subtitle of Roger Gibbins's early book *Prairie Politics and Society: Regionalism in Decline* (1980) summarized the author's major thesis. The thesis, presented as a conclusion, "is a logical extension of C.B. Macpherson's classical study of Alberta politics." Gibbins agreed with Macpherson's general strategy of interpretation: he "set the stage" for Gibbins's own more moderate and cautious work. Gibbins did not argue that economics predetermined political behaviour, but that the emergence of a "regionally distinct political style" is dependent on social and economic conditions and that politics has a reciprocal impact upon existing "socio-economic constraints." It is not necessary to detail the limitations of quantitative analysis if one follows the maxim of the great methodologist, Jesus: "for the tree is known by his fruit."

"Discussions of prairie regionalism," Gibbins said, "and particularly of western alienation," have unfortunately not relied on numbers and "attitudinal data" but on literature, history, and descriptions of "regions of the mind." As a consequence, "the mythology and even romance" of western self-understanding have obscured the serious, which means quantitative, discussion of western alienation. The mythology and romance, he said, must be "stripped away." But data and the analysis of it do much more than strip away romance and cloudiness to reveal scientific truth. They transfigure political reality as it is directly experienced and they alter the self-interpretation of that political experience. As a consequence the result is both abstract and remote from the concrete insights provided, for instance, by literature. With sufficient skill at data manipulation anyone can aggregate a data array into a "regional perspective" or a "political culture" that then can be labelled "western alienation," which leads to the sublimely meaningless conclusion: "The attitudinal component of political regionalism [is] western alienation."

This is academic silliness at its best. "Western alienation" does not express the reality experienced by Saskatchewan grain farmers or Calgary oilmen. I have never heard anyone in either province say, "I'm so proud of my political culture! I'm alienated, you know! You should be, too!" On the contrary, it is academics, particularly from beyond any formative prairie experience, who are, so to speak, alien to the subject matter they try to study. For example, J.D. House, at the time a sociologist from Newfoundland, had great difficulty in coming to terms with the fact that oilmen seemed actually to enjoy competition. "Competition as a positive value is a difficult concept to grasp," he said, "particularly for critics conditioned to think of it as an 'unnatural' human state artificially created by capitalism itself." Naturally, this did not inspire him to revise his own sociological "conditioning" by paying attention to what his interviewees had to say.

More to the point, when you look at the body of propositions, data, and measurement of a phenomenon labelled "political alienation," it turns out, in Gibbins's words, that "many of the principal characteristics of western alienation stand in direct contrast to characteristics commonly associated with more general forms of alienation." No kidding! The fact is, western alienation does not describe westerners' sense of regional identity so far as they are concerned.

So what, then, is the point of using such an inappropriate bit of Marxist and psychoanalytic jargon? It permits non-westerners to overlook the substance of western interests and pride in the regional interpretation of them; it allows non-westerners to recast the conflict of those interests and the interpretation of them into the more congenial form of a marginalized discourse. Westerners, they can say with a clear conscience, look at matters differently than we genuine, which is to say, Laurentian, Canadians. All the fuss "out there" stems from "alienation," which is both a definitive put-down because the term used to be understood as synonymous with madness (these alienated westerners better consult an alienist) and sufficiently abstract to preclude the necessity of any further investigation. In short, the insulting posture of Macpherson has been retained, though the unseemly language of Bonapartism and *petit bourgeois* false consciousness has been purged.

It is particularly puzzling when "western alienation" is used to describe the demand for increased provincial autonomy. What makes sense for the ethnic garrison of Quebec is just a symptom of alienation in the West. The historical origins, however, go back to the West as a "Roman province" as long ago as the period of Territorial government. The focus was and is on natural resources, initially land, which was reserved "for the purposes of the Dominion," later the produce grown on the surface of the land and, more recently, the subsurface minerals. Westerners have not been "alienated" from the central institutions of power in Canada so much as excluded. Initially they were excluded by subordinate legal status, then by economic subordination, and more recently by the majoritarian character of the federal government that has never reconciled conflicting regional interests so much as identified the national interest with Laurentian Canada. While the government of Stephen Harper may be preferable to its immediate predecessors, it remains to be seen whether he has the political skill and the political support to reconcile the several interests and identities of Canadians.

The most important non-political aspects of "western alienation" Gibbins identified as an "urban nostalgia for a rural past" symbolized by "a pair of attitudinal cowboy boots" that one slips on so as to be distinctive. The implication is that the attitudes expressed by wearing cowboy boots are somehow not a genuine expression of urban life, but, as with Macpherson's views on false consciousness, a pitiable irrationality. On the other hand, if one sees oneself as a westerner, the mythic dimension can very easily include boots and even spurs, and perhaps a horse. Rather than nostalgia, it might be more accurate to say that westerners find meaning by participating in a myth of local importance, to say nothing of a preference for aesthetic, comfortable, and utilitarian footwear. More grandly and aggressively, one could speak of a cultural resistance to uniformity and the homogenizing tastes retained by plastic-shod consumers of tofu.

The malign influence of the Macpherson agenda informed nearly all the polemical analyses of the 1990s directed at the Klein government. An apogee of sorts is Doreen Barrie's *The Other Alberta: Decoding a Political Enigma* (2006). According to the latest survey research, she said, there are, indeed, real regional differences in "attitudes" but they are "often overstated." Accordingly, if you ask the right questions in a properly designed survey instrument, the result is a description of uniform and comparable "core values," which leads her to conclude that "a pan-Canadian political culture does exist."

In fact, however, this notional phenomenon exists because the survey method must treat the same answer to the same question in the same way. And when a homogeneous instrument is applied to a heterogeneous reality, it is quite impossible to tell from the results that you are dealing with data gibberish. Moreover, because this alleged culture is measured by considering "values" of respondents as reflected in their "attitudes" the question concerning the reality of "values" as artifacts of method or creatures of will can never be raised. As a consequence the discourse of survey research is never, and can never be, compared to reality because it is understood to constitute it. And yet, like the alienated oilman, it is in fact an artifact. In this case, according to Barrie, "a pan-Canadian political culture does exist" because a public opinion questionnaire designed to show its existence redeems the designer's aim. By this argument as well, the Stampede—Gibbins's attitudinal cowboy boots— is as phony as a three-dollar bill. "For about ten days every July," Barrie wrote, "people who would not know the difference between a branding iron and a curling iron, dress 'Western' for the duration of the Stampede." Why they indulge in such foolishness is part of the "enigma" her book seeks to "decode."

The first reason seems to be what she calls "intellectual alienation," namely that

> prairie residents were cut off from the intellectual
> currents of the day. Without access to radio or
> television there were no pundits to keep them
> abreast of current events and tell them what to think.
> Communication was slow and the highways we now
> take for granted did not exist. Their ideas were shaped
> by what they experienced every day, and later by the
> experiences of their American counterparts.

Particularly significant is the need for pundits to explain to the poor stubble-jumpers the meaning of events beyond their ken. Otherwise they would have to rely on their own experience or on the Americans. As a symbol, "America" and "Americans" loom large in what is wrong with Alberta and especially with Calgary, "the most American city in Canada's most American province." This statement could be either "an insult meaning a Texas North with all the negative connotations that implies," or a compliment "invoking qualities like individualism, self-reliance and risk-taking." If "Texas North" is an insult, it is unfortunate that Barrie refrains from naming the unspeakable connotations; if it is a compliment, she ignores the possibility that for some of our fellow citizens even attributes such as self-reliance may be insults.

Compared to the "pan-Canadian political culture" Alberta supplies a negative stereotype, "as unsophisticated cowboys, as right-wing rednecks who care little about their fellow Canadians." They are social conservatives, homophobic, and against both abortion and "gun control." They are also in favour of capital punishment and are anti-Semitic. In the midst of this long list of alleged and real stupidities, a cowboy is described as "someone who acts without thinking and has fallen on his head too often." Even if it were true that Albertans were no more anti-Semitic than Quebeckers or no more in favour of capital punishment than Newfoundlanders, which hardly contributes to a "pan-Canadian political culture" anyhow, the interesting question is why Albertans are stereotyped the way they are. Why, if there really is a pan-Canadian political culture, is it so easy to stereotype Albertans as cowboys in the falling-on-head sense? Barrie's answer is that Alberta "elites" have provided a misleading way of framing the issues dealing with political culture and the "mass public" have followed along. The problem with this latest version of Macphersonite or Marxist false consciousness is (1) "elites" give reasons for their opinions and positions that have to be judged in terms of accuracy and adequacy; and

(2) even if elites are master manipulators, that still does not explain the stereotype nor does it explain why the arguments elites make have the appeal they do.

The deplorable consequences, however, are clear. "Many people," she said, "draw parallels between Albertans and their southern neighbours. The self-portrait flatters and obscures the true picture while driving a wedge between Albertans and other Canadians, particularly in Central Canada." In short, Alberta's cowboy culture, even if it is imaginary, a product of false consciousness instilled by ambitious (but unnamed) elites, is the great wedge issue. The ever-elusive "national unity" has been subverted by the friendliness of Albertans toward the United States. The patriotic duty of Albertans is to become as anti-American as easterners, especially Loyalist Laurentian Canadians, and to do so in the name of national unity. One way or another, "Albertans will have to adopt a more positive view of Ottawa and Central Canada." What is apparently impossible is for Ottawa and central Canada to adopt a more positive view of Alberta.

Looking back on a half-century of prejudice and narrow-mindedness one can discern a pattern. Any number of arguments have been used to insult cowboys and their great festival, the Stampede. The purpose has been to domesticate the "maverick" nature of the West, and especially of Alberta. As Aritha van Herk helpfully informed her mostly non-cowboy readers, a maverick is an unbranded calf. Unsympathetic observers adhering to the Macpherson agenda have tried in one way or another to brand the prairie West with the familiar signs of political economy as once practised at the University of Toronto.

It need not have been this way. There are real differences between western and Laurentian Canada both in interests and in self-understanding. But provincial or regional self-identification does not conflict with patriotism, and patriotism does not imply centralist politics. To repeat the obvious: even though they take pride in different things, Alberta and the West are still part of Canada, and the Canada of which Albertans and westerners understand themselves to be a part is one of conflicting political and economic interests, and a distinct mental picture of what the country looks like. This is why westerners have adopted so many different and often surprising political strategies. As David Smith at the University of Saskatchewan has said, westerners first tried working within the dominant party of the day, then through third-party persuasion of the dominant party, then through third-party balance-of-power strategies, and finally, after further interruptions and reorganizations, through the chief opposition party, that finally became the government. "No other area of the country," he said, "has experimented with so many partisan alternatives and had so little apparent satisfaction from the results." But that is simply the way of politics. Nonpolitical solutions to political complexity look simple but they have limited effectiveness because, at the end of the day, politics is devoted to the preservation of a community that is too complex to be preserved in any other way.

Perhaps now we can answer the question posed by the title to this chapter: there is no cowboy conservatism because there is no Canadian conservatism. There is, however, a political and spiritual cowboy resistance to the Canadian state and a cowboy vision to change the Canadian regime.

CHAPTER FOUR

THE EMBEDDED STATE

"The more we relate to one another through the state,
the more divided we seem to become."
—ALAN CAIRNS

A generation ago, Alan Cairns, Ed Black, Don Smiley, Walter Young, and Kal Holsti presided over the golden age of political science at UBC. When I took Cairns's class on Canadian federalism, he was working through the arguments that later appeared in print as classic articles (and then books) in Canadian political science. When they were published, I was a newly minted assistant professor. I immediately realized the amount of intellectual capital I had surreptitiously acquired as an undergraduate. Reading Cairns's work over the next couple of decades, it is impossible not to notice how he combined great elegance of style with tremendous gifts of originality and insight. As the title of one of Cairns's papers put it, he and his colleagues at UBC combined the virtues of "insiders" and "outsiders." They were insiders insofar as they were leading political scientists both in Canada (all but Walter Young, who died at age fifty-one, were presidents of the Canadian Political Science Association) and internationally; they were outsiders insofar as they lived in Vancouver, a privileged vantage point beyond the tempting but dark triangle of power formed by Toronto, Ottawa, and Montreal. In short, they were pathfinders in Canadian political science. Most of the rest of us—to continue the metaphor—are but navigators in the bomber stream, trying to follow where they led.

This chapter takes its title from one of Cairns's great papers, "The Embedded State: State-Society Relations in Canada." I would like, however, to push the insight afforded by his paper further, perhaps a lot further, than Cairns might think proper, into the space where, as he said, "the ratio of evidence to statement is precarious." In one respect, however, the ratio is anything but precarious: over the past quarter century or so political scientists have rediscovered that the state, which means chiefly officials, civil servants, or bureaucrats, is in a position to pursue policies that may well diverge from official ones sought by the elected government. Cairns's argument, to simplify, is that any set of political demands may result as easily from state action as from the action of private individuals or elected politicians.

The 1982 constitutional changes were supposed to promote Prime Minister Trudeau's vision of "national unity." In fact, they resulted in greater fragmentation both of Canadian society and of the federal state, by which is meant both orders of government, Ottawa and the provinces. The reason, Cairns showed, was that the state became increasingly "embedded" in society—by which he meant that the boundary between the state and society has grown increasingly difficult to determine.

More than ever before, the state organizes and manages society; but by so doing it increasingly limits its own flexibility and ability to govern, in the sense of steering society in a direction other than on the existing course, a course that may well be guided by the autopilot of bureaucratic inertia. Thus the state comes increasingly to exercise its own powers on behalf of (and instead of) those it claims to benefit, namely citizens. Increasing state activity (or growing embeddedness) violates the principle of limited government or of a government limited by the constitution. Remember: a limited, constitutional government is one that could do more, but does not. Canada's governments (and especially Ottawa) have come to the point where they do what they can.

The predictable result is a society of dependants who squabble over outcomes and payoffs where, if benefits do not go to you, they can come to me. This is the essence of a zero-sum game and it is played with no sense of self-restraint for the sake of the public good or even for coalition building. The condition for playing it is to ensure the state has a stake in every outcome. In other words, Cairns's argument leads to the conclusion that the regime promotes dependency in the name of serving the interests of its subjects.

Even statistics illustrate the problem. In 1867, public expenditure was under 6 per cent of GDP; by 1929 it was around 15 per cent; in 1940, 24 per cent, where it remained, more or less, until 1960, and closely approximated the comparable American figure. During the late 1960s, a trend away from the Americans began; by 1970 Canada was at 34 per cent; by 1980 Canada reached 40 per cent and continued in this direction until 1992, when it reached a peak: in that year government expenditure reached 53.4 per cent of GDP. Since then Canada has followed a downward trend and stands today at around 41 per cent. A similar picture emerges when we look at the provinces. Almost a quarter of the workforce in Canada is employed in the public sector, which means that a large number of Canadians have a dual relationship to the state, as citizens, and as employees. Even worse, there are more politicians. In 1945, there were a total of 118 cabinet ministers in Canada. Forty years later, with the addition of one small province, there were 269. The significance of this increase is not merely that there has been a multiplication of portfolios and more faces around the cabinet table, but that each of those additional ministers presides over additional functionaries scattered across the provinces and the country in a bewildering and uncoordinated variety of departments, agencies, boards, commissions, Crown corporations, and other administrative units. Some are scrutinized by ministers but others are free-standing administrative bodies— political orphans in the sense that they are relatively and sometimes fully immune from legislative or even executive oversight. This means that efforts to challenge the decisions or even the existence of such bodies are necessarily directed toward the courts because there is nowhere else to turn.

The fragmentation engendered by this proliferation has been noticed by bureaucrats who have responded by redoubling their efforts at centralization and control, which in turn has added to the strain and widened the fault lines. If one adds to these tendencies a "bureaucratic learning" in the direction of social, political, and regulatory "animation," which is discussed below, one can anticipate a well-embedded state digging itself in deeper. In short, the federal state has grown enormously since Confederation and has continued to maintain a bulky presence in our lives during the past quarter century.

For westerners, the worst example, by far, is the Canadian Wheat Board (CWB). If you grow regulated grains in the "designated areas"—the prairies, including the Peace River area of British Columbia—the CWB is the single most important determinant of your cash flow. It handles three-quarters of the wheat produced on the prairies and about a third of the barley. Measured by sales receipts, which fluctuate around $6 billion, the CWB is perennially among the top half-dozen Canadian businesses. Moreover, the powers and operations of the current CWB are essentially those of the board established in 1943 under the War Measures Act. The pre-war board was intended to help grain producers weather price fluctuations; the 1943 changes were undertaken partly in response to inflationary concerns in Canada and partly in response to requests from the U.K. government to keep wheat prices low for the war effort. In any event, the CWB was given a monopoly to buy and sell grain for the duration of the war and was designed to be an integral part of the war-making machinery of the Canadian government. It was also intended to be temporary. Like Atomic Energy of Canada Limited (AECL), the CWB is a War Measures Act legacy organization; unlike AECL, it deals not with material that goes into the production of weapons of mass destruction but with material that goes into the production of the staff of life.

Until 1967, the CWB was required by law to have its mandate renewed every five years, which at least provided the opportunity for a perfunctory debate in Parliament. Since then, it has not been subjected to any performance review or oversight by

Parliament. The Auditor General of Canada has made some cursory examinations and in 1992 Deloitte-Touche made a comprehensive management audit, but this has never been made public because, among other privileges enjoyed by the CWB, it has total immunity from Access to Information requests. Among government agencies, only CSIS is similarly sheltered from public scrutiny.

Western grain producers today are far better educated than their fathers and grandfathers. They know nothing of the anxieties of the Great Depression, they do not view the CWB as a source of benevolent help, and they do not subscribe to the moral elevation expressed by the social gospel. They are secular, confident business people, not hungry, beaten-down serfs. This is why they have taken the board to court and have defied its self-serving edicts and gone to jail. The most telling proof of the damage done by the CWB to the West came in 1989, when for a brief period a continental market in barley existed. For this forty-day window, farmers could sell directly to American consumers, especially brewers, without going through the CWB monopoly. Volumes were huge. Somewhere between half a million and a million metric tons were sold, which compares favourably with the previous maximum of 0.47 million metric tons over a year, rather than a little over a month.

The arguments regarding the purpose and performance of the CWB are, of course, a fascinating source of endless conversation in coffee shops and hotel bars across the prairie West. For critics, the CWB is objectionable chiefly because it removes decisions regarding economic well-being from the farmers and turns it over to bureaucrats. There is no obvious benefit to the producers and plenty of reasons to think that the only economic beneficiaries are CWB employees plus a few free riders among the producers. A recent (2008) study by Informa Economics commissioned by the Government of Alberta provided convincing data that the CWB's "single desk" marketing cost farmers in the designated area about $3 billion over the past five years. Meantime western grain farmers are voting with their feet. In Ontario, which is not subject to CWB control, wheat production has increased by nearly 75 per cent; in the West it has declined by almost 40 per cent. A decade ago there were nearly twice as many wheat farmers with twice the acreage planted than exist today.

The real objections, however, are based on political principles. "Most farmers," said the Western Canadian Wheat Growers,

> would never dream of telling their neighbour how to produce their crop—why then do some farmers think it is perfectly acceptable to tell their neighbour how to market their crop? We don't collectively decide what kind of tractor to drive, what crops to grow, or what type of production system we should all use. Why should marketing decisions be any different?

Or, as the president of this organization, a young (b. 1979) woman, Cherilyn Jolly-Nagel, put it:

> We don't collectively decide on when or what we are going to seed. We don't collectively decide on when or how we are going to control the weeds in our fields. And we don't decide collectively when it's time to harvest our crops. I have never understood why

people think that we have to decide collectively how to sell our wheat. There is no one better suited to make any of those decisions than the farmer who has to live with the consequences of those decisions.

This is the voice of a citizen. This is the voice of a person who understands intuitively the difference between the state and civil society. This is the voice of one who rejects the notion that remote bureaucrats, even if they have her best interests at heart, should be permitted to exercise her rights. It is probably no accident that she lives in Saskatchewan but was educated in Alberta.

The Wheat Board may be the worst legacy example of the embedded state in action, but it is far from the only one. And the others damage more than a bunch of stubble-jumpers on the prairies. During the 1960s and 1970s, the Government of Canada developed a new strategy to modify the regime by expanding the reach of the state in such a way that Canadians would adapt to increased government coercion, inducement, oversight, incentives, and obligations but in a way that the growth of the state could be turned to their own advantage and enable them to influence the policy agenda before it crystallized as legislation and regulation. In this way, the increased scope of state activities and the increased visibility of the state in selectively distributing goods and services would transmit the less obtrusive message that status, income, recognition, and power are not simply the reward of efforts in the marketplace or in the public arena, but may also be the result of administrative or bureaucratic creativity and effort directed at setting the agenda of the state. The increased size, visibility, and importance of the state in Canada is thus presented as an opportunity as much as a burden. If you are in the right place and you have the right skills, you can take advantage of everything from helping "official language minorities" to promoting sequestration of carbon dioxide in subterranean caves.

Even if, for example, there was not much of a demand for French-language poetry readings in Saskatoon, an "in-depth attack on mass apathy," as the "Social Action" branch of the office of the Secretary of State put it, would eventually result in "better understanding between the two official linguistic communities." High on the list of priorities was the creation of "animateurs" to encourage groups to organize and, eventually, to apply for government funds to promote programs that, in the beginning, only the bureaucrats in the "social animation" business considered to be important. This was a pioneer program. It was set up in response to what Les Pal, who studied these programs, called the "regime crisis" that was precipitated by Quebec, first in the Quiet Revolution and then by the separatists. It was far from the last bureaucratic response to this alleged crisis. The result, however, has been to make it worse.

A process analogous to "social animation" by Secretary of State officials has accompanied the growth of "Charter politics," only here the courts have, on occasion, ordered legislatures to spend money on issues that either otherwise would be ignored or, even more significant, having been considered by the legislature, were rejected. In addition, by using a language that linked the individual to Ottawa, the logic of the Charter has led to the "constitutionalization" of individuals by means of Charter-defined attributes. Citizens, when defined as aboriginal, female, disabled, or gay Canadians, over time come to see themselves as having acquired and occupied constitutional "niches" or "constitutional identities" that in turn can develop into the predominant self-conception or self-understanding of the individuals or groups so defined. Moreover, once rights were enshrined in the Charter, rights-holders were tempted to employ a rhetoric of non-bargaining and no-compromise. After all, a right is a right and it is con-stitutionally guaranteed. Politics may be all about prudent compromise and civility; adjudication in court produces win-ners and losers. No one compromises constitutional rights. Or so went the rhetoric.

By enhancing the state-defined, civic aspect of individual lives, rather than protecting the private or the personal, which is, after all, the traditional purpose of such documents, the chief result of the Charter has been the growth, not the retreat or the limitation, of the national state. It is not obvious in the great political scheme of things that spousal benefits, as a justiciable right, belong to lesbian couples, nor that women have a right to go topless through the streets of Kingston, or that men have a right to collect kiddie porn instead of stamps. These profound legal changes constitute what my colleagues Rainer Knopff and Ted Morton call the Charter revolution.

Revolutions, we know, have costs. The costs of the Charter revolution may not have been paid by filling public squares with the severed heads of aristocrats. But not every bill is a butcher's bill. There are some transaction costs that are simply measured, however roughly, in global increases in lawyers' fees or an expanding litigation industry. Other costs are borne by all Canadians through increased budgets to departments with increased legal costs that are necessarily paid from tax revenues. There are other less tangible costs as well, arising from the effects of the judicialization of politics within the embedded state. Among these "political costs" has been an increase in the number, scope, and importance of judicially focused interest groups.

Consider language groups. It may be difficult to recall today, but language interests were not always a matter of legal right. The two major language groups were once accommodated, more or less, by means of federalism—that is, within *divided* legislative jurisdictions—rather than adjudicated as rights within a single unified court system. Politically speaking, minority language *rights* were designed by the federal government to keep alive a symbolic notion of "French Canada" that would in all likelihood not be fostered by any of the provinces, including Quebec. The predominantly English-speaking provinces were unlikely to volunteer, and Quebec had its own counter-symbol: not French Canadians but Quebeckers. As with the operations of the Canadian Wheat Board, the action of the state in exercising as well as securing rights has been to increase fragmentation. In English-speaking Canada, bilingual signs in Smithers have been as divisive as the silliness of the language police in Quebec. To state the obvious: when courts and administrative organs become the locus for political action rather than the legislature, we are dealing with a new regime. If "Charter revolution" means anything, it certainly means changing the law.

Once again we must ask: *Cui bono?* Who are the beneficiaries of such a regime? Apart from those who administer it, it is perhaps enough to note that, in Canada, Charter-revolutionaries have been highly successful in using the opportunities afforded by the embedded state to advance their political agenda. The earliest ways of advancing interests took the form of specialization with regard to ss. 16–28 of the Charter. Today, as many observers have said, it is impossible to understand Canadian *politics* without taking interest-group *litigation* into account. But this is litigation with a difference. Instead of going to court to protect the liberty or other interests of a litigant, court action is launched in order to change policy. The results, however, are bound to be divisive. To repeat: because judicial decisions are adjudicative, they are about winning and losing, the ultimate zero-sum game, not, as in legislatures, about seeking agreement and fostering like-mindedness. As Ian Brodie observed of the Court Challenges Program, the litigious successor to aggrieved minorities seeking "social animation" with the aid of bureaucrats, it "represents the embedded state at war with itself in court." On September 25, 2006, this ill-considered program was cancelled by the Conservative government led by Stephen Harper. Ian Brodie was, at the time, serving as his chief of staff. It was a tiny step on the road to disembedding the state, and a clear indication how such programs take on a life of their own unless they are explicitly killed. Its death was mourned only by its actual beneficiaries: lawyers and spokespersons who acted on behalf of its alleged beneficiaries, the men and women the program kept dependent on the state.

In his analysis of civil libertarian supporters of the Charter, Peter Russell distinguished between old-fashioned "believers" in civil liberties who took their direction from the common law dictum that "whatever the law does not prohibit is allowed," and the "hopers," whom he identified as "egalitarians of the left" who hoped the Charter would be an instrument for reforming society. Whereas the civil libertarians believed the Charter was essential for preserving liberty, the egalitarians hoped it would bring about social equality; in general, believers favour equal opportunities for individuals, hopers favour equal results for groups. Indeed, because equal results for groups are not a present reality, equal opportunities for individuals must be suspended. Accordingly, hopers seek preferential treatment in order either to compensate groups that have been badly treated in the past (the "historically disadvantaged") or to promote group equality in the future, or both. One of the inevitable consequences of the policies advocated by hopers is more not less government spending. Nowhere is this observation more true than with respect to "First Nations."

A generation ago, Status Indians were wards of the Crown in right of Canada, "citizens minus." Today they claim to be first nations with an inherent right to self-government—"citizens plus," as Cairns put it. Behind Status Indians stand Nonstatus Indians, Inuit, and Metis ready to make the same claims. The issue to which I would draw attention in this context is not concerned with the prudence or validity of such claims. For the record, however, the notion that Metis are also "First Nations" is palpably absurd since their biological existence requires genetic material from non-aboriginals. Nor is it clear how much Indian blood is required: it is worth recalling that Peter Lougheed is more ethnic Cree than Louis Riel. And if, as the courts have ruled, adopting a primitive way of life is relevant, perhaps Grey Owl, a full-blooded Englishman, ought to be enrolled as a member of a First Nation of one. Beyond the sheer stupidity of such reflections is the more serious issue, that such stupidity has been turned into aboriginal policy by the courts.

Recall first some uncontentious facts. Section 35 of the Constitution Act, 1982, declares that "existing aboriginal and treaty rights of the aboriginal peoples of Canada are hereby recognized and confirmed." In 1981, when this particular formula was being concluded, no one knew what the effective legal and political meaning of aboriginal rights might be. Peter Lougheed wished to limit aboriginal rights to those currently in effect. Thus the inclusion of the word "existing" in section 35. For their part, spokesmen for the aboriginal groups objected to the qualification.

The Supreme Court of Canada in the 1990 *Sparrow* decision effectively extinguished this limitation by a very broad definition of "existing." Then the courts ruled that they, not legislatures, would decide if the government had upheld "the honour of the Crown." Finally, as Tom Flanagan has pointed out, the conditions for litigation, such as the admission of oral traditions and hearsay on the same basis as documents and archaeological evidence, ensure that the courts will cease to be fora for adjudication and become places where everything is up for negotiation and renegotiation—a task, as noted above, for which win-lose courts are singularly ill-equipped.

Other examples less notorious than the cwb or interest-group litigation might be briefly noted. Consider the impact environmentalists have had on Banff National Park. There are two preliminary points to be made. First, environmentalists have succeeded in changing the 1930 National Parks Act in one very important regard. Section 4 of the act stated: "Parks are hereby dedicated to the people of Canada for their benefit, education and enjoyment, subject to the provisions of this Act and

Regulations, and such Parks shall be maintained and made use of so as to leave them unimpaired for the enjoyment of future generations." This provision for preservation and enjoyment is usually called the "dual mandate." According to environmentalists, however, "a proper reading of the National Parks Act of 1930 reveals that . . . there was no dual mandate." Rather, what is now called "ecological integrity" or EI was always the one and only goal. In plain language, the purpose of enjoyment has been increasingly restricted in order to promote ever-greater preservation, now packaged as "wilderness values." This is why, for example, the Banff Park ski hills have routinely been denied permits to modernize and upgrade, even after filing extensive and expensive environmental impact reports. The only consequence has been to encourage ski-hill development outside the federal parks in nearby B.C. wilderness areas.

Moreover, this transformation of the plain meaning of the act from the dual purpose of preservation and use into the single purpose of ecological integrity has been justified in the language of wildlife biology that, on closer inspection, is based on highly questionable methodological assumptions and on population models with utterly unreliable predictive capacities. Whether from confessional honesty or regret at scientific dishonesty, one grizzly advocate and researcher allowed that "biases and values" have influenced data collection among "scientific" field workers. This regrettably unscientific wildlife advocacy, in turn, is justified by what can only be called religious commitments among the more romantically inclined of environmentalist lawyers who deliver inspirational sermons about "magic in nature" and a "spiritual hunger" that apparently is satiated by reflection on the existence of cougars and grizzlies, which have been born again as "charismatic megafauna." Snails and birds attract fewer devotions.

The problem is not that individuals should be prevented from holding (within wide limits) whatever religious views they wish, but that a belief in the "magic of nature" is not a prudent starting point for sound public policy. Nor can we expect wildlife biologists to be devoid of personal convictions. We can, however, expect that scientific research undertaken with public funds and that has a direct influence on the management of Crown lands would be carried out with the assurance that the "biases and values" of the researchers have a limited impact on their findings. In fact, unfortunately, many wildlife biologists whose work has strongly influenced the policies of Parks Canada do not meet this standard. Moreover, much of what is published as "preliminary findings," a perfectly acceptable procedure in biology or any other science, turns out to be selective findings, the purpose of which is to polarize the options: *either* increase restrictions on human activity *or* environmental desolation will inevitably follow.

Aside from ideological motives and a quasi-scientific discourse used to express them, the most striking fact about environmentalists' activities in Banff is their ability to create strategic alliances with Parks Canada officials and with universities and other NGO research institutions and advocacy organizations, that is, with civil society. As a consequence, universities are in a position to supply research to Parks Canada and in turn Parks Canada makes funds available to ensure the research is undertaken. Moreover, the connection between the "mission" of conservation biology and Parks Canada recruitment has ensured that the ranks of this branch of the state are increasingly filled with individuals whose sense of purpose has been shaped by the "values and biases" that favour reducing and eventually extinguishing human use of the parks. Environment Canada likewise funds "research" on so-called anthropogenic climate change because it is an article of faith; it does not fund "climate sceptics" because, it says (along with the United Nations) that "the science is settled." The fact is, science is *never* settled, whether it pertains to grizzly ranges in the Rockies or suv emissions melting the Greenland ice cap. Those who declare that science is settled by the same words declare they are not scientists—despite their credentials and positions in universities and the status afforded by Canada Research Chairs.

As in other areas of Canadian life, the Charter and associated jurisprudence have provided an opportunity for political action on the environmental front. Much of this litigation is funded directly or indirectly by the Sierra Legal Defence Fund (SLDF), based in San Francisco. The SLDF acts, for example, as legal adviser to the Panel on Ecological Integrity and has acted on behalf of a wide range of clients in Banff, all of whom oppose dual- or multiple-use policies for the parks. So far as I know, the vociferously left-wing Canadian nationalists have been silent about this particular mode of American imperial power.

The creation of the Parks Canada Agency illustrated another significant policy strategy, namely that fundamental reorganization can be a way of meeting specific policy problems. The use of organizational redesign as a policy instrument is intended not to effect greater coordination among "policy communities" or to improve the efficiency of a given government organ such as the Atlantic Canada Opportunities Agency (ACOA). ACOA, its predecessors, and successors have all been failures in the sense of being incapable of fulfilling their ostensible purposes. But, by reorganizing, ACOA could build in a set of mandatory policies to the "new" agency that would at least keep it in existence. Likewise, by turning the national parks service into a separate corporate entity, a new set of fundamental assumptions could be written into the bureaucratic structure of Parks Canada itself, with the consequence that thereafter anyone doing business with the new organization would, and could, do so only on the basis of the new and hereafter unquestioned assumptions.

This explains why, when the new Parks Act passed, executives in the Canadian Parks and Wilderness Society, CPAWS, expressed the hope that they would become "a partner in guiding the direction of the *entire* park system." Likewise, the Parks Canada EI Report pointed to the approaching retirement of approximately 60 per cent of the Parks Canada staff as an opportunity to improve the corporate culture or, more accurately, to recast the ideological profile of the agency's workforce. To the objection "so what?" the following answer can be made: first, the future of public policy in Banff Park, and perhaps in all of Canada's federal parks, now depends on the integration of the new EI mandate into the management protocols and operational practices of the new Parks Canada Agency.

No one would argue against the maintenance of ecological integrity in the common-sense understanding of the term; obviously it looks like an important goal for sensible parks management. But what has been consistently demanded by environmentalists is that Ecological Integrity, understood in a highly technical way that, it is alleged, only environmental experts can truly grasp and turn into policy and regulations, should be the *only* priority in the management of these public lands. The implications for human use and enjoyment and for local economies are simply not addressed. Indeed, considering such matters at all is widely considered by environmentalists to be entirely inappropriate, perhaps even obscene.

The problem, however, is that by progressively narrowing a technical definition of EI, environmentalists have succeeded in undermining the multiple-use notions that gave Canadians national parks in the first place. Without the revenue produced by human use, it is *almost* needless to add, general revenues raised from taxes will have to make up the difference. Unfortunately, no cost estimates are currently available to put a price tag on this particular piece of bureaucratic animation. Once again it is considered by environmentalists to be unseemly even to raise such issues. "It's a *park* we're talking about," they say and understand that this means further discussion of costs and benefits, or even purposes, is in very poor taste. Even so, the "dividends" resulting from direct state "investment" in EI advocacy are measured by huge bills for businesses, for property owners and lease holders, and for park users. The only obvious beneficiaries are the narcissistic environmentalists who feel good about themselves for helping the charismatic megafauna.

To the extent that the changes in the legislation governing Canada's national parks are a cautionary tale, it would seem that only wildlife biologists and other environmental scientists are at risk in having not their ecological integrity but their scientific integrity challenged. Social scientists have, in fact, been largely excluded from various panels and commissions and from studies that have had such an importance for the formation of parks policy. There were, for instance, no human geographers on the landmark Banff Bow Valley Study, even though human use of the Bow Valley west of Calgary is rather significant. Summer and winter, the park is a major recreational venue for outdoorsy Calgarians.

In the future, probably in other areas of public policy, social scientists are likely to become beneficiaries, or rather victims, of state-directed bureaucratic animation initiatives. In July 1996, the Clerk of the Privy Council launched a new program called the Policy Research Initiative or PRI. Someone in Ottawa determined there was a need "to strengthen policy capacity" in the federal civil service because of a new set of challenges. These challenges were characterized as a complex policy environment that required "greater cooperation and horizontality" on the one hand, and, on the other, "policy development [that] has become more reactive than proactive, resulting in a weakened capacity to deal with long-term strategic and horizontal issues."

Those who are familiar with the way that state policy is described these days will find the language, if not the objective, familiar. It was just such "horizontal policy" initiatives that brought ACOA into the world and that lay behind the symbiotic relationship between Parks Canada, the environmental activists, and the scientific-sounding discourse of the beneficiaries of Parks Canada's largesse. So far the results have included only a few mega-buck grants to political scientists and their consulting companies. The significance of the PRI was not that it supports building "a solid foundation of horizontal research" among some thirty government departments—no one could oppose more research, after all. The "next phase," however, would involve "building existing relationships and forging new knowledge partnerships" with "other orders of government and non-government players." These non-government players, generally speaking, are think-tanks. According to Herman Bakvis, there are about forty non-university affiliated think-tanks in Canada, nearly half of which are located in Ottawa. Of these, about a third receive between 85 and 95 per cent of their funding from Canadian taxpayers. About 10 per cent receive no government, that is, taxpayer, funding. Outside Ottawa, about half the think-tanks receive no money from the state, whether federal or provincial.

Again the obvious question: so what? It is unquestionably true that many of the people staffing the Ottawa-based think-tanks have been downsized from government departments where they used to undertake in-house research, and naturally enough, they are interested in supplementing their severance packages or pensions with contracts. Their laments, for instance, that the Chrétien government appointed no significant royal commissions during its time in office is understandable purely on grounds of self-interest. However, when a civil servant from the PRI stated that the most pressing issue in the world of think-tanks was that they were not cooperating with each other in undertaking the necessary exercises in horizontal thinking, one must raise questions about government priorities. There do seem to be more important things for these NGOs to do, such as undertake independent public policy research (from a rich variety of perspectives, let me hasten to add) than to cooperate with one another under the guidance of the PRI. And yet, since the PRI's inception, the Canadian state has dispensed some $3 million of taxpayers' money each year on it, which in turn recirculates the money into contract research, sponsored conferences, and glossy, glib publications such as the now defunct *isuma*. Perhaps some day a cautionary tale can be written of the influence of the PRI on social science.

Among other spending initiatives of highly questionable merit are those that have led to the creation of "foundations." According to the auditor general, more than $9 billion has been spent on organizations that deal with such matters as innovation, sustainable development, and "aboriginal healing." Once established on the basis of line items in a departmental budget, they become at least nominally independent and are given no further oversight either by the ministry or by Parliament. A consistent finding by the auditor general, which has been disputed by Treasury Board, is that accountability in these organizations is unsatisfactory.

No doubt there are many additional examples of the embedded state that could be discussed but the general point so far as the regime is concerned seems clear enough. In all these state initiatives, the problem is not $3 million here or $5 million there, but the multiplier effects of state-induced advocacy. And second, as Cairns said and we quoted at the beginning of this chapter, "the more we relate to one another through the state, the more divided we seem to become." That is, the greatest effect is found in the demoralization that results among ordinary Canadian citizens. If anecdotal evidence can be trusted concerning the low esprit de corps even of those who are charged with relating us all to one another, namely the bureaucrats employed by the Canadian state, not even they seem to be benefiting. Let us, therefore, enter the belly of the beast, or if you prefer, the heart of darkness, and consider directly the bureaucracy, what it does, and who pays.

CHAPTER FIVE

SINEWS OF BUREAUCRACY

*"The bureaucracy takes itself to be the
ultimate purpose of the state."*
—KARL MARX

It never troubles a wolf, how many the sheep be," wrote
Francis Bacon in his reflections on the true greatness of king-
doms and estates. "Many are the examples," he went on, "of
the great odds, between number and courage; so that a man
may truly make a judgement, that the principal point of greatness in any state, is to have a race of military men. Neither is
money the sinews of war (as it is trivially said) where the sinews
of men's arms, in base and effeminate people, are failing."
Among the many things to ponder in Bacon's terse essay is that,
when a people grows base and effeminate, money is indeed the
sinews, if not of war, then of everyday politics. It may be that
"the principal part of greatness" is the military because of the
importance of the virtue of courage, even though greatness is
subordinate to justice in the great scheme of things. But can a
people celebrate justice without ever encountering greatness?

Or to put it another way: when the sinews of men's arms are failing, can either justice or greatness ever appear in the world? This chapter is about bureaucracy, which is neither the greatest nor the most exciting topic in the world. Bureaucracy is, however, central to understanding what the Canadian regime has become. Indeed, the extent to which money has become the sinews of administration in Canada is a measure of an absence of greatness that reached its most sordid expression in the advertising scandals brought to light by the Gomery Commission, which is discussed in the following chapter. Let us begin, however, with more pleasant matters.

A constitution, it was argued, should embody principles, procedures, and institutions that do not easily go out of date and so do not need frequent amending—including amending by judges. A constitution is the supreme law, not a collection of vague principles to be craftily circumvented. Moreover, it should be above partisan advantage rather than be used for partisan advantage. It is designed to establish an equilibrium. In the first instance, it creates an equilibrium between the state and civil society, and so between the state and the citizen. That is, a constitution is designed to limit government, which is what we usually mean by political freedom. In addition, in a federal state, it creates an equilibrium between orders of government. As the great jurist A.V. Dicey pointed out in Queen Victoria's time, in a federal constitutional monarchy—and he had Canada in mind—the constitution is necessarily supreme precisely because the Crown is distributed by it into the Crown in right of Canada and the Crown in right of the several provinces. This division of legal responsibilities and the presupposition of constitutional supremacy long antedated the modern assertion by activist judges of their own understanding of what constitutional supremacy meant—namely judicial supremacy, the very opposite of what Dicey had in mind. In short, the law of the constitution establishes the framework for political action and the rules of the game. It is not meant to solve problems.

Historically, Europeans used the term *civil society* to refer to an association of individuals brought together chiefly by the rule of law that those same individuals had a hand in establishing, changing, and obeying. The word, and the reality to which it referred, has been part of the self-understanding of Western societies for nearly two hundred years. To give a famous example, in 1821, Hegel distinguished in his "textbook" on politics, *The Philosophy of Right*, the three realms of individual and family, civil society, and the state. Business enterprises, universities, churches and other religious and secular associations, newspapers, and recreational clubs were all included in civil society. A few years later Alexis de Tocqueville, in *Democracy in America* (1835), drew attention to the wide range and large number of voluntary associations in the Anglo-Saxon democracies. It was Tocqueville's argument that liberty in these countries, including what became Canada, was sustained and supported in large measure because so much of public life was lived outside the purview of the state. Indeed, modern theorists of liberal democracy have drawn on Tocqueville and his predecessors to argue persuasively and in great detail that today civil society, that arena of freedom outside state supervision, has sustained the prosperity, the technological progress, the civility, and the cultural flourishing of modern societies. These may not be the greatest of human achievements, but they are not trivial.

At the same time as civil society has sustained the liberties of citizens, it has been modified by other measures made necessary by the defence of liberty, including warfare. On occasion, additional modifications have been justified in terms of "greater liberty" by advocates of welfare. Specifically, in Canada, during World War II, the government ruled under the authority of the War Measures Act in order to mobilize the resources of the nation, the whole of civil society, in pursuit of the war effort. When the war was successfully concluded, the administrative structures established for the duration were only partly dismantled. In addition, the habits of mind developed in wartime were carried over into the post-war world. Because memories of the Great Depression had not faded from the minds of senior officials in Ottawa who were themselves schooled in Keynesian economic doctrines, the procedures and administrative interventions that had worked so well in warfare were applied over the next decades to promoting welfare.

According to J.K. Galbraith, an ardent Keynesian, Canada "was perhaps the first country to commit itself unequivocally to a firmly Keynesian economic policy." Considered from a political or a public administration perspective, the triumph of Keynesianism strengthened the hand of those who sought to embed the federal state in civil society. Moreover, by advocating the use of fiscal policy in the hope that the state could adjust economic demand, maintain high employment, and avoid inflation, Keynesianism was used to justify both increased monitoring by the state of civil society and increased and long-term deficit budgeting, which is not what Keynes had in mind. In this way, and with a clear conscience that comes when men of action tell themselves their intentions are good, the effort directed by "the Ottawa men" to improve economic and social well-being through higher spending launched the assault by the state on civil society. This change was most obviously recorded in increased state spending, increased taxation, and increased state borrowing. It was not immediately obvious who the beneficiaries would be.

The malign consequences for the autonomy and spontaneity of civil society took longer to appear in post-war Canada than occurred with the invocation of the War Measures Act in 1939, but the effects of state-directed welfare have been both more insidious and more fundamental. Civil society, and especially the economy, produces not only prosperity, but winners and losers. The formal equality of citizens before the law means that losers may be tempted to appeal to the state to extend state-secured legal equalities to the arena of civil society as well. But, as we have argued above, when the desires of the needy are turned into the political demand that the state satisfy them by providing social security, benefits, and entitlements, the result can only be to transform independent citizens into dependent subjects. In this way the purposes of civil society are eclipsed and the state enhances the dependence of the needy and extends it to those who previously had dealt with their own needs and maintained responsibility for their own independence.

For example, businesses that once were bastions of liberty under the banner of free enterprise may become constituents of a national economy regulated and directed by government, which in turn ensures their survival by protectionist measures that exclude foreign competitors. The arts, now known in Canada as the "cultural industries," are considered by some to be expressions of national "identity." Others see them as enticements for tourists to visit and spend foreign currency in Canada and so provide benefits to Canadian society as a whole. Thus they too must be protected from foreign competition whatever the cultural tastes of Canadians may be. In fact, however, the contemporary understanding of a cultural industry in need of protection refers to little more than an entertainment industry that is maintained by widely sharing the costs (through the taxation system) and tightly focusing the benefits (on Crown corporations in the entertainment business, such as CBC, for example). On this latter example, former Prime Minister Mulroney explained to Peter Newman, in colourful language, the true position of the corporation. "You've got to be right out of your mind," he said, "to think that the CBC is a public broadcaster. This is not a public broadcaster—this is a private broadcaster and it's being broadcast for the benefit of the CBC. It's conducted for the benefit of the employees of the CBC, not for Canadians." If Mulroney is correct, the actual CBC combines the worst of both the private and the public sectors, which makes it a special case.

Likewise the "knowledge industry," which used to be known as the schools, colleges, technical institutes, and universities of the country, is understood by the state as consisting of resources to be regulated and directed in response to bureaucratic initiatives and priorities usually modified by the adjective "strategic." As the state developed policies for the needy, the disabled, "visible minorities," women, aboriginal people, and so on, they instructed all sectors of civil society, from old-fashioned businesses to the newer cultural and knowledge industries, on how to order and direct their human resources. Along with this direction has come regulation and reporting requirements and responsibilities to ensure that the several regulated sectors of civil society are in compliance with state-directed administrative orders. Thus have physicians become incorporated into the national health care delivery system and social workers have become agents of the state welfare system. Often "bureaucratic animation" has not even been necessary. The mere change of regulations, of laws, or of incentives has been sufficient to transform vigilant institutions of civil society such as universities into "strategic partners" of the state. Such transformations constitute regime changes as well.

One of the reasons that the needy and even more their various and limitless needs are held in such high regard follows from the peculiar moralizing language used in Canada to discuss public policy. One way, for example, to disguise what to common sense looks like dependency and servility is to introduce the notions of "compassion" and "social responsibility." The fact is, a civil society of free and responsible individuals is at the core of modern constitutional democracy, but it is also true that human beings are capable of holding responsibilities only with respect to specific duties. We may well have duties toward our superiors, our subordinates, our neighbours and friends, but no one can have a duty toward something as protean, vague, boundless, and amorphous as "society." At best, it is a figure of speech that suggests we behave politely to strangers on the bus. At worst, it is a justification for the state to instruct us and compel us to do something we otherwise would not do.

The way a "duty to society" tends to be made effective is first to convene an assembly of busybodies, then to call them "stakeholders," and finally to "empower" them to create regulations to govern a "social partnership." These organizations, too, are occasionally exalted by being modified by the adjective "strategic." Thus a notional, but in the era of the embedded state, not a fantastic Government Task Force on Social Animation may be convened by the Office of the Secretary of State for the New Economy inspired by a bold mission statement "to create a new strategic social partnership of empowered stakeholders to determine how a well-organized civil society might best perform its social duties." Apart from the emptiness of such language, the whole purpose of civil society is subverted by bureaucratic initiatives to organize and administer it: civil society is precisely that aspect of political reality that, like play, is spontaneous. To the extent that the state is in the business of social animation, it kills spontaneity. The confusion introduced by such language is basic and akin to the notion that a tax refund is the gift of a generous government.

The other side of this confusion, which is built into the embedded state, can be seen with government support of non-government organizations or NGOs. Very often NGOs claim to represent civil society even though they are sustained by grants administered by the state. As we saw in the previous chapter, state-supported NGOs may be in the business of lobbying governments or they may go to court to provide sympathetic judges with an opportunity to issue rulings to compel the state to do what it dare not do by itself. Such NGOs, of course, are incapable of representing civil society either domestically or on the international stage. They can represent only themselves and they do so with other people's money, mostly that of taxpayers. In fact, the only way people can be represented in Canada is by voting for members of provincial and national legislatures. Accordingly, the fraudulent claims of pseudo-representation by NGOs should be understood as an attack on democratic institutions, and especially on the right to vote, not a supplement to them or an improvement of them.

These observations are meant to outline commonsensical principles, not grand theory. The political institutions that constitute the embedded state did not arise overnight and it is just as certain that they cannot be reversed easily or quickly. Canadians have, however, noticed that something significant has changed in the course of a generation or so. The decline in the confidence Canadians have in "their" bureaucracy has even been noticed by the bureaucrats. Jocelyne Bourgon, former Clerk of the Privy Council and secretary to cabinet, seemed surprised to learn that "some 32 per cent of Canadians do not believe that government is a positive force in their lives." She was surprised that the number was so high; I am surprised it is so low. Clearly she had never heard the bitter joke: "I'm from the federal government and I'm here to help you." In fact, citizen disengagement is inevitable once the state becomes too large to be held accountable. To see what is meant by "too large," we need to know what the optimal size of government is. To see what "accountability" means, we must consider the meaning of federalism. One of the reasons the state is too large is that our governments have forgotten about federalism.

Using somewhat different measures, concepts, and approaches, economists and political scientists have developed complementary measures of the optimal size of the modern state in relation to civil society. The previous chapter provided examples of how the federal state has grown since the end of World War II. Likewise, the process of making decisions has become more elaborate and complex. Federal spending has grown, along with the size of the bureaucracy, at rates significantly higher than the rate at which the Canadian population has increased.

When the state is growing, either absolutely or relative to the size of the economy—or of civil society more broadly— negative economic effects can be anticipated along with a reduction in individual liberty and responsibility in other areas of civil society. The economic argument is straightforward. In developing it, it is important to bear in mind that governments generally speaking do not spend whatever they raise by taxation. On the contrary, they set taxation levels to cover all or at least most of their expenditures. That is, spending drives taxation, not vice versa. The optimal size of the state, therefore, is directly connected to tax policy, and that is a political choice, not an economic one.

Overwhelming evidence exists that state-directed economies tend to produce lower quality goods at higher prices than market economies. The reason is that states are concerned with political as well as economic goals—chiefly the balance between welfare and warfare, or guns and butter as they used to say. The importance of welfare in state enterprises explains why they are relatively undercapitalized compared to private-sector equivalents; that is, promoting welfare reduces the search for efficiency and the tendency to substitute capital (technological improvement, for example) for labour. Monopoly tends to make matters worse, as do public-sector unions, which typically command a wage premium in conjunction with an absence of incentives to provide good service.

In the previous chapter, we noted the divergent trend in the late twentieth century between Canada and the United States on the measure of public expenditures as a percentage of GDP. The trend is even more pronounced if military expenditures are excluded. Apart from a naïve ideological faith in the possibility of government help, the assumption underlying government expansion was that beneficiaries could be accurately and easily targeted with attendant low administrative costs. In Canada, after 1960 in particular, welfare, not warfare, was the chief justification for increasing the presence and size of the state within the economy. Within the general category of welfare, transfers and subsidies to regions and individuals rather than public consumption on marble halls and grand festivals or public investment in roads or schools was the chief vehicle for expenditures. What began as a state-guaranteed social safety net became a universal entitlement and arguably a constitutional right under s. 36 of the Charter. The consequence, we know, has been the tendency to turn citizen self-respect into the self-contempt of victims and dependants.

When economists, who a decade or so ago were impressed by economic growth rates among "newly industrialized countries," calculated the optimal size of government relative to economic growth, the lowest value calculated the percentage of government expenditure of GDP at 17 per cent. The highest was double that. But even at 34 per cent, the optimal size of government is significantly less than current estimates of the state presence in Canadian civil society and of supporting Canadian tax rates.

Things look different from Ottawa because the bureaucracy constitutes an exception to the growth of passivity and dependence in civil society. The bureaucrats who make up the state and administer welfare take great pride in their own compassion, and in their willingness to do things for others. They, and the new denizens of the policy environment—the consultants and lobbyists and political hangers-on in Ottawa—are the chief beneficiaries of the embedded state. This is why Ottawa is both inflation-proof and depression-proof. The unique status of that city and of its inhabitants was emphatically brought home to me when I visited the capital in 1983 after an absence of several years, and at the height of the National Energy Program that had inflicted a terrible human and financial cost on Calgary. Ottawa was a different world, not just a different city. Subsequent visits over the years have confirmed this impression.

The federal bureaucracy has been able to claim its new place in the sun by overturning the constitutionally allocated position of the civil service in a parliamentary democracy. According to constitutional theory, the civil service has no constitutional personality or responsibility distinct from the government of the day. Ministers of the Crown direct the civil service because they have formal responsibility and are accountable and answerable to Parliament for the activities of the department over which they preside. Government delivers its programs through the line departments and agencies staffed by a single, homogeneous, and politically neutral public service, and Parliament is charged with scrutinizing everything that goes on in the departments. Formal responsibility or "responsible government" describes the minister's duty to Parliament and the corresponding duty of Parliament to know how the power of the state is being used. It does not mean that ministers invariably take the blame if bureaucrats make mistakes, but only that the bureaucrats are not directly responsible

Parliament or answerable to Parliament. It is now considered entirely appropriate, for example, for officials to answer to parliamentary committees for administrative matters, though only the minister can defend government policy in Parliament.

Once upon a time, the civil service was admired for conforming to the constitutional theory. They were respected for their professionalism, competence, frugality, loyalty, and self-effacement. Moreover, there were not very many of them; they were a poorly paid elite. The Clerk of the Privy Council was not a superbureaucrat at the head of an enormous civil service, but a clerk, a stenographer. In 1950, according to Gordon Robertson, a federal-provincial conference (today dignified as a First Ministers' Conference) would be conducted by 75 officials. Today it takes 400 to do the same job. As late as 1990, 60 per cent of the federal civil service were blue-collar workers; today 60 per cent are "knowledge workers." During the 1950s and early 1960s, politicians and civil servants operated in distinct worlds, keeping information to themselves or counting on the media to be discreet, which they were. This is one reason that Canadians trusted their government. In short, bureaucrats once were servants first of all, not empire builders or self-aggrandizing players in the policy process. They were grey and they sought anonymity. "Village life" in Ottawa was calmly conducted and sustained by an ethos of "speaking truth to power," but doing so quietly and with discretion.

The great qualitative change in Ottawa began a generation ago and has been lovingly chronicled by Donald Savoie. The bureaucrats of the line departments grew timid but the central agencies—Finance, the PMO, the PCO, and Treasury Board—grew bold. Unlike the line departments, the central agencies deliver no services. They regulate the deliverers to ensure compliance with government directives on official bilingualism, employment equity, minority language group initiatives, and so on. They watch the line departments, but no one, alas, watches them. "Governing from the centre," to use the title of one of Savoie's splendid books, meant both governing from Ottawa and using the central agencies to do it.

"Classification creep," the process of creating new senior management levels—associate assistant deputy minister, associate deputy minister, senior associate deputy minister, and the like—ensures there will be more bureaucrats available to manage "the process." In 2003, there were nineteen associate deputy ministers and three deputy secretaries in the PCO who were classified as associate deputy ministers. The impact of all this new expertise has been felt both in Parliament and in the civil service.

The need for cabinet ministers to clear legislative proposals with officials in the PMO, for example, has changed cabinet from a decision-making body, the actual seat of the executive in a parliamentary system, into a venue for information sharing where the prime minister and senior ministers present the big picture, which is then filled in by bureaucrats from the central agencies. Cabinet has become an executive in name only. In fact it is, in Savoie's apt phrase, a "focus group."

So far as legislation goes, Parliament is even less than a focus group. The replacement of cabinet-as-executive with central-agencies-as-executive has exempted Parliament from ever holding the real executive to account. Rule changes make delay of legislative timetables and the possibility of genuine scrutiny of government estimates impossible.

The decline of Parliament, which has been widely lamented for decades, has not been accompanied by the rise of the bureaucrats in the place once held by MPs. It is not a zero-sum game. In fact, the integrity and authority of the civil service have also declined, and it is no more able to deal with the problem than is Parliament. Worse, civil servants have no incentive to do so. According to the theory of parliamentary government, coordination of policy takes place in cabinet. That is the reason for the doctrine of cabinet solidarity and collective responsibility. Cabinets (in theory) act as networks rather than hierarchies and the prime minister is *primus inter pares*. But after the effective decision-making power of cabinet has been eclipsed by the central agencies of the bureaucracy so that cabinet cannot do the job it was designed for, bureaucrats are all that is left to undertake policy coordination. The term they use, which was encountered above, is "horizontality." Let's see what it means.

According to *A Brief Lexicon of Values in the Canadian Public Service*, "horizontality promotes pooled work and teamwork" and "favours the elimination of hierarchies, collaboration among levels in the hierarchy and co-operation within those levels." It also "favours multidisciplinary action in an organization." To the extent that terms such as *pooled work*, *collaboration*, or *multidisciplinarity* mean anything even in a bureaucratic context, they mean non-accountability and non-responsibility. When horizontality was confined to the central agencies, where, arguably, it made sense, it was practised only by the senior mandarins. Following the reduction in size of the line departments during the mid-1990s, the central agencies were able to infuse their own "culture of horizontality" on them. That is one reason for growth in the number of executive-class bureaucrats commanding appropriate salaries.

One of the interesting findings made by a 2007 Treasury Board report, "Expenditure Review in the Public Sector," is that, despite the cuts made in the mid-1990s, the bureaucracy in 2007 is now bigger than ever. Not only are there more bureaucrats, the place has been restructured so there are more executives and professionals making a lot more money. For example, the total compensation of an average Canadian was under $50,000 in 2004. It was nearly half again as much for a bureaucrat ($74,000). They also have more vacation time and sick days than in the past and suffer more from depression and anxiety than their predecessors. They also have worse teeth and generally poorer health and do not work overtime as they used to do.

These changes are not all consequences of "horizontality," but requiring line departments to practise it is clearly contrary to the notion of separated hierarchies. The whole point of the exercise is to create a single administrative entity, a "borderless institution," as the bureaucrats put it. What has in fact taken place as the culture of horizontality is imposed on line departments, the organizational structure of which is quite clearly vertical, is the creation of a vast jumble of bureaucratic forms. Traditional "stove-pipe" line departments sometimes contain operating agencies within them; some former line departments have become independent agencies or other kinds of arm's-length foundations; others are simply self-governing entities sustained by public funds and accountable only to themselves. To make matters even more complex and opaque, the federal state has also entered into collaborative arrangements with the provinces, the voluntary sector (which also may be sustained with public funds), and the private sector. Often this organizational dog's breakfast parcels out both authority and risk. It is a well-designed mess for what in the old hierarchical model, the model of responsible government, was called cheating and irresponsibility.

Consider how it works in practice. Starting at the top, for example, ministers might explain to their caucus that although they would dearly love to propose a bold course of action, the process—horizontality—makes it impossible. Senior bureaucrats can make the same claim and add that they can push their ministers only so far. The relationship between government agencies and the external consultants has meant that the boundaries of departments, as well as newer varieties of state organs, are both permeable and ambiguous. At the same time many public policy issues are no longer the responsibility of a single department. For example, in 2002 sixteen federal departments and forty-five federal programs dealt with children; twenty departments were involved with planning for the North. Such administrative sprawl does not allow clear lines of authority and responsibility to be drawn. In the land of the endless process, it is the bureaucratic equivalent of a miracle that anything at all gets done.

"Process," the only significant outcome of horizontality, is notoriously difficult to evaluate and appraise. When process and networks replace decisions and hierarchy, when institutions become borderless, it becomes next to impossible to determine responsibility. Administrative hierarchies have been replaced with documentary ones (strategic plans, business plans, and so on), with centres of influence rather than authority (lobbyists and government-supported think tanks), with oversight bodies outside the hierarchy of government (access-to-information processes, the office of the auditor general, the official languages commissioner), and concentrated centres of power (the PMO and the Ministry of Finance). As for the rest of the executive, it is bound by consultative, interdepartmental, and intergovernmental accommodation. In such a public policy context, it is impossible to accord a meaning to the notion of program evaluation, even though (often changing) criteria are typically supplied with each new initiative.

Ever since Brian Mulroney introduced the position of chief of staff, which is suitable in a congressional system, politicization of the bureaucracy followed in its wake, further eroding the boundaries between policy and administration. For example, Francie Ducros, after delivering her highly partisan and intemperate remarks concerning President Bush ("What a moron!"), returned to the supposedly non-partisan bureaucracy—notwithstanding the same-day characterization of her in the *Globe and Mail* as being "fiercely partisan." No one knows how many political or "exempt" staff joined the bureaucracy as Ducros did, essentially making a lateral move after a serious political indiscretion. In short, the erosion of the old notion of non-partisan merit can also be attributed to the breakdown of boundaries between administrative and policy structures.

Because it is impossible to appraise processes, it has become impossible to fire anyone for non-performance. If government managers make the effort, they are likely to end up in court. In 1999–2000, for example, 4,228 bureaucrats left government employ. They were "separated" from the public service. A grand total of 29 (0.6 per cent) were fired or "released" by the bureaucracy. A year later, the percentage had fallen to 0.4 per cent. Because assessment has, in effect, become impossible, there are no checks on administrative abuse either. Classification creep is but one of many forms of institutional rot. In an age of frequent-flyer miles and free nights at select hotel chains, no one has any interest in ensuring travel by senior officials is in fact necessary. No one, for example, is concerned about a trip to Geneva by a deputy and twenty-five subordinates even though ten might do—to say nothing of a video conference.

Until the 1960s and the great expansion, members of the civil service prided themselves on controlling costs, especially input costs. Frugality was considered an important administrative virtue. Horizontality contains no incentives for frugality and almost no checks on prodigality. Not surprisingly, therefore, the moral authority that came with the expectation (and the reality) that public servants would respect and husband the taxpayers' money has evaporated as well. Bureaucrats may not like the fact that they are widely despised by the citizens, as the polling data indicate, but they have no one to blame but themselves. The problem is not just that no new government can curb horizontality and its attendant abuses. The problem is that the bureaucracy has great incentives to work around whatever rules of accountability and transparency the executive comes up with.

Finally it is worth noting that agents of Parliament, the auditor general, the privacy commissioner, the access to information commissioner, and the official languages commissioner, are in a position not only to commit the same kind of administrative abuse as senior management in the bureaucracy but that they can make policy almost entirely outside

Parliament. On the first issue, for example, even such a folk hero as the auditor general has succumbed to mission creep. Originally the auditor general provided Parliament with financial audits, which are relatively straightforward and objective exercises, a far cry from the "comprehensive" and "value-for-money" audits of today, which are both more complex and more subjective. On the second issue, the privacy commissioner decided on his own that surveillance cameras in Kelowna violated the Constitution and ordered them removed. Likewise the official languages commissioner began an investigation of Don Cherry, a colour commentator for *Hockey Night in Canada*, for his observation, which was factually correct, that "Europeans and French guys" used plastic hockey visors more than others. Sometimes all this administrative zeal backfires: the lively investigations by the access to information commissioner have resulted in a growing reluctance of bureaucrats to leave paper trails that later may be uncovered and used to embarrass the government or the bureaucracy, which is to say, to ensure they accept responsibility for their actions. Whether they are policy or administrative actions seems to be no longer important.

Let that suffice for analysis. We know what the problem is: the state is doing too much; there are too many bureaucrats administering too many programs or managing other bureaucrats who are administering programs. Once officials were professional, neutral, parsimonious, and few; now they are partisan big spenders whose appointments are celebrated, at least in Ottawa. Above all they are many. The real issue lies not in analysis but in implementing a remedy. Obviously program reduction would diminish the size of the state, and restoring the boundaries between policy and administration could help recover the integrity that the bureaucrats have forfeited and the responsibility that politicians have abandoned. But how to do it? The fact is, the people who would be tasked with carrying out any changes are precisely the beneficiaries of the current way of doing business. This is why even so astute an analyst of the problem as Donald Savoie several times stated that "we simply cannot turn back the clock," that "the public service cannot go home again," that "there can no longer be distinct realms of political and administrative power." His was not a council of complete despair, however. "Rolling back" the size and reach of the state "will not be easy—it will require a Thatcher-like will," along with common sense. The real question is this: can Canadians and Canadian political leaders summon the required will?

To say the jury is still out is a great understatement. So far as I know there has been but one attempt. The Nielsen Task Force on Program Review, announced the day after the first Mulroney government was sworn in, September 18, 1984. It provided a genuine review of programs, unlike the bureaucratically driven exercise called *La Relève*, championed by the Clerk of the Privy Council, Jocelyne Bourgon, which amounted to tinkering with inputs in an endless process. *La Relève* was not widely viewed as a success, even among Ottawa mandarins. Erik Nielsen, however, managed both to question resource allocation, which challenged the bureaucratic competence of the administrators, and to query the actual policy results, which was an implicit challenge to his own government. On March 11, 1986, Nielsen tabled in the House of Commons the 21 volumes of his report. The cost was a reasonable enough $3.7

million, considering they examined programs that covered $92 billion in government spending and, at least according to Nielsen, "saved 135 times its cost within a year." A major conclusion was that most government programs are designed to subsidize activity, not results, effort rather than success. The argument is that of a disgruntled undergraduate who expects an "A" because she worked hard and grows distressed when you point out it is "C+" work.

The terms of reference of the Nielsen Task Force referred to program delivery rather than the formation of policy—with outputs rather than inputs. Not surprisingly the bureaucrats took offence, as they did with the Gomery Commission. One anonymous "top official" in Treasury Board declared, "It was not rigidly structured as a cost-cutting exercise. It was a government efficiency exercise." Of course, this bureaucrat knew as well as anyone that real savings would come not from "efficiencies" but from program cuts, which is to say, from changing the policy. When the Task Force Report was released, Nielsen himself went out of his way to insist that the recommendations were *not* government policy. The appropriate volumes of the report were then turned over to the relevant parliamentary committees. All of these committees, in total, spent less than 20 hours deliberating on the 15,000 pages and 3 million words of the report. There could be no clearer signal that bureaucratic conservatism and political expediency had made any serious program review impossible. In his memoirs Nielsen claimed to be shocked!

Politics and bureaucratic inertia aside, many of the recommendations are as timely today as they were twenty years ago, although the dollar amounts today are much larger. The chief lesson learned is not that it was a waste of time but that "dis-embedding" the Canadian state is far more difficult than was anticipated in the 1980s. It has not grown easier since then.

Nielsen expressed reservations about the inappropriateness of "universal subsidies," although there was no discussion of such major universal subsidies paid to individuals as family allowances and pensions. Nor was anything said about the most egregiously harmful and regionally focused "universal subsidy," the equalization program paid not to individuals but to provinces. The latter program in particular violated both the general strictures made against universal subsidies and it violated the principled statement in favour of decentralization, which is to say, federalism. Equalization is still a major problem. Let us see how.

James Buchanan, 1986 Nobel Laureate in Economics, is often identified as the "father of equalization" on the basis of his 1948 Ph.D. thesis and a number of early technical articles. The original theory argued that citizen-taxpayers in relatively high-income provinces would be better off if they offered fiscal inducements in the form of lower taxes to their fellow citizen-taxpayers in low-income provinces. In effect, individuals living in wealthy provinces would use the tax system to bribe people in poorer provinces to stay home rather than move to a wealthy province and become a burden on the welfare system there.

The actual system of Canadian equalization is not an inter-individual transfer but an intergovernmental one. Government-to-government transfers, as Buchanan has often pointed out, introduce major new inefficiencies by artificially establishing a bureaucratic "rent," namely a vested bureaucratic and political interest in maintaining the system in place. If no one is encouraged to move to Fort McMurray to work when they can stay at home in Happy Valley and collect a handout, policies that have regional redistributive effects increase regional disparities. Thus spending money raised from productive taxpayers on unemployed workers keeps the latter unproductive. Moreover, the provinces that receive transfer payments are also harmed.

Indeed, transfer payments have been called a welfare trap for provinces. An example shows how the welfare trap works. Let us say that an individual welfare recipient can make $100 a week and still receive welfare benefits. If she makes more than this preset minimum, however, benefits are reduced; at some point she will have to pay taxes and lose other government-administered benefits—free child care, for example. It is thus entirely possible that increased earnings can result in net reductions in total compensation, whether in cash or in kind. Thus welfare recipients, by following only their interests or, as economists say, by acting rationally, choose not to work or even to look for work. As is always the case when interests alone drive action, pride, self-worth, self-esteem, and eventually even professional skills, which once were a source of pride, deteriorate. The possibility of ever gaining future employment likewise is diminished. An analogous welfare trap operates in a similar manner with provinces in receipt of transfer payments.

What began in 1957 as a modest initiative by the federal government has turned into a program of such complexity that, as Peter Holle said, perhaps only thirty people in the world understand it; Paul Boothe added that even among those who do understand it, no one can predict what actual transfers will be, which plays havoc with financial planning in recipient jurisdictions. On those grounds alone, therefore, it is a prime candidate for program extinction. Two examples will show just how perverse incentives are built in to the equalization program.

First, a major mineral deposit was discovered a few years ago in Voisey's Bay, Labrador. At the time, Premier Brian Tobin refused to allow Inco to begin developing the deposit unless it built a smelter as well. Inco considered this requirement to be uneconomic, although the company was prepared to invest $180 million to see if local chemical processing of the ore made economic and business sense. This investment was insufficient to win the approval of the Newfoundland government. Had the mineral deposit been located in northern Ontario, there is no question the development would have gone ahead quickly even without a smelter. Moreover, Newfoundland had little incentive to proceed with the development in the first place because over 80 per cent of the increased revenues would be deducted from the equalization payment. This aptly named clawback meant that a hundred million dollars of tax revenue that the same development would provide rich Ontario would be worth less than $20 million to poor Newfoundland.

In addition, Tobin pressed for the construction of the smelter because, during construction, workers would be paying taxes to the province and because, once it was completed, the now redundant construction workers would be eligible for employment insurance payments. As a consequence, the development of the Voisey's Bay deposit was delayed, skilled workers were idle or left the province, tax revenues were postponed along with opportunities for public investment or tax reductions. In short, as a result of the equalization program, unnecessary economic inefficiencies were imposed on Newfoundland and on Canada.

A second example is even more of an insult to sound economic policy. The western sedimentary basin does not end at the Alberta–Saskatchewan border. Chiefly as a result of public policy decisions taken in Regina, the energy resources of Saskatchewan are underdeveloped compared to Alberta. Even so, there is a significant oil and gas industry in Saskatchewan. In 2000–01, for example, Saskatchewan's energy revenues were over a billion dollars. Saskatchewan is as much a "have" province in terms of energy as Alberta. Alberta, however, is excluded from the formula by which equalization calculations are made. Saskatchewan is not. One of the purposes of the equalization program is to offset unequal resource-based fiscal capacity, which is why oil and gas royalties are included in the equalization formula. Saskatchewan is, however, a "have-not" province in every other measure of fiscal capacity but resource revenues.

Bearing this in mind, when the formula is applied, Saskatchewan loses revenue because it has developed its energy resources, however modestly. According to one economist's calculations, between 1998 and 2001 revenues increased by $668.3 million and equalization payments decreased by $835.3 million. This amounts to a clawback of 125 per cent. In fact, the effective rate is even higher because Saskatchewan has to pay to collect the energy resource revenues before it can pay again to have them deducted from the equalization payment. This is not just inequitable, it is harmful. Of course, Saskatchewan has pursued several policies all on its own that helped prolong its "have-not" status. The point, however, is that confiscation by the federal government of resource revenues is making an already bleak picture even worse. Thus a well drilled a hundred feet to the west of 110 degrees helps enrich Alberta, but an identical well drilled 100 feet to the east of 110 degrees helps impoverish Saskatchewan.

The results of the federal assault on Saskatchewan's energy sector have influenced the rest of the province's economic environment as well. One most obvious and widely lamented consequence has been out-migration by young and well-educated Saskatchewan citizens, chiefly to Alberta. This is why when the Stampeders play the Riders, McMahon Stadium is filled with as many green-and-white–clad fans as those wearing red, and nearly all of them are Calgarians. Moreover, when own-source resource revenues actually impoverished the province, there was no reason for Saskatchewan to pursue resource development at all. A second-worst strategy would be to pursue economically inefficient policies in the resource sector, such as maximizing employment. Lastly, when Saskatchewan finally did become a "have" province and the effective tax on resource revenue fell from 125 per cent to zero, the cumulative effects of the current policy ensured that the province inherited a highly inefficient energy industry.

These two examples indicate that the equalization program does not transform poor provinces into self-sustaining ones but rather locks them into dependency relationships with Ottawa and encourages them to pursue perverse policies that combine high taxes and poor services. The political effects are even worse. Evidence from other countries—Sweden, Australia, and Belgium—indicates clearly that eventually the donor regions come to resent subsidizing the recipients. And the recipients, made more dependent by the transfers, feel no gratitude to the donors. In other words, the much-touted "glue" that equalization is supposed to supply to the federation has just the opposite effect. This is not to say that no have-not province can ever change its status. The example of Saskatchewan shows that it can be done. But notice that the condition for the change was a major increase in energy prices and a new government committed to changing the local political culture. The change, in short, had nothing whatsoever to do with the equalization program delivering on its promises.

At the end of the day, Ottawa has created what Tom Courchene called "hourglass federalism." It didn't happen overnight, but the three bureaucratically driven steps can be clearly distinguished. First, policy responsibility for oversight of forestry, mining, tourism, fishing, and energy, the economic engine of the old "nation-building" model of federalism, was transferred largely to the provinces. Second, Ottawa balanced the federal budget by off-loading its deficit onto the provinces, especially via the Canada Health and Social Transfer cuts, starting in 1995. Third, because these cuts in transfers could not be followed by cuts in health services, largely as a result of a massive, Ottawa-led PR campaign about the importance of health care to the definition of Canadianness, the provinces had to pick up the tab, which meant they had less money to spend on other things. So, as medicare payments take up ever larger shares of provincial budgets, Ottawa has more money to spend.

The problem then is that Ottawa is in a position to undertake spending in areas of provincial constitutional responsibility. Thus a final issue to explain the triumph of the

BARRY COOPER / 181

federal bureaucracy is generally called the "spending power." Hourglass federalism was designed initially to co-opt the cities and their citizens into acquiescing in an extra- or unconstitutional regime. The result has been to squeeze the provinces, like the centre of an hourglass, in the middle of a division-of-powers bottleneck. Off-loading fiscal responsibilities onto the provinces in order to free up money for federal spending initiatives in areas of provincial responsibility is nothing more nor less than a Machiavellian move by the Ottawa bureaucrats to retain power over citizens. Thus the educational initiatives of the 1990s—the Canada Research Chairs, the Millennium scholarships—along with daycare spending and the so-called cities initiative, were all undertaken by Ottawa in areas of provincial jurisdiction. All the provinces, including Alberta, were trapped. The only way out is to change the big-ticket item, medicare, by uploading it to Ottawa, which would make matters much, much worse. Another possibility is to reinforce failure by increasing transfer payments from Ottawa to the provinces. And a third is to download it onto citizens. This last option, also called privatization, is quite sensible. The only problem is symbolic, but that is a very big problem given the success of the federal propaganda campaign that conveys the message that Canadians are defined by the government-funded services they consume, especially medical services.

In short, both the growth of the state and perverse and wasteful policies such as the equalization program are enabled by the spending power. Ottawa would be unable to undertake such policies in the absence of the widespread acceptance of the view that, in effect, Ottawa has an unlimited power to spend. Apart from the bureaucracies that administer programs that rely on the spending power, there are no other beneficiaries. Indeed, the use of the spending power and the strategy of "hourglass federalism" serves no other purpose than to maintain and augment central bureaucratic power—the heart of the Canadian regime. The interesting question is how they ever got away with it.

The three major objections to the doctrine that Ottawa has an unlimited power to spend provide an explanation, but do not indicate the underhandedness of what the federal bureaucrats have done. The first is that, until recently, there was no pretence of constitutional authority for it, which means it was simply claimed or demanded by Ottawa. It is, in a word, an innovation for which there may be no legal basis. Second, it undermines the central element of responsible government. And third, it is contrary to the basic principles of federalism.

On the first problem, it is sufficient simply to cite the views of prominent legal authorities. In 1981, E.A. Driedger noted: "I have been unable to find the expression 'spending power' in any Canadian judicial decision or statute." A few years later, in the midst of the megaconstitutional negotiations regarding Meech Lake, Peter Hogg noted that although Parliament can spend money raised through taxes, borrowing, and other means, "curiously, this spending power is nowhere explicit in the Constitution Act, 1968." The reason for this rare approach to unanimity among lawyers is found in a 1935 decision of the Judicial Committee of the Privy Council (JCPC) in the Employment and Social Insurance Act reference where Lord Atkin stated, "Assuming that the Dominion has collected by means of taxation a fund, it by no means follows that any legislation which disposes of it is necessarily within Dominion competence" because such legislation may "affect the classes of subjects enumerated in s.92" and thus would be *ultra vires* the Dominion government, and thus unconstitutional. This decision was politically, though not necessarily constitutionally, changed. The fact is, no one knows if the spending power *today* is legal because it has not been challenged in court.

From Confederation until World War II, the courts, constitutional scholars, and politicians all agreed that a clear division of political responsibilities between the two coordinate orders of government was the basic characteristic of the Canadian state. Apart from "statutory subsidies," which are specified, and unconditional grants to specific provinces, there are no provisions in the Constitution Act (1867) giving Parliament the authority to transfer money to the provinces. As early as 1867, however, Parliament did provide additional money to Nova Scotia, but as with the statutory subsidies, it was unconditional. This "classical" federalism depended on a clear set of responsibilities for each order of government along with financial independence. As Don Smiley warned many years ago, "If one level became to any significant degree financially dependent on the other to carry out the functions assigned to it by the constitution, there would be at least the possibility of a shift in *de facto* authority from the receiving to the granting jurisdiction." That is precisely what has happened.

The foundations for the eclipse of "classical federalism" were laid down during the war when the provinces agreed to abandon the personal and corporate income tax fields to the exclusive levy of Ottawa. In exchange, Ottawa assumed the provincial debt, increased the level of unconditional grants, and accepted responsibility for supporting unemployed

Canadians. As with so many aspects of civil society regulated by the War Measures Act, this arrangement was supposed to be temporary. Instead of securing a constitutional amendment as recommended by the 1940 Rowell-Sirois Report, the 1945 "Green Book" proposals contemplated unilateral fiscal intervention in areas of provincial jurisdiction. Ontario and Quebec did not agree to the "tax-rental" agreement embodied in the Green Book. The other provinces, however, agreed to limit their share of inheritance, corporate, and personal income taxes, which necessarily enhanced the share of Ottawa. And the Ottawa mandarinate was already committed to Keynesian intervention during a period of extensive post-war economic expansion and social spending.

For example, in 1939 federal taxes from personal and corporate income were about 22 per cent of budget revenue ($123 million). A year after the tax-rental agreements ended in 1963, federal revenues from these taxes stood at $3.6 billion and over 50 per cent of budget revenue. That is, at the same time as Ottawa increased its take by a factor of 30, the provinces increased theirs by about half as much. Once having secured access to a large source of revenue, Ottawa proceeded to spend it through conditional grants to the provinces for everything from the Trans-Canada Highway to the Hockey Hall of Fame. In 1945, conditional grants were less than 1 per cent of federal expenditures; thirty years later they constituted 20 per cent, a level maintained well into the 1980s.

Consider first the implications of this "administrative federalism," as Edwin Black called it, for responsible government. The fundamental principle of responsible government is political accountability—of the executive to the legislature and of the legislature to the voters. The golden thread of responsibility transforms a regime that in form is a monarchic despotism into a constitutional democracy. For responsible government to work in a federal constitution, citizens must have an under-standing of the powers of the provincial and the national governments. An electorate ignorant of which order of govern-ment bears responsibility for what policy lacks the capability of expressing its political will. As Smiley said over forty years ago, when the provinces have primary constitutional responsibility and the federal government makes conditional grants available, "it is almost impossible to enforce accountability" because it is impossible to tell whether the federal government had provided insufficient support or the provinces have squandered it.

As the notorious example of the Canada Health Act shows, conditional grants, which are tributary to the exercise of the spending power by Ottawa, do not shift responsibility from the provinces to the federal government but hide it. A former NDP attorney general of British Columbia, Andrew Petter, said that reliance on the spending power to overcome jurisdictional problems in a federal system creates "the worst of all possible worlds." The consequences for federalism are at least as bad as they are for responsible government. The essential attribute of federalism as noted in the 1937 JCPC decision quoted above is that Parliament cannot dispose of money raised by taxes "in any manner that it sees fit," but only in accordance with its own responsibilities. Accordingly, disposing of funds in an area of provincial responsibility would be illegal. That is, the 1937 deci-sion clearly indicated that Ottawa cannot use taxing and spending as a way to circumvent the division of responsibilities under ss. 91–2 of the Constitution Act (1867).

After World War II, the JCPC position was most vociferously maintained by Quebec—notably in the Royal Commission on Constitutional Problems, better know by its result, the 1954 *Tremblay Report*. As a result of the aggressive assertion of provincial responsibility Frank Scott, a formidable opponent of the Quebec government of the day, a centralist, and a socialist, advanced a novel judicial doctrine based not on the law of the constitution but on the common law:

> All public monies that fall into the Consolidated
> Revenue Funds of the federal and provincial govern-
> ments belong to the Crown. The Crown is a person
> capable of making gifts or contracts like any other per-
> son, to whomsoever it chooses to benefit. The recipient
> may be another government, or private individuals....
> These simple but significant powers... derive from doc-
> trines of the Royal Prerogative and the common law....
> Generosity in Canada is not unconstitutional....
> Because one type of government alone has jurisdiction
> over a class of subject under the B.N.A. Act, does not
> mean that the other may not make gifts to persons
> whose activities fall within that class.

In one form or another, Scott's argument has been adopted by the federal government and by a substantial number of legal writers. The assumption of Scott's disciples seems to be that spending or "gift-giving" is a form of government activity unique by reason of the fact that it has no need of constitutional limitation. Andrew Petter, however, noted that such views "have a sense of unreality about them" for the obvious logical as well as historical reason that expenditures are related to taxation. By long-established law, Parliament cannot raise taxes for provincial purposes and it therefore would be consistent that it not spend for provincial purposes either. Again the reason is obvious and commonsensical: spending for provincial purposes deprives the provinces of resources that they themselves need to act within their own jurisdiction.

By 1969, however, Ottawa had grown so accustomed to using the spending power to act in areas of provincial jurisdiction that it could with confidence advance the claim that "the modern state" has become so complex "that it has become quite impossible to think of government policies and programs as affecting the people within the jurisdiction of the particular government responsible for these policies." So far as division of powers is concerned, "the difficulty with this tidy approach to federalism is that it does not accord with the realities of a Twentieth Century state." This argument, issued in the name of Prime Minister Trudeau, had been contradicted by Professor Trudeau a few years earlier. In any event, what this statement means is that it has "become quite impossible" *for Ottawa* to think about a "tidy approach" to federalism. As Lawrence Martin, *Globe and Mail* columnist and Ottawa insider, observed, this understanding of centralization is now a Canadian "tradition," and Prime Minister Harper's very modest dissent is some sort of revolution. In any event, for Canadians living outside Ottawa, when stress is placed, in everything from child care at the beginning of life to medical care at the end, on "national standards," they are correct in concluding that the term means simply the imposition of Ottawa's standards on policy areas that belong constitutionally to the provinces.

A second consequence is the now famous use of "opting out" provisions that often accompany such program delivery. These provisions do not in fact "give" the opting-out province genuine autonomy. Peter Hogg, whom as I mentioned is a supporter of the federal spending power, noted that the opting-out province gets the "trappings" of autonomy, not the reality because compensation still requires the province to maintain comparable programs. All the province gets is administrative responsibility because the conditions for payment for opting out are still in place. Incidentally, the opting-out conditions indicate the fraudulence of the gift-giving justification for federal spending in areas of provincial jurisdiction. Even if the Crown in right of Canada could bestow gifts constitutionally, how can this justify forcing a province that *declines* the "gift" to abide by the same conditions as a province that accepts it?

There have been a few editorials and some half-hearted and inconclusive efforts to limit the spending power. The first in recent history came with the initial round of negotiations leading to the 1971 Victoria Charter. The latest decree on the spending power is in the 1999 "Social Union" document negotiated between Ottawa and the provinces *sans* Quebec. It declared that "the use of the federal spending power under the constitution has been essential to the development of Canada's social union." The feds promised to negotiate with the provinces, but required only a majority to reach an agreement. This means that the six have-not provinces could, at least in theory, launch a new spending initiative that the big three would have to pay for. This was the "national standards" argument with a pronounced left-wing vengeance. Naturally it was rejected by Quebec, which invented the new doctrine of 9-1-1 federalism. Nine provinces agree with Ottawa and one gets "asymmetric" treatment, which in turn is seen by the gang of nine as *de facto* special status. Thus, once again, the federal use of the spending power, which was justified in terms of "national unity," ends up encouraging the opposite.

Debate surrounding the use of the federal spending power is really about the integrity of the federal system. This means that those who side with Scott and his disciples may be compelled logically to deny the federal character of the Canadian Constitution. The chief consequence of exercising the federal spending power, and especially the use of conditional grants, is to enable Ottawa to flex its fiscal muscle and influence (or distort) provincial decision making. This subverts both federalism and responsible government. It adds opacity to government and demoralizes citizens. It empowers bureaucrats in their Ottawa-based empires and leaves the provinces with unsustainable liabilities once official attention moves on to another area and federal funds move with bureaucratic whim. If, for example, the Canada Health Act is followed by the Canada Cities Act, we can expect even further incentives to bigger and badder government.

The solution to this vexing issue is as simple as it is difficult: a constitutional prohibition of conditional grants. The answer to the gap between provincial responsibility and provincial revenue can be bridged simply by leaving the provinces sufficient tax room. In that way the sinews of the embedded state can be cut, one by one. All it takes is will. As we will argue in the next chapter, the cost of avoiding regime change will be more problems along the lines that the Gomery Commission brought to light.

CHAPTER SIX

THE FRUITS OF GOMERY

"Chrétien's reading is limited. He has an instinctive approach."
—BRIAN MULRONEY

Following an extended debate, the Gomery Commission found *le mot just* for the English term "culture of entitlement." They agreed upon *"la culture du tout m'est dû"* which can be retranslated into English as "the culture of everything is mine by right" or "everything is owed to me." In whatever language the phenomenon is described, it is a long way from anything concerned with public service. Adscam, the vernacular term referred to by Gomery as "the Sponsorship Program and Advertising Activities," was not just about money— though, of course, greed and venality were prominent motivations all around. In both instances one also finds the articulation of a political culture, and a regime.

The Gomery Commission was announced by the new Martin government a few days after the February 2004 report of the auditor general was tabled in the House of Commons. After conducting a custom-designed and very expensive poll,

Martin concluded a more or less independent commission was the best way to manage the fallout. He also thought that his predecessor would wear most of the blame, which is why many members of the Chrétien government, including John Manley and Eddie Goldenberg, to say nothing of Alfonso Gagliano and other members of Chrétien's "Roman guard," thought the investigation of the Sponsorship Program to be supremely misguided.

In May 2004, Gomery announced the rules of engagement, and six months of public hearings began in Ottawa in September, followed by hearings in Montreal, which ended in June 2005. Twenty-five participants, including three political parties, were granted standing. One hundred and seventy-two witnesses appeared over 136 days of hearings. All of their testimony is available electronically. This was a "fact-finding" exercise, and Gomery was explicitly directed not to make any conclusions or recommendations regarding civil or criminal liability.

That is, the commission was constrained to describe what happened and answer this question: how did a government program, the Sponsorship Program, become a scandal, Adscam? Because the testimony of witnesses and other evidence was sometimes in conflict, Gomery had to resolve the discrepancies by accepting some and rejecting other evidence. Naturally, his conclusions in this respect were bound to be controversial because he was, in effect, attributing veracity to some witnesses and denying it to others. Gomery was untroubled by his responsibilities. He was a judge, after all.

The Sponsorship Program began in fiscal year (FY) 1994–95, prior to the Quebec independence referendum. The proposal was to subsidize high-profile events such as car races in Montreal in exchange for advertising displays of federal government departments and agencies. It looked like a charm offensive on the so-called national unity file, the central symbol of the self-understanding of Laurentian Canada.

Within the mythology of "national unity," the logic of events that eventually resulted in the Gomery Commission can be simplified and summarized as follows:

- The Rowell-Sirois Commission understood that to implement Keynesian anti-cyclical policies the central government would have to be able to spend money in areas of provincial jurisdiction and responsibility. Hence the centrality and importance of the spending power.
- It was impossible to pass a constitutional amendment to achieve that objective.
- As a result, a series of extra-constitutional, political agreements were struck between Ottawa and the provinces during the twenty-five years after the end of the war. One consequence of the effective operation of federalism was to obscure political responsibility by enhancing bureaucratic power, not least of all in sheer size. In response, another consequence was the establishment, in Quebec first of all but also in the other provinces, of a competent clerical or bureaucratic cadre to deal with Ottawa. Moreover, in Quebec the bureaucrats understood themselves as guardians of the nation in more or less the same fashion as had the ecclesiastical clerics who preceded them, whereas in Ottawa the new mandarins saw themselves as guardians of Canada and "national unity."

- The effort to formalize the new status of Quebec and of its clerks within Canada by constitutional amendment met the same fate as the Keynesian economists' proposal forty years before.
- Faced with the impossibility of constitutional (not political) recognition of Quebec's distinctiveness within Canada, and unwilling to contemplate a genuine deconfederation—notwithstanding the Clarity Act, which allows Ottawa or its creature, the Supreme Court of Canada, to rule on whether the threshold of "a clear majority on a clear question" regarding independence has been met—the federal parties, and especially the Liberal Party of Canada, and the ambitious, and politically sensitive federal bureaucracy, suitably polished by the requirements of bilingualism, were simply not prepared to permit the secession of Quebec.

The great irony is that, absent the notion that Ottawa had an obligation to manage the post-war peacetime economy as it had managed the country under the War Measures Act, the centrality of Quebec on the national agenda and of the politicization of its social transformation may never have arisen.

Of course, there would have been dislocations. No society has changed from an agrarian and religious community to a secular and industrial one without disruptions; no society, moreover, has done so as quickly as Quebec. The logic of the path not taken, namely the politicization of an already disruptive social change, suggests that those changes and dislocations would have been confined to Quebec to a much greater extent than, in fact, they have been. Indeed, as many observers have pointed out, by imposing their own problems on the rest of the country, by insisting that Manitobans or Newfoundlanders have a major stake in "national unity," which means they have a stake in how Quebec constitutes itself as a political body, the result has been to reduce the ability of the rest of Canada to sympathize with the very real changes Quebec has undergone and even less to acquiesce in formal, constitutional acknowledgement of that reality. Hence the notion that Quebec is the spoiled brat of Confederation. Finally we must note the crucial role of exempt staff, these statutory orphans, as they have aptly been called. They are the unelected, often ill-trained and uneducated individuals, devoid of professional qualifications, but invariably ambitious and energetic ministerial advisers. Two such people, Pierre Tremblay, chief of staff to Alfonso Gagliano, former Minister of Public Works and Government Services, and Isabelle Roy, his special assistant, were central to the operation of the sponsorship program, especially after they accepted employment in the federal bureaucracy.

The imperatives of the bureaucrats and of the political staff are bound to be different: the former live for the rules governing program and financial administration; the latter are concerned with "getting it done," to use the title of Derek Burney's memoir. When you add to this institutional conflict the discrepancy between the age and experience of the two parties, conflict seems inevitable and not necessarily a bad thing. At its best the tension could be a creative tension. But things do not always work for the best, and the alternative in this case turned out to be acrimony and blockage.

One way of reducing or perhaps eliminating the tension between these conflicting institutional imperatives of officials and political staff is to recruit bureaucrats who no longer care very much about the rules or are too cowardly or incompetent to object when they are being broken either by the exempt staff or by other bureaucrats. This solution was hit upon in the administration of the sponsorship program. It was aided by the ability of exempt staff to join the bureaucracy on a preferential basis under the appropriate terms of the Public Service Employment Act. Thus ministerial staff were able to switch to the bureaucracy at the equivalent level at which they were hired by a minister. Such is the embedded state in action.

To see the implications of all this, recall the response of the Chrétien government to the October 1995 Quebec referendum. One of the first acts was to appoint a committee under Marcel Massé, a former Clerk of the Privy Council who was then serving as intergovernmental affairs minister. His committee was to come up with a promotional strategy for national unity. Hence the plan to advertise the benefits of remaining in Canada on Quebec billboards.

The reason for the ad campaign, according to both Prime Minister Chrétien in his testimony before Gomery and his long-time assistant, Eddie Goldenberg, was that the Quebec government was engaged in an extensive campaign of "subliminal advertising" in favour of the independence of the province. The term was coined by James Vicary in 1957 and referred to flashing slogans at 1/3000 of a second on a movie screen to stimulate popcorn sales. The practice was subsequently declared illegal in the United Kingdom, Australia, and the United States. Vicary's results, unfortunately, were non-reproducible and he later admitted to having made up the data showing increased popcorn consumption. Concerns about subliminal advertising today are confined to conspiracy theorists, hypnotists, and various kinds of fundamentalists worried about recording diabolical messages backwards on rock music songs. The only example cited (by Goldenberg) was, in fact, a play on words. A Quebec campaign promoting the use of seat belts used the slogan "*on s'attache au Quebec*," which means both "in Quebec we buckle up" and "we belong to Quebec." Goldenberg said, presumably with a straight face, that Chrétien "wanted to counter it with similar federal messaging." The genesis of Adscam, if we can believe Goldenberg, is found in prime ministerial anxieties over a pun.

In any event, the decision to "sponsor" community, cultural, and sporting events was taken at a cabinet meeting on the first and second of February 1996. At the same time, it is clear from the minutes of that meeting (made available to the Gomery Commission) that the participants did not clearly distinguish between the federal government and the Liberal Party, which is to be expected. But neither did the report, which is unusual. This is what it said:

> Ministers recommend a substantial strengthening of the organization of the Liberal Party of Canada in Quebec. This means hiring organizers, finding candidates, identifying ridings that are winnable in the next federal election, and using the most modern political techniques of reaching targeted voters.

François Perreault, who served as media liaison for Gomery, reported that the Prime Minister's Office, and especially the

Clerk of the Privy Council, Alex Himelfarb, strongly resisted Gomery's request for the minutes of the February cabinet meeting. The documents were produced only under threat of a court order.

The reason is clear: cabinet committees are formally the source of recommendations to the representative of the sovereign. They are, of course, partisan bodies but only informally so. It may be proper for the Government of Canada to promote Canada, that is federalism, in a province that nearly voted to separate from Canada, though sovereignists would dispute this. It is not at all proper for the Government of Canada, which obviously includes the Crown in right of Canada, to support a political party. In partisan terms, the government, the cabinet of which was Liberal, was declaring that only the Liberal Party of Canada could promote federalism in Quebec.

The testimony of both the prime minister and the executive director of the Liberal Party of Canada in Quebec before the Gomery Commission supported this view. The PMO knew that this was improper, which is why it resisted making the February cabinet minutes public. From the beginning of Gomery, therefore, the bureaucracy was complicit at the highest level in improperly protecting the government and the party. As for members of cabinet, both Stéphane Dion and Pierre Pettigrew said they were "surprised" by the Massé report. Massé himself allowed that it was "incongruous," but only "in theory." When Gomery asked Jean Pelletier, Chrétien's chief of staff, for his views on the Massé report he replied: "I think, Mr. Commissioner, that I have been clear enough. I think one would be suffering from *angélisme* if one thought that elected people, responsible for governing the country, ceased to have partisan commitments. They always stay partisan." Certainly they avoided pretending they were angels.

The Canada Information Office was to be funded from the Unity Reserve fund, a non-budget or off-books account that was available for discretionary executive spending on "national unity." In his testimony, Alex Himelfarb, Clerk of the Privy Council, described these next-to-invisible pots of money in the following way:

> The way a reserve works is that a provision would be put in place in the fiscal framework to capture a liability, a contingency, or a priority where specific spending decisions have not yet been made and cannot yet be voted.... So the reserves aren't exactly managed. They are an accounting procedure to set aside money to capture—it is an accounting procedure.

Commission co-counsel Neil Finkelstein cut through this thicket of bureaucratic nonsense with an obvious observation: "Well, except for this, sir. They are a source of funds, right?" to which Himelfarb replied:

> The fiscal framework is a source of funds and parts of the fiscal framework are notionally set aside either for liabilities or contingencies on the one side or for priorities not specified on the other.
> MR. FINKELSTEIN: Right.

When he was called back to testify in Montreal, Himelfarb allowed as using the Unity Reserve as a source of funds for sponsorships was not a "serious issue." Indeed, he said, "I am not even sure why it is an issue now"—apart from the ill-informed publicity given to funding the program from sources that never were discussed in Parliament or even it seems in cabinet. Accordingly, in his testimony, when asked directly whether ministers knew sponsorship money came from the Unity Reserve and, after having had it pointed out to him that "the answer is either yes or no," Chrétien avoided answering. In his testimony Stéphane Dion hit upon the perfect formula: using the Unity Reserve fund to pay for sponsorships was not secret but "I think the prime minister maybe didn't want it talked about too much in order to maintain his flexibility."

The irregularity of the source of funds within the "fiscal framework" was not the only oddity surrounding the Canada Information Office. The individual nominally in charge of this office, Jean Collet, even though chosen by the prime minister, had no experience either in starting an agency from scratch or working in an ongoing advertising firm. The mandate he was given, coordinating federal/Liberal advertising in Quebec, was very similar to that of the advertising section in the Department of Public Works, which had been run since 1994 by Joseph Charles "Chuck" Guité.

In July 1996, the Canada Information Office announced it had money available and that those seeking federal subsidies for an event or a project should apply to Collet's office. He was swamped with requests but had no clue what he should do. He called upon Guité, and the two mid-level bureaucrats agreed that Collet's Canada Information Office money would be turned over to Guité in Public Works. Eventually Collet was relieved of his responsibilities and his office was incorporated in Communications Canada, along with Guité's operation.

In retrospect, it looks as if Prime Minister Chrétien picked Jean Collet to handle the "flexible" off-book spending from the Unity Reserve. It is not clear why, but the default position for most of Jean Chrétien's appointments was loyalty. In the event, Collet proved sufficiently incompetent that Chuck Guité had to be recruited. It then turned out that Guité's section of the federal bureaucracy was too small and also too inexperienced to manage the new and expanded program so Guité contracted with private-sector ad and communications companies to administer the government-approved sponsorships. In exchange, these companies would receive commissions and the production costs for creating the ads would be billed to the government. On paper this looks like a straightforward contract for services between the government and a service provider.

Gomery, however, was concerned about how the money actually got under Guité's control so that he could authorize cheques be cut and services accepted and monitored. For example FY 1996 began on April 1; the money Guité would spend on sponsorships was not in the Public Works budget. Somebody had to tell Guité that his office would be in charge of implementing the new visibility program decided at the February meeting, but who? None of the witnesses called before the Gomery Commission could recall. In his report, Gomery said it was "extraordinary" that no one knew what took place between early February and the first documented meeting between Jean Pelletier and Guité on April 16, 1996. "It is impossible to believe that there were no meetings or discussions involving the Prime Minister and his staff during that period concerning the implementation of the decision [made by Cabinet], but Mr. Pelletier purports to have no recollection of what happened." Gomery was incredulous, which is a polite way of saying he thought Pelletier may not have been telling the whole truth.

By April 22, 1996, it had been determined that about $17 million would be needed by Public Works for advertising the next year. This money came from the Unity Reserve; transferring the money to Public Works was authorized by the prime minister against the advice of the Clerk of the Privy Council, Jocelyne Bourgon, who warned Chrétien that, because there was no way of evaluating the submissions, he should not sign the authorization. If he did, she said, the government would, in effect, be buying a pig in a poke. At one point in her testimony, Bourgon tried to suggest that the Sponsorship Program was not, properly speaking, a program because it lacked bureaucratic oversight. It was more a collection of "projects" or contracts associated with the Government of Canada, a "strategy," perhaps, or a "file."

However it was to be named, two aspects of the process by which contracts were let ensured that any quality control was impossible. First, once an ad agency was on an "approved list," which, according to Guité, meant that, by definition, though not necessarily in fact, a "competition" had taken place, then the agency could be awarded a contract without any additional scrutiny. Guité was well aware that this procedure violated Treasury Board guidelines though he told his administrative superiors that he was following them to the letter. In fact, some agencies received contracts without being on the "approved" list. Guité could provide no explanation of how this ever could have happened.

Second, price was not to be considered as a criterion for deciding which agency was awarded a contract. Chrétien testified he was unaware of this violation of Treasury Board guidelines, dismissing the entire issue as an "administrative" triviality. Guité explained in his initial or Ottawa testimony that creativity was more important than price so it was acceptable to exclude price. In his later testimony in Montreal he said the decision to do so was "politically driven," which, he explained, meant it was done in order to give post-election contracts to ad agencies that worked for or otherwise had supported the Liberals during a prior election.

Notwithstanding these irregularities, Chrétien signed off on the program, which introduces another unusual practice. It was not an ordinary procedure for the prime minister to co-sign with the minister responsible for a program, in this instance the minister of Public Works, a request to the Treasury Board to release funds. This initial tranche of money would be used to subsidize everything from professional car races to the Montreal Canadiens, a professional hockey team, and the Ottawa Rough Riders, a professional football club. "Free" tickets to the Canada Grand Prix in Montreal, for example, cost taxpayers $246,000. They were paid for by a Montreal ad firm, Groupaction, using sponsorship funds. The tickets were used by, among others, Chuck Guité and his family, Jean Pelletier and his family, and Jean Carle, Chrétien's director of operations, and his family, all in service of national unity.

Several witnesses indicated that having the prime minister as well as the minister responsible both sign a request for funds from Treasury Board was unprecedented. They also explained why Chrétien did it: to signal to the bureaucracy that he was a strong supporter of the spending initiative. Every bureaucrat concerned got the message loud and clear: question the sponsorship program at your peril. The boss likes it. He is behind it. And, in fact, the minister responsible, Diane Marleau, did not have a clue what her nominal subordinate, Guité, was doing.

Marleau may not have been the most impressive of Chrétien's ministers, but she did insist on running her department by the book. Several witnesses testified, as did Marleau, that she would not deal directly with Guité and that he was to report through the chain of command to the deputy minister, with whom Marleau would deal (as would every minister in a normal department). That is, in a well-run department, political input by the minister or, even more, by political staff, including the chief of staff, would be recorded at meetings with the deputy minister and the action requested would be tracked and sometimes evaluated. In this instance there was neither a paper trail nor any effort at determining the effectiveness of the program.

The absence of documentation, particularly under the management of the Public Works Department by Marleau's successor, Alfonso Gagliano, also attracted the attention of the commission. On this question the testimony of Gagliano's secretaries and office staff pointed to deliberate precautions taken by Guité and his political masters to avoid scrutiny by anybody.

Several individuals indicated directly and indirectly that asking questions about the sponsorship program was taboo. Joanne Bouvier, a special assistant to Gagliano, observed that "when I asked a question, I didn't get any answers. So after a while I stopped asking questions." Huguette Tremblay, chief of special projects in Gagliano's office, was asked to process invoices without documentation. When she asked the ad agencies to supply it, Guité told her not to be concerned. On reflection she said, "Call it naïveté, call it misplaced loyalty, I don't know, stupidity, if you want, but you get used to it.... At a certain point you don't ask any more questions because there aren't any answers anyway." Ghislaine Ippersiel, secretary to two of Gagliano's executive assistants, had little information about the program to share with the commission. When she asked her boss, Isabelle Roy, what the criteria were and how they were to be applied to the applications for sponsorship funds, Roy said, "Tell them to call me and I'll take care of it." For her part, Roy could not recall why notes of meetings between Guité and Gagliano were not kept.

MS. ROY:... I do not remember the reason behind it.

THE COMMISSIONER: Ms. Roy, I am asking you to try a little harder....

MS. ROY:... it is probably because I did not want any traces to be left.

THE COMMISSIONER: That is probably the explanation, right?

MS. ROY: Yes.

When Don Boudria replaced Gagliano as minister of Public Works, Ippersiel and two other secretaries were called upon to purge all the files of Post-it stickers that recorded the actual decisions on who received sponsorship money. Jean-Marc Bard, Gagliano's executive assistant, helpfully explained that destroying handwritten notes was a "common practice" after a cabinet shuffle.

The lines of responsibility were, to say the least, blurred. Normally, as they say in the text books, a middle-level bureaucrat such as Guité would report up the chain of command to the deputy minister. As just noted, this was the procedure that Marleau insisted upon until she was replaced by Gagliano, who reverted to the practice of Marleau's predecessor, David Dingwall, who also dealt directly with Guité. Bourgon told the commission that it was permissible for Guité to speak with the minister so long as he reported what he discussed in the meeting to his deputy minister. But as Huguette Tremblay said, "I know that Mr. Guité did not meet often with Mr. Quail [the deputy minister], and on several occasions, Mr. Guité told me that Mr. Quail was not involved... that... his [Guité's] relationship was directly with the minister's office."

The deputy, Ranald Quail, did not insist that Guité keep him in the picture. Guité, he testified, had "unique" access to Gagliano even though he, Quail, was "responsible" for all departmental procedures. This "unusual" relationship, he said, was not "inappropriate" and was in any case Gagliano's "prerogative." This meant that Quail never knew how the ad agencies were selected but that he "trusted" that Guité was following the rules. The temptation to consider Quail merely naïve or incompetent is easily resisted given his shrewd advice to Gagliano to bury $40 million in sponsorship money in general estimates rather than have it listed as a line item in the budget of Public Works. If anything, this senior bureaucrat, who never pushed back when he saw that things were being conducted in a "unique" way, looks both supine and complicit.

Under cross-examination by Gagliano's lawyer, Bourgon said that it was permitted for the minister to delegate authority to Guité, but only "theoretically." In his initial testimony before Gomery, Bourgon's successor, Alex Himelfarb, also explained that the delivery of instructions and "input" takes place "normally through the deputy minister." Even so, he continued, "there is a huge amount of flexibility in our system about who interacts with whom.... In many cases it is encouraged for logistical reasons, for other reasons." As a logistical reason, Himelfarb gave the example of a minister interacting with a junior official when travelling outside Ottawa. As for "substantive" and "detailed" communications between senior political staff and junior bureaucrats, you do not need a Ph.D. in Administrative Science to know that the notion that political staff would be directing discretionary spending is simply a recipe for abuse, especially when there were no guidelines or criteria by which decisions should be made. Himelfarb allowed as he thought a deputy minister would likely be "uncomfortable" with such an arrangement. Such a person would also have to possess sufficient spine and backbone to resist the demands of his or her minister for greater "flexibility." In the event, for the next three and a half years the program was Chrétien's responsibility, and it was paid for entirely from the Unity Reserve. It was not until 2000 that an item for $40 million for "special programs" was included in the budget for Public Works and so came before Parliament. Before then it was all done in secret.

The 25,000 pages of testimony recorded before the Gomery Commission, of which the foregoing remarks summarize only a sample, reveal a great deal about what the Canadian regime had become at the end of the millennium. Not only do the witnesses describe an institutionally corrupt organization but they do so in such a manner that their own personalities, which are central to any regime, are clearly exposed. The most important individuals to testify, apart from the prime minister, were members of cabinet, especially the minister of Public Works and his staff, and the prime minister's chief of staff, Jean Pelletier. To see the impact of these strong personalities on the regime we must consider how these responsible officials acquitted themselves before the commission.

To start at the top: unless one seriously believes that Jean Chrétien was spooked by subliminal advertising, the corrupt use of the program was its intended use. In that respect it was a spectacular success. All it took to succeed, at least for a time, was adherence to norms and conventions of mendacity. This is so obvious a conclusion from Gomery's report that it is an equally obvious explanation why Chrétien filed a motion in the Federal Court of Canada first to force Gomery to recuse himself, then to shut down the inquiry, and finally to suppress the publication of the report. It also explains why he has carried on an extensive PR campaign in the press to discredit Gomery. In the criminal justice system, such tactics are typically used by the defence, particularly when guilt or innocence is determined by the facts of the case, because it shifts the grounds for argument to procedural or constitutional issues. That was, no doubt, Chrétien's intent as well.

It is equally significant to note that by and large Chrétien was successful, not least of all because Gomery was a bit of a naïf when it came to speaking to reporters such as Don Martin. In 2004 Gomery gave an interview to Martin that characterized both the running of the sponsorship program and the personalities of key players, including Guité, Chrétien, and Pelletier, in accurate but unflattering language. In due course, Chrétien brought suit against Gomery, and Federal Court Justice Max Teitelbaum found that Gomery was biased. Looking back on the original interview, Martin recalled that Gomery's "quips and quotes... had me pinching myself in disbelief while nervously eyeing the tape recorder to make sure it was catching every word." It would have been too much to expect a journalist to act responsibly when interviewing a judge who was clearly unacquainted with the ways of the Ottawa media, and that too tells us something about the Canadian regime because the media are an integral part of it. As the name suggests, they are right in the middle.

In his testimony, Jean Pelletier told Gomery he had nothing to do with advertising firms and certainly had nothing to do with any donations to the Liberal Party of Canada. All he had was "input" into the program in order to ensure lots of "presence" of Canada in Quebec, especially in the separatist parts of the province. He may have made "some strong recommendations" but never made a decision. Moreover, it was appropriate for the Chief of Staff to the prime minister to be giving advice regarding events worthy of sponsorship and the level of support they deserved because "the national unity file was a very special file." It was also acceptable for Guité to talk directly with Pelletier, Pelletier said, without going through the deputy minister because "silence equals consent" and Quail was silent, never once complaining to his boss, the Clerk of the Privy Council.

According to his own version of his place in the decision hierarchy, Jean Pelletier claimed that he simply gave passive approval to lists of events to be sponsored that were drawn up by Guité. He explained that one such list, in his own hand-writing, of events to be approved was compiled to assist Guité in remembering what Guité had proposed. Gomery allowed it was "improbable" that Pelletier, chief of staff to the prime minister of Canada, would act as secretary to a middle-management bureaucrat. It is more than improbable. The notion is preposterous. In the more polite language of Justice Gomery, his "testimony concerning this document is not credible."

A little farther down the PMO food chain sits Jean Carle, director of operations. He is generally regarded as a protégé of Jean Chrétien. He and Warren Kinsella had been pals for many years, having risen from the ranks of the Young Liberals. Carle had been the representative of the prime minister in the secu-rity negotiations concerning the APEC summit in Vancouver a couple of years earlier. He had been instrumental in giving political direction to the RCMP on that occasion, but then denied it before a judicial inquiry. As Gomery found with Pelletier, the judge on that occasion, Mr. Justice Hughes, did not find Carle's testimony credible. The reason, no doubt, was that Carle, like Pelletier, had a bad memory. Carle testified he could not remember fifty-two times, second only to Isabelle Roy with eighty-one forgets (Jacques Corriveau claimed to have suffered a memory loss following anaesthesia so must be excused from the forgetfulness competition). On matters other than those concerned with sponsorship, however, he had an "accurate and vivid memory."

By March 2000, Carle had moved on to the presidency of the Business Development Bank of Canada (BDC). In his testi-mony, he told of a deal between the BDC, the Communications

Coordinations Services Branch, or CCSB, which at the time administered the money inside Public Works, and an ad agency call L'Information essentielle. The ad agency would be paid $125,000 to sponsor a TV mini-series called *Le Canada du Millénaire*. There was no contract between the two parties, but CCSB had no further money for this project. An official at CCSB phoned Carle to tell him that "the government" owed the ad company $125,000 and would the BDC please write the cheque instead because, as the CCSB official said, we have spent too much on the project anyhow. Carle said BDC was just acting as "a conveyor belt for the final payment." At this point, Judge Gomery intervened and asked Carle why he hid the transaction with such a roundabout method. Carle said he got free advertising simply by acting as an "intermediary."

> GOMERY: Well, if it was a drug deal, it would be called money laundering. It is the same principle, is it not? Am I mistaken?
> CARLE: No, you are not mistaken.

BDC paid L'Information essentielle and then invoiced Public Works. Commission counsel observed, "It was a phony operation?" Carle agreed, L'Information essentielle "hadn't delivered any services."

Testimony from cabinet ministers indicated that, in effect, no one knew anything. One is reminded of a remark by Senator William Saxbe (R-Ohio) who observed of the Watergate conspirators that they were "like the piano player in the cathouse who had no idea what went on upstairs." When the auditor general's report was published in February 2004, for example,

Paul Martin said, "I have no idea what was going on here." He was, however, the Finance minister who routinely signed off on the $50-million Unity Reserve. He explained that it was part of the "fiscal framework" about which Himelfarb had spoken at such length. That is, because it was not new money but "minor" multi-year funding, it was "simply grouped with a whole bunch of other items under one—the descriptive line such as 'other spending.'" Although he approved of the Unity Reserve, he said he knew nothing at all about how the money would be used. He knew the government sponsored events in Quebec but he had no idea it was part of the "national unity" strategy. He "never" discussed sponsorships with Gagliano and sponsorships were "never" discussed in the Quebec caucus. And yet somehow he knew where to send the letter asking for sponsorship money, as was brought out in examination.

> MR. FINKELSTEIN: But how would you have known
> that the minister [to whom a letter dealing with spon-
> sorships should be sent] would be Mr. Gagliano?
> THE RT. HON. PAUL MARTIN: Well, to be honest, I have
> no idea....

And yet, in June 1999 Martin had a senior aide ask Gagliano's office, because he was minister in charge, why one of his friends in Montreal had not received a reply to his request for $600,000 in sponsorship grants. In testimony before Gomery, Joanne Bouvier, an aide to Gagliano, said that Marielle St. Germain from Martin's Montreal constituency office requested $3,000 from the sponsorship program for a volleyball tournament. A $3,000 request may have been undertaken without Martin's awareness—"handled by the Correspondence Branch," as he put it—but not one for $600,000.

It seems evident that Paul Martin knew how the Sponsorship Program worked and that Gagliano was at the top of the decision-making apparatus. Gilles Duceppe, leader of the Bloc, made an obvious point: Paul Martin is a meticulous man who is familiar with details of how the Canadian economy or Canada Steamship Lines operates. "I'm not saying he knew what was really happening but I'm saying that he didn't want to know what was happening," Duceppe said.

Stéphane Dion, then minister of Intergovernmental Affairs, said that Martin was present in cabinet when the sponsorship money was discussed, but neither he, nor Chrétien, nor Dion himself knew anything about the "difficulties" involved. Dion added that he "didn't believe" in the program at all and really knew very little about it. But Jean Chrétien testified he was "surprised a great deal" to learn that Dion knew nothing of the program. Jean-Marc Bard, chief of staff to Gagliano, said it was well known, especially in the Quebec caucus. Gagliano himself said Dion was aware of the Sponsorship Program since its inception in 1996. "Mr. Dion was a Quebec minister," said Gagliano. "He was participating. He was very active in the Quebec minister tours and he would receive a request. And definitely he knew. And everybody else. I believe it was once, a couple of times, discussed in cabinet committee, I believe in 1999."

And as for Gagliano himself, becoming a minister of the Crown capped a successful career. A November 18, 2004, New York *Daily News* article reported a leaked FBI interview with Frank Lino, a Mafia hit man turned state's evidence. Lino said that Gagliano attended a meeting "in the nineties" in Montreal where New York mobsters informed their Canadian associates that Joe Massino was now the boss of the Bonanno organization. Lino said that only "made members" were at the meeting.

In 1994, the RCMP undertook a security check on Gagliano, as they do with all potential cabinet members. It took two years to complete, which is considerably longer than usual. In the 1970s, Gagliano was the personal accountant to Agostino Cuntera, a nephew of Pasquale Cuntera, who is a major player in the Cuntera-Carvana crime family whose business operation focused on international drug smuggling and money laundering, just the sort of business in need of a sharp accountant, and rather like the Sponsorship Program in that respect. Gagliano was also the accountant to another Cuntera-Carvana associate, Dima Messina, who worked with Vito Rizzuto, a Cuntera-Carvana family mobster. So the structure has turned into a pattern: Gagliano would work for a fella who would be close to another fella who happened to be a mobster. In 1999, Gagliano's office aided the immigration of the wife of an Italian mobster, Gaetano Amodeo, who then joined her in Canada on the family reunification program. Amodeo was wanted by Interpol and was charged with murder in Italy.

Gagliano's testimony, generally speaking, was obstructive and evasive. For example, there was evidence that Liberal fundraisers in Quebec were also conduits for information on government programs. Gomery suggested to Gagliano that this might appear improper.

THE COMMISSIONER: If they are generous with their contributions, they're going to have a better chance of accessing those programs?

THE HON. A. GAGLIANO: Mr. Commissioner, with all due respect....

THE COMMISSIONER: I asked you a question, you don't see any problems?

THE HON. A. GAGLIANO: No, I don't see any.

Gagliano was asked whether the Order of the Sons of Italy in Canada, which received a sponsorship, had any separatist members. Gagliano answered by talking about the Italian community where, he said, "they're not all federalists." Gomery had to ask him three times to answer the question. He didn't know the answer because he didn't know "the names on the membership list." But some Italian-Canadians were separatists, just as is true in any other community, "and I thought that in Canada everyone was equal."

Did he know how many sponsorships went to fight the separatists in Bloc Québécois leader Gilles Duceppe's riding as compared to his own riding of St. Leonard? Gagliano again played the ethnic card, accusing Gomery of insulting "the entire Italian community" but also claiming not to know how many sponsorship dollars were spent in the separatist leader's riding to fight separatism.

Gagliano had earlier said he made no decisions: that was Chuck Guité's job. All he did was, like Pelletier, provide "input" or "suggestions," but his political staff could not recall an example when his suggestion was not complied with. He claimed he met with Guité only rarely, less often than once a week. Unfortunately, his appointment diaries, which might have confirmed the frequency of his meetings with Guité, had disappeared. He also made a curious admission in response to a question by commission counsel Bernard Roy, who asked why the government did not simply publish a list of events that the government sponsored. If they did that, he said, it would become propaganda. That is, the Sponsorship Program was useful so long as no one knew that it came from the federal government. Everything was proceeding according to plan "until the auditor general published her report and this commission was created." Then the cat was out of the bag, sponsorship turned into propaganda, and so it became ineffective. This explained the need for secrecy.

As for Chuck Guité, he admitted to having lied to the auditor general when he told her that he controlled the Sponsorship Program, but said he told the truth to Gomery and did take direction from his political masters, Gagliano, Pelletier and, through Pelletier, Chrétien. Thus Gomery had to assess which, if any, of Guité's testimony was credible. As criteria he used corroborative testimony, documentary evidence, and plausible explanation, which is to say, common sense. In this regard, Gomery believed his account of his relationship with Gagliano and Pelletier. His refusal to follow the required guidelines, Gomery said, was "shocking" and, no doubt, "his testimony reveals him to be a man without scruples." Gomery further inferred that if he were unscrupulous in his actions, he would also be unscrupulous in telling the truth about those actions. In particular, Gomery did not believe Guité's account of the work he had done after his retirement for ad agencies with whom he had previously been contracting on behalf of Public Works. Gomery concluded that Guité was paid handsomely by several ad agencies after retirement for favours dispensed while he was a civil servant.

To no one's surprise, neither Guité nor the principals in the ad agencies said anything useful on this topic.

Two matters emerge from the often spectacular testimony of the ad men. First, they were happy to cheat the government all on their own, and second, they were part of what, under Canadian law, is a criminal conspiracy, the other parties to which were officials and fundraisers of the Liberal Party of Canada in Quebec.

On the first point, two ad agencies, Coffin Communications and Gosselin Communications, often sent Public Works invoices for work not done. This is straightforward fraud. Two other ad men, Luc Lemay and Jean Brault, indicated that, as a condition for doing business with the government they were required to assign money to Jacques Corriveau, a good friend of the prime minister and long-time Liberal Party organizer and fundraiser. Some of that money was handed to the party; some of it stuck to Corriveau.

There were plenty of shady characters on the periphery as well. One, Alain Renault, in exchange for a cool million helped the ad firm, Groupaction, land meetings with Jean Carle and Gagliano. In explanation he offered the following insight: "Friends work with friends, and that is not about to change." The person to whom Brault said he delivered cash in plain brown envelopes and a good friend of Gagliano, Guiseppe Morselli, had been under RCMP surveillance for some time. When he died in March 2006 a lot of Mounties were disappointed that their work had been in vain.

All these illegal activities were summarized by Christie Blatchford in a column in the *Globe and Mail*. She mentioned an offhand remark by MP and former Crown prosecutor, Peter

MacKay, that the Liberal Party was, in effect, a criminal organization akin in this respect to a biker gang. "Take these boys out of their good suits," she wrote, "and dress 'em in leathers, switch the red ties for red do-rags, line them up with some biker gangs, and bets are, you won't be able to tell the difference."

From the apotheosis of smarmy and premeditated deceit in the testimony of Jacques Corriveau, art lover, to the "comprehensive and candid" testimony of Jean Brault, street fighter, it is clear to all but the willfully blind that the money-laundering and kickback schemes implicated the individuals around Chrétien and Gagliano, and drew connections to Paul Martin by way of Francis Fox, a former cabinet minister in the Trudeau government and later Martin's principal secretary, and Georges Farrah and John Welch, whom Brault put on his Groupaction payroll, and who later served as exempt staff in Martin's government.

The corrupting effect of the Sponsorship Program on the bureaucracy was also significant. I will mention three instances: the ethics commissioner, the RCMP, and the PMO. The ethics commissioner, like the auditor general, is an officer of Parliament. One incumbent, Bernard Shapiro, said that the sponsorship scandal can be viewed either as "a triumph of entrepreneurship" or as "a triumph of theft." It all "depends on how you look at these kinds of things." And that is how the ethics commissioner looked at it. He elaborated, "I don't believe we have a bunch of criminals who are trying to get away with something. But what we've got is a bunch of people who are trying to do exactly the right thing who sometimes do the wrong thing." This was Chuck Guité's (unsuccessful) defence at trial as well.

Second, there is the RCMP. The Mounties, of course, are not only a "guardian" agency akin in this respect to the Canadian Forces and the judiciary, they are for most Canadians a symbol of all that is good about the country. In the last report I completed for the Fraser Institute, I discussed in detail the illegal acts of the RCMP, the evasiveness of senior management, the deliberate use of inaccurate statements to cover up their awareness of payment of illegal commissions to ad agencies, the use of sponsorship funds to help pay for a full-dress RCMP party, and so on. The involvement of the federal police in the sponsorship scandal simply violated the expectation that they are independent of both the criminal and the political community.

When the Clerk of the Privy Council, Alex Himelfarb, tried to prevent the release of notes of the cabinet meeting of February 1–2, 1996, it had nothing to do with cabinet secrecy because the prime minister had, in effect and formally, waived that right. It seems more likely that the Clerk and PMO officials were acutely aware of the improper use of taxpayers' money to support the Liberal Party in Quebec. According to François Perreault, this attitude of non-cooperation continued throughout the period the commission received testimony. Indeed, the hostility of the senior mandarins in the Ottawa bureaucracy was well known among the Ottawa press corps. Jocelyne Bourgon, for example, had to be asked three times whether she knew Guité was in charge of a $2.6-million billboard campaign. Alex Himelfarb was unhappy to be recalled to Montreal to testify. Moreover, his testimony was greeted with a degree of scepticism to which eminent persons such as he were unused. The very idea that a mere judge was asking questions about the conduct and operations of government and public administration was not only without precedent, the very notion was an insult to the bureaucracy itself, its integrity, dedication, and so forth. Exactly. No wonder Himelfarb was incensed, especially when Gomery characterized his behaviour regarding Chrétien as a "don't ask, don't tell" policy, a "sort of conspiracy of silence."

Himelfarb fought back the way that mandarins do: by indirection and damage control. The story broke in the *Ottawa Citizen* on May 24, 2005. It seems that on February 18, 2004, a few days after the commission was established, an "intergovernmental coordinating group" was set up at the Privy Council Office under the direction of Guy McKenzie, who reported directly to the PMO and to Himelfarb. At a cost of over a million dollars for FY 2004, the purpose was to prepare responses for Liberal politicians who had to deal with Adscam in Parliament but, more importantly, to defend "the reputations of high-ranking civil servants, many of whom had been promoted to their positions during Prime Minister Chrétien's ten-year reign." That its real purpose was bureaucratic camouflage is indicated by its official non-existence on paper and its entirely misleading name. Among other things, this "group" undertook to divert attention from what Gomery was uncovering by releasing to the media exaggerated estimates of the cost of the commission.

Gomery concluded on the basis of the evidence and his commonsensical inferences that the sponsorship program was run by Pelletier from the PMO; Pelletier had been tasked directly by Chrétien and had chosen to run the operation through a middle-level bureaucrat in a regular line department. That meant bypassing the minister if, as with Marleau, she did not cooperate and then replacing her with somebody who did. Gomery's broader conclusion can be summarized as two points: (1) Ottawa does not enforce its own rules, and (2) there are few incentives in place that are supportive of good conduct.

In his second appearance, Himelfarb mentioned "disciplinary actions" twice. Gomery asked: "What disciplinary actions?" None were named. The uniformed bureaucrats in the RCMP made the same empty promises. At one point Gomery said that the experience of listening to how government "really works" amounted to a loss of innocence. A lengthy parade of individuals who embodied cynicism, cowardice, ass-covering, opportunism, lack of respect for rules and procedures, lack of concern for inefficiency and waste, a climate of deception, secrecy, favouritism, and contempt for Parliament and the public interest signified precisely the "culture of entitlement" that Gomery found so offensive. The sum of his recommendations were not to impose new rules but to create a new "political culture." Judge Gomery was calling for regime change.

The Gomery Commission report, testimony, and research studies brought to light three main reasons that the Sponsorship Program turned into the sponsorship scandal. First, Gomery repeated what some leading Canadian political scientists, including his director of research, Donald Savoie, have said for several years: the centralization of power in the PMO is an invitation to abuse. As Antonin Scalia, Associate Justice of the U.S. Supreme Court, observed: "No government official is 'tempted' to place restraints upon his own freedom of action, which is why Lord Acton did not say 'Power tends to purify.'" Second, this concentration of power was facilitated by the refusal of cowardly bureaucrats to exercise oversight over ruthless ones who were determined to act in secrecy. Third, the political leadership—Chrétien, Pelletier, and Gagliano—found in that combination of ruthlessness and timidity just what they were looking for. Gomery brought to light the nadir of the Canadian regime. Now what?

CHAPTER SEVEN

CONCLUSIONS FOR THE FUTURE

"Canada has no claim to immortality."
—PIERRE TRUDEAU

George Grant used to distinguish regularly between the love of one's own and the love of the good. At its widest, love of one's own applies to the regime, our regime, the Canadian regime. Unlike love of the good, one's own regime never receives unqualified love, first because no regime is simply just, but more importantly because "our own" embodies things closer to us, including family and that mythical place called home. And home for many Canadian citizens is concretely some other place: the upper Fraser Valley, Ricardo Ranch, the Downtown East Side, Prince Albert, perhaps even the Eastern Townships, Halifax, Heart's Content, or *la nation de Québec*. In contrast, one's status as citizen is legal only, and so is defined by the regime. Some citizens admire the regime more than others; the sentiments that bind citizens to the regime are unquestionably stronger in some parts of the country than in others. This distinction between citizenship and love of one's own, of home, is another way of making the distinction between identity and place on the one hand and a political understanding of the regime on the other. However the problem is approached, it is a real distinction or a distinction within reality. Moreover, I do not believe it is going away anytime soon, even if Stephen Harper's Conservatives become Canada's naturally governing party.

It seems to me equally true that there comes a time, as the regime declines from rule by what Toynbee called a "creative minority" to rule by a "dominant minority," that sentimental (and so, in fact, weak) attachments to the regime snap. Increasingly one finds that what is one's own, whether we like it or not, is unworthy of anyone's love. Whether we have reached this point, Canadians will quietly decide on their own. Certainly a significant number of Quebeckers are there and, in part as a result of the ineptness, the malice, the endless Machiavellian cunning so beautifully brought into focus by the Gomery Commission, many thoughtful Canadians elsewhere are ready for some serious regime change. Albertans are not excluded from their number and, at least anecdotally, their numbers are growing. In any event, no one who is alive to Canadian political reality could possibly be unaware of the malign consequences of the changes to the Canadian regime over the past two generations.

The Canadian regime is hardly unique in this respect, not even in North America. Americans have argued, for example, that republican government, which meant the election of decent representatives, has been circumvented during about the same period of time by national party platforms, plebiscites, and mandates given force by the electorate and put into operation by the administrative state. The Canadian equivalent was built by the post-war mandarinate along with party discipline and rule from the centre. In both countries, the growth of administration has diminished the possibilities for political action, innovation, and glory. At the same time, it has eroded the respect that democratic citizens owe the Constitution. These two changes for the worse, we showed, are connected. In the modern bureaucratic state, the rule of law, especially the law of the Constitution, is an impediment to cozy relations between the favour-seekers and the trustees of the nation's bounty. Within this perhaps global and certainly North Atlantic commonality, the malaise we endure is clearly our own. So, even while we bear in mind that the decline or the degeneracy of the Canadian regime is to be regretted, it also provides an opportunity for regime change that almost necessarily will be for the better.

The argument of this essay has already drawn a few conclusions. This is not surprising because the point of analysis is to reach a conclusion, to come to a judgment, to distinguish actual practices from professed ones, formalities we seek to live up to from mere behaviour. Drawing together a few themes may be redundant. It would be premature to call them conclusions, even though one has to stop somewhere.

I began this essay with reference to a nearly universal sentiment that Canadians, as other citizens in democracies, are uncertain about their future but also dissatisfied by their uncertainties. If we ask whether these dissatisfactions are reasonable, we soon enough encounter the importance of the regime. At the very least, the arguments made above suggest that by losing respect for the Constitution, and with that loss of respect for the rule of law, we have lost respect for much else besides. If so, the answer to our dissatisfactions is obvious: restore the Constitution.

Unfortunately, this simple structure, that of problem and solution, which is generally preferred by engineers, is almost never to be found in politics. Politics nearly always involves the unexpected, the unprecedented, and brand new. Leaving aside the current problem of constitutional interpretation, which is that the Constitution is what the judges on the Supreme Court of Canada say it is, I do not wish to suggest that Canadians and their governments should set about "recovering" the original Constitution, the "ancient constitution," as the British sometimes have said. First of all, skilled Canadian political leaders, as noted above, have tried and failed to change the Constitution and they are unlikely to embark on megaconstitutional change again unless they are compelled to do so.

But more to the point of this essay, it would be foolish to embrace the seductive temptations of romanticism—that, for example, we were better off with the old BNA Act and without the Charter, so that is where we must aim to return. It may be true that Canada in 1947 was a happier place, but that does not mean that the old ways are by definition the good ways. Our childhoods may well have been happy and glorious, but even Bruce Springsteen knows the glory days are gone and they cannot be relived.

If it is accepted that constitutional change has been undertaken not chiefly by formal amendment but more often surreptitiously and for reasons of expediency justified by high-sounding, moralistic, but ultimately sophistic abstractions—such as Frank Scott's gift-giving capability of the Crown—it is certainly true that expediency can be undone only by invoking the reasons of principle.

Here are two: first, the old way was public and transparent. Change had to be argued about. It was explicitly and deliberately political, not "settled" and not at all a backroom administrative deal. If governance is to be improved, the forms of politics, though not necessarily of earlier practices, must be recovered. Second, crises, chiefly depression and war, lead to big government of one sort or another. We know that governments do not shrink when the crisis is over and we know why: because they come to govern in their own interests.

From classical political science we also know that the name of such a regime is tyranny. However needful the recovery of non-tyrannical practices may be, removing tyranny is difficult in the extreme because it is not for the faint of heart. To compound the difficulty, as Hannah Arendt once pointed out, administrative tyranny is worst of all, because it is the rule of rules, a tyranny without a tyrant, and thus cannot be extinguished even by the desperate remedy of tyrannicide. This is why the replacement of the Liberal Party of Canada, however welcome, does not address the fundamental issue of the regime. The end of Liberal government was merely a necessary but far from a sufficient change. Moreover, should the Liberals return, they will come armed to the teeth this time not with the silliness of national unity—the crises of which their governance assured—but some even more fraudulent issue such as "global warming" and what Canadians must do about it.

Whatever awaits us on that score, political science is unpredictive. Looking only to the recent past, we can begin the process of understanding what went wrong only by first acknowledging a basic fundamental fact: there is not now, nor has there ever been a Canadian identity. All the efforts by the Government of Canada and its various agents, from the CBC to the CWB, have failed to do anything but reinforce the reality of our limited, local, and regional identities, things that are "our own" that we love a lot more than we love the regime. Moreover, there is no way to destroy these limited identities without destroying what is cherished by those who hold to them. We must accommodate one another politically or go our separate ways.

I have indicated that respect for the constitution is a good place to begin the endless business of accommodation, but today that may prove impossible. Even if we merely recollect what the constitution once was, namely the law of a federation, that insight would help extinguish once and, with luck, for a very long time the great fraud called "national unity." Because of the reality of our limited identities, it is no wonder that every time Ottawa seeks to push us in the direction of "national unity," the consequence is greater fragmentation. The reason is obvious; ask yourself the question: concretely, who advocates "national unity" with such loud and hectoring voices? None but the bureaucrats on the banks of the Rideau, their captive audience of politicians, and cheerleaders in the CBC and associated media.

In reality, and in contrast, regional myths and federal constitutional formalities harmonize with one another and are reinforcing. Our chief problems therefore stem from the refusal of the regime to accommodate itself to these realities in civil society. Students of Canadian federalism will see in this argument a restatement of that made by William S. Livingston in his classic study half a century ago. Perhaps. But perhaps Livingston was right.

The integrity of local identities has been most obvious in recent years in the politics of Quebec and of Alberta (tomorrow maybe Newfoundland?), both of which share the rejection of the myths of Canadian identity and national unity, but for different reasons reflecting the different historical experiences of Quebeckers and Albertans. For Quebeckers, resistance is burdened with the residua—the spiritual mortgage, if you prefer—of ethnicity, even if it is mentioned only to be denied. Indeed, even when ethnicity or ethnonationalism is said to have been replaced by civic nationalism of some sort, this historical change can no more escape the historical past than a girl can jump over her shadow. This history of Quebec is saturated with ethnicity, just as it is with religion, language, and myths of defeat.

In contrast, the history of the western territory and provinces has been from the beginning political, as the history of resistance was and is bound to be. In this respect, but also in others, western or just Alberta sovereignists have a great advantage: they are serious. They are not threatening to leave in order to get someone else to pick up the tab so their "distinct society" can have an external taxpayer-supported daycare or an external taxpayer-supported aeronautics industry.

Whether Alberta or Quebec gains independence or not, the anti-American heritage of the Loyalists and especially of those who consider themselves the spiritual heirs of Loyalism, the nationalist left centred chiefly in Ontario, needs strongly and fundamentally to be reconsidered if not entirely rethought and repudiated. Certainly as a practical matter, Canada is an independent country that, on occasion, has fought for its independence—though not recently. Today any serious and principled (or worse, any ideological) argument favouring "an independent foreign policy" for Canada and similar generally left-wing fantasies is particularly misguided. At one time, in the eighteenth century, the Loyalists and the Patriots may have drawn distinct practical conclusions from the same principles. But even two centuries ago that was just a pragmatic, not a principled, choice.

Notwithstanding the existence of His Lordship, the Duke of Mississauga, who, I have heard, is an insurance salesman, transplanting the "image and transcript" of British society to the backwoods of British North America was never a serious proposition and quite ridiculous today. Likewise reliance on Sir John A. Macdonald's rhetoric regarding the United States is simply anachronistic. So, to the infantile anti-Americans in our midst I say: Stop it! Right now! Disagreeing with any particular American policy is one thing. Specifically, it is akin to disagreeing with some specific policy of the government of France or of Romania. Anti-Americanism, however, has always been more than a policy disagreement. It is an ideological conceit, a thoughtless and disagreeable prejudice of which Canadians, whether Tories or socialists, ought to be ashamed. To introduce a little sobriety into their hot tempers, anti-Americans had better bone up on some elementary eighteenth-century North American history or take a shortcut and ask themselves: Whom would you prefer to have as neighbours? North Korea? Germany? Argentina?

And speaking of history: Laurentian Canadians need to expend the effort to understand their other great prejudice, their distaste for prairie politics. That is, they need to come to grips with western and, especially, Albertan self-understanding. A useful beginning would be to reflect on the fact that no Canadian would like to be considered a "Roman provincial." They need to see what is objectionable in monopoly, whether the "monopoly clause" of the Canadian Pacific Railway or the cwb monopoly of western wheat and barley.

The effort expended to overcome prejudice will be repaired not merely by a growth in understanding, but by a growing sense of moderation and appreciation of one's fellow citizens whose interests as well as the things in which they take pride are not always shared. Remember as well that the alternative of transforming provinces into sovereign states will impose great transaction costs on us all. It is probably obvious to Laurentian Canadians who is best positioned to pay those costs with the least long-term damage: Alberta, not you.

If such mental experiments are too taxing, here is another shortcut. This one was proposed by my colleague at the University of Alberta, Leon Craig. If Alberta were currently independent, is it likely that it ever would decide to join Canada as it is today? What would be the advantages? Seeing none, now ask yourself, why would Alberta want to stay?

The Canadian regime involves more than myths, of course, though its current fractiousness exists largely because the several myths do not harmonize with one another but rather conflict head-on. Nowhere is the institutional dominance of Laurentian Canada, which has treated and still aims to treat Alberta and the West as a Roman province, more obvious than in the phenomenon we have called the embedded state. The chief effect of this aspect of the regime is that an entrenched bureaucracy is capable of following its own advice with greater fidelity, if it thinks it must, than it needs to follow the direction of the politically elected executive. As a result of this effective but non-responsible rule, Canadian society has been fragmented and Canadian politics has been embittered far beyond the sensible political divisions created by a federal constitution. Once again, that is, by attempting to create a spurious "national unity" by organizing the integral but dispersed provinces and regions into some sort of administrative unit, the bureaucracy has simply created additional divisions.

To conclude that the results, namely fragmentation, dependency, and the frustrations of impotence, were the consequences of a deliberate bureaucratic strategy of dividing the country in order to rule it would be to ascribe Machiavellian cunning to a shabby collection of self-interested intellectual mediocrities. Besides, as Leo Strauss once said in a similar context, Machiavelli's teaching was graceful, subtle, and colourful. Of recent Canadian politicians only Pierre Trudeau approached the Machiavellian ideal, and he fell far short. Even so, the Canadian regime today, though achieved chiefly by happenstance and opportunism, may appear in retrospect as if it were the achievement of designing minds. No doubt a succession of Clerks of the Privy Council would like to think they created something great or at least enduring. The fact is, they merely took advantage of the fears of politicians to assume their public responsibilities, all the while avoiding public responsibility themselves.

The theoretical implications of the embedded state are

obvious: to the extent that it exercises rather than protects rights of citizens, it creates dependency and subservience. It may do so with high motives, low ones, or practically no motives at all. The result in every instance is that power and authority gravitate to the state and away from citizens. The most objectionable aspect of the embedded state is the practice of bureaucrats and, let us be frank, judges undertaking to create constituencies for their own administrative advancement.

The "Social Action" branches of government may be a thing of the past and the power of the Canadian Wheat Board may be under serious scrutiny, but when judges, and especially the crimson-and-ermine-clad sages on the Supreme Court of Canada, make rulings that further fragment society by, for example, supporting special privileges for Indians, or women, or Indian women, the result is no different than the explicit aims of "bureaucratic animation." That is, judicial decisions no less than bureaucratic initiatives serve the interests of those who make them. No judge is so politically naïve as to think that a particularly creative decision is likely to result in anything but further litigation and thus greater enhancement of judicial authority. Again one need not ascribe Machiavellian motives to the judiciary to understand the effective and thus Machiavellian consequences. In any event, political life further recedes into the background and a somewhat inchoate, because inarticulate, citizen discontent grows.

It is important to reduce the attractiveness of interest-group litigation. Extinguishing taxpayer support for any group that seeks to advance its "charter interests" (as distinct from the political interest of citizens) would be a first step. It will also take a judiciary with a proper and restrained understanding of the genuine and real limits to litigation and adjudication to correct this malfunction in democratic self-government.

The non- or extra-constitutional expansion of Ottawa at the expense of provincial responsibility has undermined both the federal constitution and the conventions of parliamentary government. For decades the constitutional divisions that are elaborated chiefly in sections 91–2 of the Constitution Act (1867) provided a workable framework for both federal variants and experimentation and for more-or-less responsible government. Initially the Keynesian doctrines promising smooth economic growth supplied the rationale for engrossing the power of Ottawa. Today there is little beyond the fears and anxieties of politicians, which they adroitly communicate to citizens, and the self-interest of the bureaucracy to justify the enormous disproportion between the capacity to raise revenue and the responsibility to spend it on public policy. Paul Wells recently remarked: "There was [and is] a rock-solid consensus among bureaucrats in the federal Finance department that the fiscal imbalance was a province-built bogeyman designed to extort money out of federal coffers." And federal coffers are, to the mandarins in the Department of Finance, their special focus of concern. No one in that department is interested in reducing the size of federal coffers. Indeed, it is no great exaggeration to say that, to these people, because the government prints the money, all revenues generated by the Canadian economy are, properly understood, theirs to use for what they alone are in a position to determine is the greater national good. It is true that our bureaucratic masters and the enforcers in Revenue Canada, as by an act of grace, permit us to retain and spend as we wish some of our income. But that privilege can (and will) be revoked if we do not do what is entrusted to us in a manner that meets with their approval.

If any proof were needed beyond what has been presented above, it is the handling of income trusts by the Harper government. Granted, they did not engage in what was likely criminal behaviour regarding rulings on income trusts as had the Liberals, but the same anxiety about "lost revenue" animated the senior mandarins in Finance to frighten the new minister, an excitable and pugnacious lawyer, not a priestly economist or even a businessman who may be presumed to be able to understand the concept of the bottom line. In fact, revenue leakage to Ottawa was minimal, since the flow-through beneficiaries or "unit-holders" would pay taxes on the income received from the trusts. What the creation of income trusts did illustrate, however, is that business people could outsmart bureaucrats. That was simply not tolerable.

To add insult to injury, energy trusts, which were centred chiefly in Calgary, were the main beneficiaries. Who did they think they were? It mattered not a bit to the feisty little Toronto lawyer that energy trusts contributed enormously to the Canadian economy, that they helped ensure Canadian ownership of energy companies, and that they were just about the only vehicle available to exploit mature and declining reservoirs. Who cares? Off with their heads!

As we have seen, the effect of maintaining a large state revenue flow to Ottawa is not to defend Canadian national interests by, for example, reasonable expenditures on military training and equipment, but merely to reproduce the large and inefficient state. Economists may make poor political analysts, but they are pretty good at calculating social optima. There is absolutely no doubt or question that the Canadian state is about twice as big as optimally it needs to be.

Given that Canada is a federation, a reasonable compromise that would foster experimentation would leave the provinces room to do as they please with regard to the size of bureaucracy they wish to support in order to administer whatever social programs they choose. But these same provinces must pay for their choices. If PEI wants "free" child care for everyone on the island, fine. And let them pay for it. Likewise with medical care, which is, of course, the biggest elephant in the forum. Or unemployment insurance or welfare. Let a hundred flowers bloom! Let governing from the centre end! George Grant was fond of quoting a Spanish proverb: "Take what you want, said God; take it and pay for it." The proverbial Spanish God was clearly a federalist. She was not a supporter of transfer payments or equalization. No sensible human being, let alone a divine one, is.

In this respect it might be helpful to recall that Canada began as a kind of experiment in living, much as the great nineteenth-century liberal J.S. Mill recommended. The several provinces entered into the confederation on quite different terms and by means of different legal instruments, from Imperial to Canadian statutes. Some constitutional lawyers have argued that these different constitutional positions do not amount to special status, but others are more impressed by the "asymmetries." Is the glass half-full or half-empty? Historically, it seems clear, Canada has had a rich variety in the modes of its governance. On occasion these variations appeared in unexpected quarters.

In 1934, for example, in the midst of the Great Depression

but prior to the triumph of Keynesian orthodoxy, the Government of Nova Scotia engaged Norman McLeod Rogers, a political scientist at Queen's, to argue before the Nova Scotia Royal Commission of Provincial Economic Inquiry, better known as the Jones Commission, that the colonies that came together as Canada were "distinct entities" that retained their distinctiveness owing to the "tenacity of local sentiments," particularly in the historically more established settlements such as Nova Scotia. Rogers, and Premier Angus Macdonald who accompanied him, quoted (somewhat inaccurately) the image of James Bryce in *The American Commonwealth* that the national government may be compared to a church erected on the site and foundation of earlier houses of worship. As Jennifer Smith commented, "The implication of the endurance of distinct identities was that the federation did not produce one, new identity out of them. It did not submerge them in a national identity."

The point was made again thirty years later in much the same way in the Tremblay Report. During the course of Canadian history, the myths of Canadians' various and occasionally antithetical identities find expression in demands to recover, to restore, or, in any event, to change political institutions. As the Nova Scotia submission of Professor Rogers concluded so many years ago, "A federation exists not to destroy but to maintain the distinct identity of its component communities."

It is historically true as well that Ottawa has done its level best to destroy distinct identities whenever and wherever they raised their heads. The most recent effort was the accounting trick, which Tom Courchene called "hourglass federalism." First, use the spending power to tempt provinces to accept "gifts" from Ottawa. Then off-load debt onto the provinces chiefly through cutting health care transfers while at the same time mounting an enormous PR campaign, second only to "national unity," promoting state-run health care as the very marrow of Canadianness. When the provinces had to pay for health care, their discretionary spending was extinguished. Ottawa gets fat; the provinces are emaciated. Hence the "fiscal imbalance." More important, however, is that power of the federal bureaucracy never declines.

From the objections of Nova Scotia in the 1930s (and even earlier, truth to tell) to the perverse tricks of hourglass federalism, the growth of the federal state has been the source of so many discontents and the site for the orchestration of so many anxieties among Canadian citizens. If the optimal size estimates of economists are accurate within an order of magnitude, it follows that good governance in Canada requires a 50 per cent reduction in the size of the federal bureaucracy.

Finally, consider the lessons Judge Gomery and his inquiry can teach us about Canada's regime. All regimes, but especially democracies, because of their variability and dynamism, are influenced by the character of their political leaders. The iconic remark of David Dingwall, that he was entitled to his entitlements, was discovered by Gomery not to be a dishonourable personality trait but the attribute of a "culture." It is clear from the testimony heard before the commission that the several people involved exemplified what Andrew Coyne called "the moral rot that has taken hold of Ottawa over the past three decades." After all, institutions do not exist apart from the individuals who staff them.

Accordingly, the argument that Adscam was an aberration,

the result of a few rogue bureaucrats and misguided or greedy admen, is absurd. It is the end point of a lengthy historical development. The Chrétien governments brought to perfection the extra-constitutional politics that began with pragmatic incremental steps back in the days of Pearson or even St. Laurent. Moreover, the triumph of pragmatic incrementalism over constitutional provisions was bound to end in criminal politicians looting the wallets of taxpayers for their own benefit and the benefit of their parties. Once you need not refer to the law of the constitution, which is for politicians what the criminal law is for citizens, where else could it end? Once you become accustomed to circumventing, for example, the provisions of ss. 91–2 of the Constitution Act (1967) by making political deals because it is easier than amending the constitutional law, why not make another deal? Pretty soon there is no need even to look at the letter of the law because the spirit of political deal making has superseded it.

This is not, however, to place an equally naïve faith in the Constitution on the grounds that the real problem is corruption of human beings sown in the hearts of men and women. Regime change is more than changing the Constitution; even Gomery saw that, which is why he spoke of a culture that had to be changed. That is, the link between corrupt human beings and a corrupt regime does not mean that the answer lies in a counsel of perfection and enlightenment that would find a remedy in an "accountability act," however pleasant such legislation is to contemplate. In fact, I am far from believing the enlightened Kantian notion that with a proper constitution a race of devils could live together in peace and justice. They could not. The first thing they would do is amend the constitution in order to proceed with their devilry. Second, however, people who disparage following the constitution in order to pursue "flexible" public policy usually have an imperfect and often half-baked and misguided grasp of what a constitution is, namely the grounds for the rule of law.

It was certainly clear from the Gomery hearings that "Ottawa," which is to say the federal bureaucracy, does not enforce its own rules. Moreover, it was equally evident that the regime "endlessly," as Andrew Coyne said, suppressed evidence, intimidated institutions it did not already control, and even prepared a counterforce strategy to use against Gomery. It is one of the major oddities of the response to Gomery by the Martin government that it immediately passed 238 new rules and made provision for associated auditors and comptrollers to monitor the great heaving organism. The problem was not the absence of rules or inadequate rules; the problem was that a significant number of individuals broke the rules.

Nor should we lose sight of the most important aspect of Adscam: it was a made-in-Quebec problem. Whether one believes or not the superstitious nonsense of "subliminal" advertising by the separatists, it is undoubtedly true, as Antonia Maioni said, that "the spirit behind the sponsorship program was one of blind panic about Quebec." There is, however, a fine and subtle dialectic at work in getting into a panic "about Quebec," which is to say, about Quebec separatism. Supposing no one was in a panic about Quebec separatism? Supposing we had a prime minister who said, as Bercuson and I said in the closing words of *Deconfederation*, "Bon voyage et bonne chance." And we did not mean "au revoir." But what then?

The conventional response is, more or less, Canada cannot

be governed without electoral support from Quebec. To which one can only reply: not since the days of John Diefenbaker has it been tried. And anyhow, is governing *with* the support of Quebec, along with the blackmail, the eclipse of serious priorities, the constant anxieties that occasionally erupt into "blind panic" that comes with that support—indeed, that is essential to "understanding" what makes Quebec so special and thus what, in the minds of people who think this way, makes Canada so special—is all this dreamy, narcissistic avoidance of reality really, truly, at the end of the day, worth it?

In this concluding chapter I have spoken easily and frequently of necessity, of things that must be done, including taking a hard look at whether we, whoever we think ourselves to be, can remain part of the same regime as Quebec. Necessity is a major category of Machiavellian, and thus of modern, political science. If we do not heed the imperatives of necessity, the world will not end. Necessity does, however, bring into relief some stark alternatives. We can, of course, continue along the road of bureaucratic tyranny, blaming others, especially Americans, for our own servility, telling ourselves how much Quebec makes us unique in the world, distinct, and so very, very special. But for many of us, perhaps especially because of the myths and culture of the cowboy west, the bleak prospects of never-ending bureaucratic tyranny will be rejected along with the self-serving narcissism. This regime change will bring an end to the country. Who will lament its passing?

I began this essay on the regime by describing its origin on a cattle-buying trip with Sandy Soutzo to Medicine Hat. As the book was nearing completion, some nine calving seasons later, I joined him again, this time in High River. We were sitting in the stands, and Soutzo explained to me that a couple of years ago he had discovered that fully 90 per cent of the cow-calf operators were over fifty years of age. By 2008, 90 per cent are over sixty. He found this demographic fact troubling. What lay ahead? Could the industry continue?

"Why is this happening?" I asked.

"The young guys just aren't interested," he said. "They think it's just too hard. Look around."

As the lots of preg-tested cows were brought in, an older cowboy seated on the other side of him said, "I see you're buyin'."

"A few," said Soutzo.

"Got quite a few?" he asked.

"Yup. Quite a few," he replied.

"Oh, you've probably got lots of help," the cowboy said. "Help's hard to get nowadays. At least help that knows what they're doin'," he went on. "What've you got for help?"

"Well, I'll tell you," said Soutzo. "The kid that helps me calve just turned sixty-nine."

"Ha! You think that's something?" said the cowboy. "The kid that helps me is eighty-one! And you know what? I hope to get another ten seasons outta him."

At which comment yet another cattleman sitting behind the three of us snorted, and we turned around. Soutzo said, "Well, what about you?"

"Oh," the old veteran replied, "I do it myself. I only got 500 cows."

LEGENDS OF THE CALGARY SCHOOL, THE INSTITUTE, AND THE UNIVERSITY

On April 1, 2006, Tom Flanagan posted a notice in *News and Notes*, a newsletter circulated within the Political Science Department at the University of Calgary. It announced a talk he was giving that afternoon at the radically left-wing think-tank at the University of Alberta in Edmonton, the Parkland Institute. The title of his talk was "Tales of the Calgary School: The Guns, the Dogs, and the Women they Loved." At first I wondered why the Parkland Institute would have invited a known operative from Stephen Harper's electoral team. Then I noticed the date.

It would have been an interesting talk, though not everyone who is said to belong to the Calgary School has a gun or a dog. Flanagan, for example, has neither. In April 2006, following the Harper victory earlier in the year, journalists, especially in Laurentian Canada, were desperate to find the right kind of spin to apply to the Harper phenomenon, and so they consulted their own. In particular, an article in the Toronto glossy mag, reeking with Laurentian self-importance, called *The Walrus*, had run a feature in October 2004 by Marci McDonald called "The Man Behind Stephen Harper: Everything You Should Know—But Don't—about Tom Flanagan and the Calgary School." On the basis of McDonald's article, Flanagan had been pestered by journalists for weeks to provide insight into what it all meant. So had I. Such attention illustrates the importance of legends and tales more than it says anything significant about this so-called school. So let me set the record straight.

First of all, university departments, as other institutions, go through a kind of natural history. Young scholars of promise are recruited; they begin their careers, publish books, grow in maturity, and fade away into emeritusness. Sometimes young scholars do not do anything of significance after completing their Ph.D. theses. They are called deadwood, and university departments have their apportioned lot.

Second, university departments, as other institutions, including think-tanks such as the Fraser Institute, are governed by distinct regimes. Usually they are one-person regimes, which means that the personality of the administrative head of these comparatively small organizations matters a great deal.

In my university department, starting in the 1980s, or perhaps slightly before, a series of department heads recruited and maintained a productive and fairly harmonious faculty. We wrote mostly for other scholars on topics that only such oddballs could care about—the poetry of the young Louis Riel was one of Flanagan's early works; I wrote about obscure French and German thinkers; Ted Morton and Rainer Knopff were beginning their work on the courts; and David Bercuson had made the switch from Canadian labour to Canadian military history. Flanagan and I had known one another since graduate school; in the late 1980s Bercuson and I started writing together. Morton and Knopff had been in graduate school together at the University of Toronto; the three of us began hunting together in the early 1980s. A few years later, Bercuson, Flanagan, and I started fishing together, in the north and on the west coast. In short, we were more a collection of reasonably accomplished scholars who shared recreational interests than a coherent school.

What changed things slightly, at least for the political scientists, was regime change in the department. It would be unkind, but not inaccurate, to describe this change as the triumph of deadwood, but something had definitely been altered. In 1992, when Jeff Simpson wrote a column in the *Globe and Mail* about the "Calgary mafia," some of our colleagues wrote an angry letter to the editor pointing out that the persons named by Simpson did not represent the department. Bercuson, being a historian, was spared this indignity. One of the consequences of departmental regime change is that Knopff went into higher administration in the university, Flanagan spent more time downtown with Preston Manning, Morton eventually became a senator-elect, then an MLA and cabinet minister, and I eventually became the managing director of the Calgary office of the Fraser Institute. Two others, not linked to the Calgary School, Roger Gibbins and Keith Archer, also found gainful employment outside an increasingly fractious department.

The effect, one way or another, was to increase the public profile of each of us. We continued to do our academic work

but, having been more or less purged from internal departmental self-administration, we had more time for popular
writing and political activities, according to taste.

Then, in 1996, an American academic from Johns Hopkins,
David J. Rovinsky, wrote a paper for the New England Political
Science Association (NEPSA) called "The Calgary School: The
New Motor of Canadian Political Thought." Flanagan happened to attend the meetings of the NEPSA and picked up a
copy. When he returned, he came into my office and
announced with a grin, "We are now a school." This was, I suppose, more respectable than the other collective name we had
given ourselves, *les bonhommes du lac Hearne*, after a place we
fished. Rovinsky and Zagos Madjid-Sadjadi published another
paper on "Canadian Neoconservatism" that added to the public certification of the "school." Then journalists picked up the
label and the die was cast. Recognition, even if a bit misguided,
is always flattering.

In 2000, we were called "the bad boys of Canadian acade-
mia," our home the "Department of Redneckology." It was only
when Stephen Harper was approaching the prime ministership
that friendly banter turned to serious and usually hostile attention. Hence the McDonald article in *The Walrus*, followed by
others in the *Toronto Star* and the *Globe and Mail*, but also by
spirited defences of this "school." The Laurentian conclusion
to all this attention, as John Ibbotson put it, is that the Calgary
School has "shaped, and now dominates, the thinking of the
new Conservative Party." Prime Minister Harper, he said, is "the
finest flower" of the school. The blogospheric material paints
an even more astonishing picture.

The mere facts of the case, however, are more modest. We all know one another and generally get along. Some of us are better friends than others. We are an informal social network, not an organization. Several pair-wise teams have done work together; we disagree on a wide range of issues, from same-sex marriage to the war in Afghanistan and the policies of the Harper government. If "schools" are supposed to have a consistent and internally coherent view of the political landscape, then the Calgary School does not exist beyond the imaginative world of journalism. The label, however, is an indication of precisely the importance of myth and legend.

So far as my affiliation with the Fraser Institute is concerned, it all began in 1998 when Ralph Hedlin, a respected old-school journalist, proposed to some institute supporters in Calgary that the "Calgary School" be affiliated with the institute. The theory was that the political analyses we had undertaken would complement the economic analyses of the Vancouver people. He put me in touch with some of his associates to fund a feasibility study. Initially we called this virtual organization the Chinook Institute on the grounds that we would be, as Flanagan put it, "a warm zephyr melting the icy dogmas of received opinion." Norm Wagner, former president of the University of Calgary, disagreed: "It sounds too much like hot air from over the mountains," he said.

My initial efforts were directed at establishing an institute of some sort within the University of Calgary. The barriers to entry were high. The chief problem was oversight by the senior administration and the necessity to fundraise through the University Development Office, neither of which I wished to endure. The chief obstacle to creating an institute outside the university was the reluctance of Revenue Canada to recognize think-tanks as charities for tax purposes. As part of the feasibility study, I had visited the Fraser Institute to discuss this question with its founding and long-time executive director, Michael Walker. I had known him for several years and had placed one of my former students, Lydia Miljan, with the Vancouver operation. She was running a division of the institute called the National Media Archive and, had she not decided to move to the University of Windsor, would no doubt have been included among the members of the Calgary School. Walker suggested that we consider affiliating with the Fraser Institute; this then turned into an offer to my colleagues and me to do research for, and publish with, the institute.

Some of the others were more enthusiastic than I was, but it did solve the barrier-to-entry problem. In retrospect, my misgivings concerned not what Walker or the institute had written or said but, as my thesis supervisor once observed of a prominent American conservative, "I just don't like his tone of voice." It was, however, a compromise I thought I could live with— part of the cost of doing business, as they say. Miljan became the first managing director of the Calgary office and, after she moved east, I became the second. Again in retrospect, it is clear that, by having a credible operation in Calgary, the institute would be able to mollify several of its major supporters in the city who were not entirely happy with sending money across the Rockies and receiving little institute attention to the problems and interests they thought were important.

Even after the Calgary office opened, fundraising remained a difficult issue. In 1999 Walker told me, "Barry, fundraising is the most important aspect of the whole activity and is one of the most difficult ones to, in fact, get right." It turned out that "getting it right" was not just a matter of raising money to support projects undertaken by the Calgary office, even though this was the chief reason for opening the office here. Rather, the objective was to raise money for general revenues, as they say in government, or the bottom line, as they say in business and at the institute.

General funding is much preferred by the central administration over project funding. General funding can be allocated according to the priorities of the institute, whereas project funding (minus overhead) is to be spent only on the project for which it was raised. This was an ongoing problem because Calgary supporters, generally speaking, wanted money raised in Calgary to be spent on Calgary projects. Like everyone else, Calgary businessmen also love their own. Vancouver Central wanted Calgary to be a money cow they could milk. In the event, project-specific money was often appropriated to the bottom line anyway, and end-of-year surpluses mysteriously vanished, even when donors made it very clear the money was for the Calgary office and Calgary projects. I had more than one sharp exchange with the director of development on this question because it was a matter of respecting donor intent. When I convinced a Calgary oilman to donate $10,000 to support projects I had been discussing with him, such as the Canadian military or relations with the United States, I considered it both dishonest and insulting to use his or her money to support another project that somebody on the coast considered more important.

On April 25, 2001, I officially joined the Fraser Institute as a "budget holder," which is to say, a member of the management committee. Half my teaching time was bought out from the university and the remainder of my time would be devoted to Fraser Institute affairs. I agreed to be in the office in the Grain Exchange Building in downtown Calgary half of every working day. In fact, when I measured my hours (at Walker's request), my half-time job worked out to take between thirty and thirty-six hours a week. I also undertook projects that were not connected with the institute, such as writing a newspaper column and other academic work.

I proposed to Walker that I could contribute to fundraising, having several friends in the business community. These terms were also acceptable to the university. To my surprise, I enjoyed the fundraising meetings with Barry McNamar who, to use a baseball analogy, was a superb closer. After a year or so, the long-term strategy the two of us developed, often in opposition to the people in Vancouver, proved to be a great success. About a third of my time was devoted to administrative tasks, focused on Vancouver, which was not as much fun as it sounds. I enjoyed the public policy research and associating with interesting individuals—Gordon Gibson, Martin Collacott, Ken Green, Laura Jones, Suzanne Walters, and Jason Clemens. Few of them are still associated with the institute. Indeed, after Ken Green and I were fired, Ken suggested we establish FIASGO, the Fraser Institute's Analysts' Support Group Organization. On the whole it was a satisfying experience.

Walker prepared to become the head of the Fraser Institute Foundation and relinquish the title of executive director of the institute during 2005. On July 11 of that year, as his elevation was nearly complete, out of the blue he proposed that I develop a "transition" plan. I left the meeting puzzled and asked one of my business pals in Vancouver what that meant. He told me I had just been fired. A conversation with one of my fishing buddies who was also a lawyer said the same thing. He suggested, as lawyers tend to do, that I demand a significant settlement package or plan to go to court. That struck me as a great waste of time. My initial reaction of surprise was followed by a certain degree of anger, not so much at being fired but at the mendacious euphemism of a "transition," designed clearly to avoid the discomfort of both a severance payment and a firing.

The reasons Walker offered to explain why he thought this was a good idea turned out to be bogus. In conversations over the years, he had expressed his dissatisfaction at the way I managed the Calgary office, with its profile in the city, with the productivity of the office, or with all three of these alleged failings. In fact, the culture in the Calgary office was that it was friendly, harmonious, and productive, as many visiting institute analysts from Vancouver and Toronto noted. I knew for a fact we were highly productive and later created an index to measure productivity: Calgary turned out to be the most productive unit in the institute. Regarding profile, Walker's remarks were plain silly—as is evident by the much lower institute profile in Calgary today.

So what was going on here? Without getting into too much inside baseball, of interest chiefly to gossips, there are a couple of things related to the institute as a regime that may be worth noting. First, Walker was well known for following Machiavelli's advice that it is always better to blame than to praise. Accordingly, I usually dismissed his criticism as simply the expression of his management style.

In fact, more was involved. I had often noticed a kind of low-key resentment that found expression, for example, in Walker's remarking on my monthly appearance in Vancouver, "Aha, Doctor, Professor, Fellow-of-the-Royal-Society Cooper." To pretend it exuded warmth and camaraderie or even good humour would be ridiculous. Another analyst would call me regularly and express mock surprise "that a university professor would be in his office." Once I asked him why he called me in my office if he found it so surprising to find me at work.

A second problem stems from the limitation of economics as a discipline and of an economic view of politics or of social reality more broadly. Marketeers have no understanding of virtue outside of market-set value. You may value courage or value hockey but neither is judged to be a virtue. Their focus, of course, is quite properly on interests, but they also sneak in a position of moral rectitude in the form of faith that the market is in all things efficient. But why? If you are doing okay, that is what matters, not the efficiency of the market. This combination of technical soundness regarding the economic benefits of markets with moralizing rhetoric about the virtue of markets was simply incoherent and was badly obscured by a strident, not to say dogmatic, insistence on economic doctrine.

The social implication with respect to doctrinal and moralizing economists is that it is impossible to enjoy a conversation with them, let alone make a joke. A doctrinal mind that knows its doctrine really is like a steel trap. As Derek Burney observed with respect to Treasury Board concepts of program management and quantifiable objectives, the focus turned into an obsession with measurement rather than a concern with what was important. Just as with the measurement of public opinion, this approach necessarily ignores the importance of importance. There were a few exceptions, but generally speaking measuring media hits for the tenth edition of a study of hospital waiting times or a report card on elementary schools in Alberta were seen as far more significant than any serious innovation.

When I was at the institute, we published several papers on the Canadian military and security policy. Defence and security provisioning are not market-rational activities because they protect markets and enable them to operate. I found this an extremely difficult notion to get across; it was easier to explain that the Auto Pact was a result of Canada having sufficient troops to stand between the Greeks and the Turks on Cyprus, thus ensuring the southern flank of NATO remained intact. That made sense to economists as a payoff.

I came reluctantly to the conclusion that, although these institutions are called think-tanks, intellectually speaking they are more accurately described as dogma-tanks or formula-tanks. In the case of the Fraser Institute, the dogma is not simply that markets and prosperity are associated across the globe, which I consider an empirical fact not a moral or political achievement, but that markets can effectively trump other institutions everywhere and always. The formula is to measure even what to common sense is without metric. At one point there was a serious email exchange on a project to measure happiness. Indeed, one of my initial disagreements with Walker concerns index construction the result of which is to treat what is essentially nominal or ordinal data as interval data. This is a fundamental mistake that I learned in an undergraduate course in methodology. I was told: "Well, Barry, 'yes' or 'no' is a kind of measurement." The conclusion I drew from this piece of sophistry is that the dogma regarding the formula is that measurement equals science. The undoubted fact that other so-called think-tanks, especially on the left, are even more dogmatic does not excuse what the Fraser Institute does, though it makes some of their activities more intelligible.

Budget-holders were responsible for drawing up a five-year plan. I had thought such exercises fell out of favour sometime after 1928 when the first such document was demanded from GOSPLAN by the Central Committee of the Communist Party of the Union of Soviet Socialist Republics. Silly me. There was also an annual planning session, a mid-year planning session, a monthly management committee meeting, a weekly Monday morning meeting, as well as monthly reports to the executive advisory board, and quarterly reports to the board of trustees. Perhaps the constant demand for reporting and meeting was modelled on the federal Department of Finance where Walker once worked. The idea that holding meetings among interesting people such as themselves saves time is, shall we say, not proven. Moreover the people were generally not as interesting as they thought they were. I was told early on that Walker "did not react well to surprises," which is one reason for all the planning—except when Walker wanted to "surprise" the analysts, which was an entirely different matter.

The Fraser Institute is well known for its advocacy of free market solutions—but not internally, with events management, for example. There everything is done in-house so there is no competition. When I asked about this, I was told about economies of scale, which is the one economic factor absent from a small in-house shop. One of my most unpleasant experiences at the institute came in the aftermath of an enormously successful "announcement dinner," held at the Fairmont Palliser Hotel in 2002, the purpose of which was to let the Calgary community know the Fraser Institute was in town.

We secured Bjørn Lomborg, author of the recently published *The Skeptical Environmentalist*, as the dinner speaker. The events and development people in Vancouver claimed he was too expensive. I replied that the Calgary office would assume the risk and keep the profits. Vancouver agreed, but their chief anxiety was not to tell Walker. The event was expensive to stage and the tickets were expensive to sell but we filled the hotel's ballroom and made a considerable profit for the Calgary office. The following week after the management meeting, Barry McNamar and I were summoned by Walker into a very tense meeting with the heads of events and development and told in no uncertain terms we were never, ever, to do that again. On the plane back to Calgary, we figured out how to evade the incompetence (and nepotism) of the events department, at least for important occasions where serious money was involved.

The Fraser Institute also has the reputation of being a highly libertarian outfit. There are (or were) a few libertarians in the organization, but there is even more pressure in the direction of external conformity, particularly regarding "professional attire," which included the specific prohibition against the wearing of jeans, clearly an anti-cowboy prejudice. In the spring of 2004, the dress code again came under scrutiny. It seems that some of the senior staff had taken offence at the revealing attire of some of the younger women in Vancouver and, instead of addressing the issue directly, turned to the bureaucratic solution of a mandated policy. It was never made clear whether these were elderly gents inflamed by visible flat tummies or women of a certain age envious because their tummies were no longer flat. The response in Calgary to my report on this new anxiety from Vancouver was both risible and measurable.

This nonsense was tolerable because in Calgary we could work around it and still get our work done. Even so, the summer of 2005, just prior to Walker's own "transition" to a higher plane, was like being a junior officer on the USS *Caine*, prior to the mutiny. The details are both mundane and boring: the email traffic grew more abusive, and it was clear that the cost of doing business with Walker was approaching the red line, which was probably the purpose of it all.

As the Walker regime came to a close, there was an intense debate about "rebranding." This involved arcane discussions, undertaken with great seriousness regarding the "mission statement," the "vision statement," the "slogan," the "elevator pitch," and so on. I argued that it was far better to have the right people disliking what the institute did for all the wrong reasons. No one thought it funny when I pointed out that, where I come from, rebranding was done by rustlers. Considering the evolution of the Fraser Institute as a regime, it is probably just as well that the third managing director of the Calgary office will properly enforce the manual of procedures, especially the dress code and the correct use of coat racks. He also thinks it important to keep the noise down.

So I returned full time to the university about the same time that Flanagan ended his stint as campaign manager for the Conservatives. The regime in the department had been changed for the better, and it was a fairly pleasant place to work once again. The university regime had also changed. Today the focus is on growth, particularly in the number of buildings, on fundraising, especially for new and, to my mind, highly questionable programs dealing with environmental anxieties, and on alleged efficiency, such as not letting the students pay for their courses by using credit cards. And, of course, there are lots of new and important senior administrators, and endless new processes for reporting that are made possible by computers. Indeed, in the short five or so years I was partially gone from the university, it has become as bureaucratic as the nightmare world of Ottawa.

Years ago I was asked to prepare a report for the dean of graduate studies that depended on distinguishing the several parts of the university and the level at which graduate students were funded. I argued that there were academic faculties, which used to be called arts and sciences, professional faculties such as engineering, law, and medicine, and what I called certification faculties—chiefly social work and education. I argued that students should receive funding chiefly in academic faculties, because this was the centuries-old heart of the university, and not at all in the certification faculties, because, in effect, the university was simply doing the bidding of, for example, the teachers' unions.

I did not expect this proposal to win the approval of my colleagues in education, but it did bring a little clarity to the discussion. And that, after all, is what those of us who have the opportunity to work within the university asylum are supposed to do. Whether we actually do provide clarity depends not a little on the university regime, just as clear thinking can be encouraged or retarded by the regime operating in other institutions in civil society.

REFERENCES

Autobiographical Prelude

Bercuson, David, and Barry Cooper. *Deconfederation: Canada Without Quebec*. Toronto: Key Porter, 1991.

——. *Derailed: The Betrayal of the National Dream*. Toronto: Key Porter, 1994.

Cooper, Barry. "Weaving a Work," in Ronald Beiner and Wayne Norman, eds., *Canadian Political Philosophy: Contemporary Reflections*. Toronto: Oxford University Press, 2001, pp. 374–85.

Cooper, Barry. "Some Implications of the Embedded State in Canada," in Gerald Kernerman and Philip Resnick, eds., *Insiders and Outsiders: Alan Cairns and the Reshaping of Canadian Citizenship*. Vancouver: UBC Press, 2005, pp. 104–16.

Elofson, Warren M. *Cowboys, Gentlemen and Cattle Thieves: Ranching on the Western Frontier*. Montreal: McGill-Queen's University Press, 2000.

——. *Frontier Cattle Ranching in the Land and Times of Charlie Russell*. Montreal: McGill-Queen's University Press, 2004.

Macpherson, C.B. *Democracy in Alberta*. Toronto: University of Toronto Press, 1953.

Mallory, J.R. *Social Credit and the Federal Power*. Toronto: University of Toronto Press, 1954.

Mansfield, Harvey. *America's Constitutional Soul.* Baltimore: Johns Hopkins University Press, 1991.

Voegelin, Eric. *The New Science of Politics: An Introduction.* Chicago: University of Chicago Press, 1952.

——. *Hitler and the Germans.* Tr. and ed. by Detlev Clemens and Brendan Purcell. Columbia: University of Missouri Press, 1999.

Chapter One

Arendt, Hannah. *The Human Condition.* Chicago: University of Chicago Press, 1958.

——. *The Life of the Mind: Vol. I, Thinking.* New York: Harcourt Brace Jovanovich, 1971.

Bloom, Allan. *The Closing of the American Mind.* New York: Simon & Schuster, 1987.

Codevilla, Angelo M. *The Character of Nations: How Politics Makes and Breaks Prosperity, Family, and Civility.* New York: Basic Books, 1997.

Cooper, Barry. "Some Implications of the Embedded State in Canada," in Gerald Kernerman and Philip Resnick, eds., *Insiders and Outsiders: Alan Cairns and the Reshaping of Canadian Citizenship.* Vancouver: UBC Press, 2005, pp. 104–16.

Cooper, Barry, and Lorna R. Marsden. "Stating the Problem of Equality and Justice: What's a Fair Share?" in Emer Killean, ed., *Equality in the Economy: A Synthesis of the Proceedings of a Workshop.* Montreal: IRPP, 1986, pp. 1–4.

Flanagan, Tom. *First Nations, Second Thoughts.* Vancouver: UBC Press, 2000.

Hayek, Friedrich. *The Road to Serfdom.* Chicago: University of Chicago Press, 1946.

Hayek, Friedrich. *The Constitution of Liberty.* Chicago: University of Chicago Press, 1976.

Kinsella, Warren. *Kicking Ass in Canadian Politics*. Toronto: Random House, 2001.

——. *Fury's Hour: A (Sort-of) Punk Manifesto*. Toronto: Random House, 2005.

Malcolmson, Patrick, and Richard Myers. *The Canadian Regime*. Peterborough: Broadview, 2002.

Mansfield, Harvey. *America's Constitutional Soul*. Baltimore: Johns Hopkins University Press, 1991.

Oakeshott, Michael. *Rationalism in Politics and Other Essays*. Indianapolis: Liberty Press, 1991.

Strauss, Leo. *What Is Political Philosophy? And Other Studies*. Glencoe: The Free Press, 1959.

Voegelin, Eric. *Collected Works*, vol. 16, *Order and History, vol.* III, *Plato and Aristotle*. Columbia: University of Missouri Press, 2000.

Chapter Two

Ajzenstat, Janet. "Decline of Procedural Liberalism: The Slippery Slope to Secession," in Joseph H. Caerens, ed., *Is Quebec Nationalism Just? Perspectives from Anglophone Canada*. Montreal: McGill-Queen's University Press, 1995, pp. 115–31.

Atwood, Margaret. *Survival: A Thematic Guide to Canadian Literature*. Toronto: Anansi, 1972.

Bashevkin, Sylvia B. *True Patriot Love: The Politics of Canadian Nationalism*. Toronto: Oxford University Press, 1991.

Burnet, Jean. *Next Year Country: A Study of Rural Social Organization in Alberta*. Toronto: University of Toronto Press, 1951.

Cameron, Silver Donald. *Seasons in the Rain*. Toronto: McClelland & Stewart, 1978.

Carpenter, David C. "Alberta in Fiction: The Emergence of Provincial Consciousness." *Journal of Canadian Studies*, 10:4 (1974), 1–20.

Davey, Frank. *Post-national Arguments: The Politics of the Anglophone-Canadian Novel Since 1967.* Toronto: University of Toronto Press, 1993.

DeSouza, Mike. "More Canadians Put Province First." *Calgary Herald,* June 30, 2007, p. A4.

Doull, James. *Philosophy and Freedom: The Legacy of James Doull,* eds. David G. Peddle and Neil G. Robertson. Toronto: University of Toronto Press, 2003.

Duffy, Dennis. *Gardens, Covenants and Exiles: Loyalism in the Literature of Upper Canada/Ontario.* Toronto: University of Toronto Press, 1982.

Dumont, Fernand. *Genèse de la Société québécoise.* Montreal: Boreal, 1993.

Elkins, David. "British Columbia as a State of Mind," in Donald E. Blake, ed., *Two Political Worlds: Parties and Voting in British Columbia.* Vancouver: UBC Press, 1985, pp. 47–68.

Frye, Northrop. *The Bush Garden: Essays on the Canadian Imagination.* Toronto: Anansi, 1971.

——. *Divisions on a Ground: Essays on Canadian Culture.* Toronto: Anansi, 1982.

Granatstein, J.L. *Whose War Is It? How Canada Can Survive in the Post-9/11 World.* Toronto, HarperCollins, 2007.

Grant, George. *Lament for a Nation.* Toronto: McClelland & Stewart, 1965.

Harrison, Dick. *Untamed Country: The Struggle for a Canadian Prairie Fiction.* Edmonton: University of Alberta Press, 1977.

Johnson, William. *Anglophobie, Made in Quebec.* Montreal: Stanké, 1991.

——. *A Canadian Myth: Quebec between Canada and the Illusion of Utopia.* Montreal: Davies, 1994.

Keefer, Janice Kulyk. *Under Eastern Eyes: A Critical Reading of Maritime Fiction.* Toronto: University of Toronto Press, 1987.

MacGregor, Roy. *Canadians: A Portrait of a Country and Its People*. Toronto: Viking, 2007.

MacMechan, Archibald. *Headwaters of Canadian Literature*. Toronto: McClelland & Stewart [1924], 1974.

Martin, Patrick, Alan Gregg, and George Perkin. *Contenders: The Tory Quest for Power*. Toronto: Prentice-Hall, 1983.

McCourt, Edward A. *The Canadian West in Fiction*. Toronto: Ryerson, 1949.

Nemni, Max. "Post-Ethnic Nationalism in Quebec: A Promise of History." Paper presented at the 66th Annual Meeting of the CPSA, Calgary, June 1994.

O'Flaherty, Patrick. *The Rock Observed: Studies in the Literature of Newfoundland*. Toronto: University of Toronto Press, 1979.

Powe, W.B. *Towards a Canada of Light*. Toronto: Thomas Allen, 2006.

Resnick, Philip. *The European Roots of Canadian Identity*. Peterborough: Broadview, 2005.

Ricou, Laurence. *Vertical Man/Horizontal World: Man and Landscape in Canadian Prairie Fiction*. Vancouver: UBC Press, 1973.

Stephens, Donald. "Introduction" to Stephens, ed., *Writers of the Prairies*. Vancouver: UBC Press, 1973, pp. 2–10.

Taylor, Charles. *Multiculturalism and the "Politics of Recognition."* Princeton: Princeton University Press, 1992.

———. *Reconciling the Solitudes: Essays on Canadian Federalism and Nationalism*. Montreal: McGill-Queen's University Press, 1993.

———. *Modern Social Imaginaries*. Durham: Duke University Press, 2005.

Thomas, Lewis H. *The Struggle for Responsible Government in the Northwest Territories, 1870-97*. Toronto: University of Toronto Press, 1978.

Whittaker, Reg. *The Government Party: Organizers and Financing the Liberal Party in Canada.* Toronto: University of Toronto Press, 1977.

Wilson, Edmund. *O, Canada: An American's Notes on Canadian Culture.* New York: Farrar, Strauss and Giroux, 1965.

Wiseman, Nelson. *In Search of Canadian Political Culture.* Vancouver: UBC Press, 2007.

Chapter Three

Ajzenstat, Janet, et al., eds. *Canada's Origins: Liberal, Tory or Republican.* Ottawa: Carleton University Press, 1995.

———. *Canada's Founding Debates.* Toronto: Stoddart, 1999.

Ajzenstat, Janet. *The Once and Future Democracy: An Essay in Political Thought.* Montreal: McGill-Queen's University Press, 2003.

Bailyn, Bernard. *The Ideological Origins of the American Revolution.* Cambridge: The Belknap Press of Harvard University Press, 1967.

———. *The Ordeal of Thomas Hutchinson.* Cambridge: The Belknap Press of Harvard University Press, 1974.

Barrie, Doreen. *The Other Alberta: Decoding a Political Enigma.* Regina: Canadian Plains Research Centre, 2006.

Bell, David, and Lorne Tepperman. *The Roots of Disunity: A Look at Canadian Political Culture.* Toronto: McClelland and Stewart, 1979.

Caldarola, Carlo. "The Social Credit in Alberta," in Caldarola, ed., *Society and Politics in Alberta.* Toronto: Methuen, 1979, pp. 20–41.

Camp, Dalton. *Points of Departure.* Toronto: Deneau and Greenberg, 1979.

Careless, J.M.S. "'Limited Identities' in Canada." *Canadian Historical Review,* 50 (1969), 1–10.

Christian, William. "A Note on Rod Preece and Red Tories."
Canadian Journal of Political and Social Theory, 2 (1978),
115–36.

———. "Was George Grant a Red Tory?" in Ian Angus, et al., eds.,
*Athens and Jerusalem: George Grant's Theology, Philosophy,
and Politics.* Toronto: University of Toronto Press, 2006.

Cooper, Barry. *The Klein Achievement.* Toronto: University of
Toronto Press, 1996.

———. "Adam Smith's Defence of Capitalism." *Fraser Forum*,
November 2005, 4–5.

Cooper, Barry, and Mebs Kanji. *Governing in Post Deficit Times:
Alberta in the Klein Years.* Toronto: University of Toronto
Press, 2000.

Creighton, Donald. "Macdonald and the Anglo-Christian
Alliance." Reprinted in *Towards the Discovery of Canada:
Selected Essays.* Toronto: Macmillan, 1972, pp. 205–30.

Elton, David, and Roger Gibbins. "Western Alienation and
Political Culture," in Richard Schultz, Orest M. Kruhlak,
John C. Terry, eds., *The Canadian Political Process*, 3rd. ed.
Toronto: Holt, Rinehart and Winston, 1979.

Farthing, John. *Freedom Wears a Crown.* Toronto: Kingswood
House, 1957.

Fellows, Jo-Ann. "The Loyalist Myth in Canada." Canadian
Historical Association, *Historical Papers*, 1971, 94–111.

Forsey, Eugene. "Canada and Alberta: The Revival of Dominion
Control over the Provinces," in his *Freedom and Order:
Collected Essays.* Toronto: McClelland and Stewart, 1974,
pp. 190–215.

Gibbins, Roger. *Prairie Politics and Society: Regionalism in
Decline.* Toronto: Butterworths, 1980.

———. *Regionalism: Territorial Politics in Canada and the United
States.* Toronto: Butterworths, 1982.

Hartz, Louis. *The Liberal Tradition in America*. New York: Harcourt, Brace and World, 1955.

Horowitz, Gad. "Conservatism, Liberalism, and Socialism in Canada: An Interpretation." *Canadian Journal of Economics and Political Science*, 32 (1966), 143–71.

House, J.D. *The Last of the Free Enterprisers: The Oilmen of Calgary*. Toronto: Macmillan, 1980.

Hutchinson, Thomas. "Dialogue Between an American and a European Englishman." Bernard Bailyn, ed., *Perspectives in American History*, xi (1975), 341–410.

Jaffa, Harry. *How to Think About the American Revolution*. Durham: Carolina Academic Press, 1978.

Kendall, Willmoore, and George W. Carey. *Basic Symbols of the American Political Tradition*. Washington: Catholic University of America Press, 1995.

Lingard, C. Cecil. *Territorial Government in Canada: The Autonomy Question in the Old Northwest Territories*. Toronto: University of Toronto Press, 1946.

Lutz, Donald S. "The Relative Influence of European Writers on Late Eighteenth-Century American Political Thought." *The American Political Science Review* (1984), 180–95.

Macpherson, C.B. *Democracy in Alberta: Social Credit and the Party System*, 2nd. ed. Toronto: University of Toronto Press, 1962.

Mallory, J.R. *Social Credit and the Federal Power*. Toronto: University of Toronto Press, 1954.

McRae, Kenneth. "The Structure of Canadian History," in L. Hartz, ed., *The Founding of the New Societies*. New York: Harcourt, Brace and World, 1964, pp. 219–47.

Morton, W.L. "The American Revolution: A View From the North." *Journal of Canadian Studies*, 7:2 (1972), 30–50.

——. "The Bias of Prairie Politics (1955)," in A.B. McKillop, ed.,

Contexts of Canada's Past: Selected Essays of W.L. Morton.
Toronto: Macmillan, 1980, pp. 145–62.

Norton, Mary Beth. *The British-Americans: The Loyalist Exiles in England, 1774-1789.* Boston: Little, Brown and Company, 1972.

Oakeshott, Michael. "Rationalism in Politics," in *Rationalism in Politics and Other Essays,* ed. Tim Fuller. Indianapolis: Liberty Press, 1991, pp. 6–42.

Panich, Leo. "The Role and Nature of the Canadian State," in Panich, ed., *The Canadian State: Political Economy and Political Power.* Toronto: University of Toronto Press, 1977.

Pencak, William. *America's Burke: The Mind of Thomas Hutchinson.* Washington: University Press of America, 1982.

Potter, Janice. *The Liberty We Seek: Loyalist Ideology in Colonial New York and Massachusetts.* Cambridge: Harvard University Press, 1983.

Preece, Rod. "The Myth of the Red Tory." *Canadian Journal of Political and Social Theory,* 1 (1977), 1–18.

——. "The Political Wisdom of Sir John A. Macdonald." *Canadian Journal of Political Science,* 17 (1984), 449–64.

Richards, John, and Larry Pratt. *Prairie Capitalism: Power and Influence in the New West.* Toronto: McClelland and Stewart, 1979.

Sandoz, Ellis, ed. *Political Sermons of the American Founding Era.* Indianapolis: Liberty Press, 1991.

Scruton, Roger. *The Meaning of Conservatism,* 2nd. ed. London: Macmillan, 1984.

Smith, David A. "A Comparison of Prairie Political Movements in Saskatchewan and Alberta." *Journal of Canadian Studies,* 4:1 (1969), 17–25.

Smith, Peter J. "The Ideological Origins of Canadian Confederation." *Canadian Journal of Political Science,* 20 (1987), 3–29.

Taylor, Charles. *Radical Tories: The Conservative Tradition in Canada*. Toronto: Anansi, 1982.

Upton, Leslie. *Revolutionary versus Loyalist: The First American Civil War, 1774-1784*. Waltham: Blaisdell, 1968.

van Herk, Aritha. *Mavericks: An Incorrigible History of Alberta*. Toronto: Penguin, 2001.

Ward, Norman. "One Prairie Province: Historical and Political Perspectives," in David K. Elton, ed., *One Prairie Province?* Lethbridge: Lethbridge Herald, 1970, pp. 163–85.

Wise, S.F. "Sermon Literature and Canadian Intellectual History." *Bulletin of the Committee on Archives of the United Church of Canada*, 18 (1965), 1–17.

——. "Upper Canada and the Conservative Tradition," in *Profiles of a Province: Studies in the History of Ontario*. Toronto: Ontario Historical Society, 1967, pp. 11–31.

——. "Conservatism and Political Development: The Canadian Case." *South Atlantic Quarterly*, 69 (1970), 228–39.

——. "Liberal Consensus or Ideological Battleground: Some Reflections on the Hartz Thesis." Canadian Historical Association, *Historical Papers* (1974), 1–14.

Wrong, George M. *Canada and the American Revolution: The Discussion of the First British Empire*. Toronto: Macmillan, 1935.

Chapter Four

Bakvis, Herman. "Rebuilding Policy Capacity in the Era of the Fiscal Dividend." *Governance*, 13 (2000), 71–103.

——. "Think Tanks and Political Parties: Competitors or Collaborators?" *isuma*, 2 (2001), 107–13.

Bercuson, David J., and Barry Cooper. *The Monopoly Buying Powers of the Canadian Wheat Board: A Brief History and Analysis*. Edmonton: Alberta Agriculture, 1997.

——. *The Legislative Evolution of the Monopoly Buying Powers of the Canadian Wheat Board, 1943-1967.* Winnipeg: Thompson, Dorfman, Sweatman, 1998.

Brodie, Ian. *Friends of the Court: The Privileging of Interest Group Litigants in Canada.* Albany: SUNY Press, 2002.

Brodie, Janine. "The Women's Movement Outside Quebec: Shifting Relations with the Canadian State," in Ken McRoberts, ed., *Beyond Quebec: Taking Stock of Canada.* Montreal: McGill-Queen's University Press, 1995.

Cairns, Alan. *Reconfigurations: Canadian Citizenship and Constitutional Change,* ed. Douglas E. Williams. Toronto: McClelland and Stewart, 1995.

——. *Citizens Plus: Aboriginal Peoples and the Canadian State.* Vancouver: UBC Press, 2000.

Carter, Colin, and Al Loyns. *The Federal Government and the Prairie Grain Sector: A Study of Over-Regulation.* Toronto: University of Toronto Press, 1998.

Cooper, Barry. "Some Implications of the Embedded State in Canada," in Gerald Kernerman and Philip Resnick, eds., *Insiders and Outsiders: Alan Cairns and the Reshaping of Canadian Citizenship.* Vancouver: UBC Press, 2005.

Cooper, Barry, and Sylvia LeRoy. *Off Limits: How Radical Environmentalists Are Shutting Down Canada's National Parks.* Public Policy Sources, No. 45. Vancouver: The Fraser Institute, 2000.

Cooper, Barry, Sylvia LeRoy, and Jason Hayes. *Science Fact or Science Fiction? The Grizzly Biology Behind Parks Canada's Management Models.* Critical Issues Bulletin. Vancouver: The Fraser Institute, 2002.

Flanagan, T.E. "The Manufacture of Minorities," in Neil Nevitte and Allan Kornberg, eds., *Minorities and the Canadian State.* Toronto: Mosaic, 1985, pp. 107–24.

Flanagan, Tom. *First Nations? Second Thoughts*. Montreal: McGill-Queen's University Press, 2000.

Grubel, Herbert, ed. *How to Use the Fiscal Surplus: What Is the Optimal Size of Government*. Vancouver: The Fraser Institute, 1998.

Informa Economics. *An Open Market for cwb Grain*. Winnipeg: Informa Economics, June 2008.

Inglehart, Ron. *Culture Shift in Advanced Industrial Society*. Princeton: Princeton University Press, 1990.

Knopff, Rainer, and F.L. Morton. *Charter Politics*. Toronto: Nelson, 1992.

———. *The Charter Revolution and the Court Party*. Peterborough: Broadview, 2000.

Lermer, George. *Probing Leviathan*. Vancouver: The Fraser Institute, 1984.

Loyns, R.M.A., and Colin A. Carter. *Grains in Western Economic Development. Discussion Paper No. 272*. Ottawa: Economic Council of Canada, 1984.

Pal, Leslie. *Interests of State: The Politics of Language, Multiculturalism and Feminism in Canada*. Montreal: McGill-Queen's University Press, 1993.

Russell, Peter. *Constitutional Odyssey*, 2nd. ed. Toronto: University of Toronto Press, 1993.

Savoie, Donald J. *Governing from the Centre: The Concentration of Power in Canada*. Toronto: University of Toronto Press, 1999.

———. *Breaking the Bargain: Public Servants, Ministers, and Parliament*. Toronto: University of Toronto Press, 2003.

Skocpol, Theda. *Bringing the State Back In*. Cambridge: Cambridge University Press, 1985.

Chapter Five

Aubry, Jack. "Spending Power on Agenda." *National Post*, October 10, 2007, A4.

Bender, Keith. "The Central Government–Private Sector Wage Differential." *Journal of Economic Surveys*, 12 (1998), 177–220.

Black, Ed. *Divided Loyalties*. Montreal and Kingston: McGill-Queen's University Press, 1975.

Boothe, Paul. *Modest but Meaningful Change: Reforming Equalization*. Halifax: AIMS, 2002.

Bryden, Joan. "Harper Risks Backlash to Woo Quebec with Spending Limits." *Calgary Herald*, September 23, 2007, A4.

Buchanan, James M. "Federalism and Fiscal Equity." *American Economic Review*, 40 (1950), 583–99.

——. "Federal Grants and Resource Allocation." *Journal of Political Economy*, 60 (1952), 208–17; 536–38.

——. *Fiscal Equalization Revisited*. Halifax: AIMS, 2002.

Campbell, Robert A. *Grand Illusions: The Politics of the Keynesian Experience in Canada*. Peterborough: Broadview, 1987.

Chao, Johnny C.P., and Herbert Grubel. "Optimal Levels of Spending and Taxation in Canada," in Grubel, ed., *How to Use the Fiscal Surplus: What Is the Optimal Size of Government?* Vancouver: The Fraser Institute, 1998.

Courchene, Thomas J. "Confiscatory Equalization: The Intriguing Case of Saskatchewan's Vanishing Energy Revenues." *Choices*, 10:2 (March). Montreal: Institute for Research on Public Policy, 2004.

Crowley, Brian Lee. "Silent Partner in Voisey's Bay." *Globe and Mail*, January 18, 2000, A19.

Delacourt, Susan. "Dion Fears Result of Bid to Limit Federal Powers." *Toronto Star*, September 24, 2007, A1.

Dicey, A.V. *Introduction to the Study of the Law of the Constitution,* 4th ed. London: Macmillan, 1893.

Doms, Olivier. "In Flanders' Fields the Transfers Grow: Equalization Policies Fraying Belgian Federation." *Frontier Background,* April. Winnipeg: Frontier Centre for Public Policy, 2004.

Driedger, E.A. "The Spending Power." *Queen's Law Journal,* 7 (1981–82), 124–34.

EKOS. *Rethinking Government 1994: An Overview and Synthesis.* Ottawa: EKOS Research Associates, 1995.

Franks, C.E.S. *The Parliament of Canada.* Toronto: University of Toronto Press, 1987.

Granatstein, J.L. *The Ottawa Men: The Civil Service Mandarins 1935-1957.* Toronto: Oxford University Press, 1982.

Grossman, Philip. "Government and Economic Growth: A Non-Linear Relationship." *Public Choice,* 56 (1988), 193–200.

Gunter, Lorne "Federal Government Is Bigger than Ever." *Edmonton Journal,* August 5, 2007, A18.

Hardin, Garrett. "The Tragedy of the Commons." *Science,* 162 (December 13, 1968), 1243–48.

Hayek, Friedrich. *The Road to Serfdom.* Chicago: University of Chicago Press, 1944.

Hogg, Peter. "Analysis of the New Spending Provision (Section 106A)," in K.E. Swinton and C.J. Rogerson, eds., *Competing Constitutional Visions: The Meech Lake Accord.* Toronto: Carswell, 1988, pp. 155–62.

Holle, Peter. "How Equalization Harms Have-Not Provinces: Anti-Growth Policies Supported by Alberta Transfers." Policy Briefing, April 15, 2004. Calgary: The Fraser Institute, 2004.

Hood, Christopher. "Relations Between Ministers/Politicians and Public Servants: Public Service Bargains Old and New," in B. Guy Peters and Donald J. Savoie, eds., *Governance in the*

Twenty-first Century: Revitalizing the Public Service. Montreal: McGill-Queen's University Press, 2000, pp. 178–206.

Kent, Tom. *A Public Purpose: An Experience of Liberal Opposition and Canadian Government*. Montreal: McGill-Queen's University Press, 1988.

Lajoie, Andrée. "The Federal Spending Power and Meech Lake," in K.E. Winston and C.J. Rogerson, eds., *Competing Constitutional Visions: The Meech Lake Accord*. Toronto: Carswell, 1988, pp. 175–85.

Martin, Lawrence. "A New Vision for the Country?" *Globe and Mail*, July 31, 2008, A13.

May, Kathryn. "Public Servants Multiply Despite Cuts." *Calgary Herald*, July 30, 2007, A4.

McMahon, Fred. *Retreat From Growth: Atlantic Canada and the Negative-Sum Economy*. Halifax: AIMS, 2000.

Nahan, Mike. "The Tasmanian Devil Is in Equalization's Details." *Frontier Background*, April. Winnipeg: Frontier Centre for Public Policy, 2003.

Nielsen, Erik. *The House Is Not a Home*. Toronto: Macmillan, 1989.

Olson, Mancur. *The Rise and Decline of Nations: Economic Growth, Stagflation, and Social Rigidities*. New Haven: Yale University Press, 1982.

Osborne, David, and Ted Gaebler. *Reinventing Government*. New York: Plume, 1992.

Petter, Andrew. "Federalism and the Myth of the Federal Spending Power." *Canadian Bar Review*, 68 (1989), 448–79.

Rae, Bob. "Why Something Called the Spending Power Matters." *Globe and Mail*, October 1, 2007, A10.

Robertson, Gordon. *Memoirs of a Very Civil Servant: Mackenzie King to Pierre Trudeau*. Toronto: University of Toronto Press, 2000.

Savoie, Donald J. *Governing From the Centre: The Concentration of Power in Canadian Politics*. Toronto: University of Toronto Press, 1999.

———. *Breaking the Bargain: Public Servants, Ministers, and Parliament*. Toronto: University of Toronto Press, 2003.

Scott, F.R. "The Constitutional Background of Taxation Agreements." *McGill Law Journal*, 2 (1955), 1–10.

Simon, Herbert A. *Administrative Behavior: A Study of Decision-Making Processes in Administrative Organizations*, 3rd. ed. New York: Free Press, 1976.

Smiley, Donald V. *Conditional Grants and Canadian Federalism: A Study in Constitutional Adaptation*. Toronto: Canadian Tax Foundation, 1963.

Sutherland, S.L., and G. Bruce Doren. *Bureaucracy in Canada: Control and Reform*. Vol. 43. *Collected Research Studies, Royal Commission on the Economic Union and Development Prospects for Canada*. Toronto: University of Toronto Press, 1985.

Theakston, Kevin. *The Civil Service Since 1945*. Oxford: Blackwell, 1995.

Tiger, Kristan. "Sweden's Equalization Milk Cow." *Frontier Background*, April. Winnipeg: Frontier Centre for Public Policy, 2003.

Chapter Six

Aubry, Jack. "Liberals Gauged Scandal Reaction with $127K Poll." *Globe and Mail*, November 8, 2004, A4.

———. "Taxpayers Paying $1M for Liberals' Gomery War Room." *National Post*, May 24, 2005, A5.

———. "Ad Scam: Triumph of Theft, Ethics Commissioner." *National Post*, September 16, 2005, A4.

———. "Media 'Seduced' Judge, Say Chrétien's Lawyers." *Calgary Herald*, October 29, 2007, A4.

Auditor General. *Report of the Auditor General of Canada.* Ottawa: Office of the Auditor General, 2003.

Benoit, Liane E. "Ministerial Staff: The Life and Times of Parliament's Statutory Orphans," in "Commission of Inquiry into the Sponsorship Program and Advertising Activities, Restoring Accountability," *Research Studies,* vol. I, *Parliament, Ministers and Deputy Ministers.* Ottawa: Public Works and Government Services, 2006, pp. 195–252.

Benoit, Liane E., and C.E.S. (Ned) Franks. "For Want of a Nail: The Role of Internal Audit in the Sponsorship Scandal," in Commission of Inquiry into the Sponsorship Program and Advertising Activities, Restoring Accountability, *Research Studies,* vol. 2, *The Public Services and Transparency.* Ottawa: Public Works and Government Services, 2006, pp. 233–303.

Bercuson, David J., and Barry Cooper. *Deconfederation: Canada Without Quebec.* Toronto: Key Porter, 1991.

———. *Derailed: The Betrayal of the National Dream.* Toronto: Key Porter, 1994.

Burney, Derek H. *Getting It Done: A Memoir.* Montreal: McGill-Queen's University Press, 2005.

Clark, Campbell. "Mint Chairman Spent $26,351 in Three Months." *Globe and Mail,* October 4, 2005, A7.

Clarkson, Stephen. *The Big Red Machine: How the Liberal Party Dominates Canadian Politics.* Vancouver: UBC Press, 2005.

Commission of Inquiry into the Sponsorship Program and Advertising Activities, *Transcripts of Public Hearings.* Available at: www.gomery.ca/en/transcripts/index.asp

Cooper, Barry. *Bureaucrats in Uniform: The Politicization and Decline of the Royal Canadian Mounted Police.* Fraser Institute Electronic publication. 2006. Available at: www. fraserinstitute.ca/shared/readmore.asp?sNav=pb&id=833

Cosh, Colby. "The Liberals' Original Sin." *National Post,*

November 2, 2005, A14.

Coyne, Andrew. "The Mindset He Betrays." *National Post,*
February 9, 2005, A1.

———. "Straining Credulity to the Breaking Point." *National Post,*
February 12, 2005, A12.

———. "The Scandal's What's Legal." *National Post,* March 12,
2005, A12.

Daly, Brian. "Cash Drop in Chrétien's Riding: Inquiry."
Canadian
Press, May 10, 2005. Available at: Canada.com/
components/printstory/printstory4.aspx?id=12cb7664-18c7-
4660-86c4-bc6bidf. (13/05/2005)

Dawson, Anne. "Martin 'Didn't Want to Know,' Duceppe Says."
National Post, February 11, 2005, A5.

Gagliano, Alfonso. *Les Corridors du Pouvoir.* Montreal: Du
Méridièn, 2006.

George, Peter. "Jean Chrétien Awarded Degree for Distinguished
Public Career." *Hamilton Spectator,* June 4, 2005, A8.

Goldenberg, Eddie. *The Way It Works: Inside Ottawa.* Toronto:
McClelland & Stewart, 2006.

Gomery, John H. "Who is Responsible?" in Commission of
Inquiry into the Sponsorship Program and Advertising
Activities, *Fact Finding Report.* Ottawa: Public Works and
Government Services, 2005.

———. "Restoring Accountability," in Commission of Inquiry
into the Sponsorship Program and Advertising Activities,
Recommendations. Ottawa: Public Works and Government
Services, 2005.

Ha, Tu Thanh. "Chrétien Friend Bragged about 'a Little
Scheme.'" *Globe and Mail,* October 21, 2006, A8.

Hamilton, Graeme. "Italian but No Godfather, Morselli Says."
National Post, May 27, 2005, A5.

Hughes, E.N. (Ted). *Commission for Public Complaints against the RCMP, RCMP Act—Part VII, Subsection 45.45 (14), Commission Interim Report Following a Public Hearing into the Complaints Regarding the Events That Took Place in Connection with Demonstrations During the Asia Pacific Economic Cooperation Conference in Vancouver, BC, in November 1997 at the UBC Campus at the UBC and Richmond Detachments of the RCMP.* Ottawa: RCMP Public Complaints Commission, 2001.

Kinsella, Warren. "Sponsorships Are Good (No, Really)." *National Post*, May 2, 2005, A16.

Kinsella, Warren. "A Tell-all That Shouldn't be Told." *National Post*, February 2, 2006, A14.

Laghi, Brian, and Campbell Clark. "Chrétien Asks Court to Quash Gomery Report." *Globe and Mail*, December 1, 2005, A8.

LeBlanc, Daniel. "Globe's Sponsorship Probe Led Ottawa to Invent Rules." *Globe and Mail*, October 15, 2004, A1.

LeBlanc, Daniel. *Nom de code: Ma Chouette.* Montreal: Libre Expression, 2006.

Love, Rod. "Not the Rules, It's the Culture." *Calgary Herald*, November 2, 2005, A12.

Maioni, Antonia. "Showing the Flag: The Origins and Consequences of the Sponsorship Scandal." *Policy Options* 26:5 (June 2005), 22–25.

Mallory, J.R. "The Minister's Office Staff: An Unreformed Part of the Public Service." *Canadian Public Administration*, 10 (1967), 1–30.

Marsden, William. "Exonerate Chrétien, Leader 'Betrayed,' Lawyers Urge Gomery." *Calgary Herald*, July 7, 2005, A12.

——. "Gagliano Ties MPs to Sponsorship." *Calgary Herald*, December 19, 2005, A4.

Martin, Don. "Better Be Careful What You Wish For." *Calgary Herald*, January 26, 2005.

———. "Canada's Watergate." *National Post*, April 8, 2005, A4.

———. "Liberals Dogged by Bad Luck, Worse Timing." *Calgary Herald*, April 20, 2005, A7.

———. "Gomery, a Judge of Injudicious Truthfulness." *National Post*, June 27, 2008, A5.

McCullagh, Declan. "US Blogger Thwarts Canadian Gag Order." CNET News.com. 2005. Available at: news.com.com/ U.S.+blogger+thwarts+Canadian+gag+order/2100-1028-3-5656087.html. (4/5/2005)

Morton, Desmond. "Reflecting on Gomery: Political Scandals and the Canadian Memory." *Policy Options* 26:5 (June 2005), 14–21.

Nanos, Nick. "The Sponsorship Scandal: Chrétien's Mess, Martin's Inheritance." *Policy Options* 25:5 (June 2005), 41–42.

Naumetz, Tim. "Don't Let Chrétien Make Mockery of Court: Gomery Lawyer." *National Post*, June 26, 2005, A6.

O'Connor, Lauretta. "Chief of Staff." *Policy Options* 12:3 (April 1991), 22–25.

O'Neill, Peter, and Kathryn May. "Gomery Must Go: Chrétien." *National Post*, January 26, 2006.

Pelletier, Jean. "Open Letter to Mr. Justice John Gomery." *Globe and Mail*, November 22, 2005, A17.

Perreault, François. *Inside Gomery*, tr. Carl Angers. Toronto: Douglas and McIntyre, 2006.

Russell, Peter. *Constitutional Odyssey: Can Canadians Become a Sovereign People?*, 3rd. ed. Toronto: University of Toronto Press, 2004.

Savoie, Donald. "The Minister's Staff: The Need for Reform." *Canadian Public Administration*, 26 (1983), 507–24.

————. *Breaking the Bargain*. Toronto: University of Toronto Press, 2003.

Smith, David E. "Clarifying the Doctrine of Ministerial Responsibility as It Applies to Government and Parliament in Canada," in "Commission of Inquiry into the Sponsorship Program and Advertising Activities, Restoring Accountability," *Research Studies*, vol. 1, *Parliament, Ministers and Deputy Ministers*. Ottawa: Public Works and Government Services, 2006, 101–43.

Smith, Greg B. "Stoolie: Canada Pol in Mob." *Daily News*, November 18, 2004.

Steele, Kevin. "What Did We Know About Gagliano and When Did We Know It?" *Western Standard*, 20 December 20, 2004. Available online at: http://www.westernstandard.ca/website/index.cfm?page=print.print_article&article_id=474 (27/11/2005)

Taber, Jane, and Campbell Clark. "Martin and MPs Applaud Chrétien Testimony." *National Post*, February 10, 2005, A1.

Tellier, Paul. "Pour une Réforme des Cabinets des Ministres fédéraux." *Canadian Public Administration*, 11 (1968), 420–30.

Travers, James. "There's a Bigger Story than Chrétien's Testimony." *Toronto Star*, February 8, 2005, A12.

Woods, Allan. "Grits Accused of 'Criminal Conspiracy.'" *National Post*, April 8, 2005, A5.